The Action
of Ben Jonson's
Poetry

The Action
of Ben Jonson's
Poetry

Sara J. van den Berg

DELAWARE
Newark: University of Delaware Press
London and Toronto: Associated University Presses

Associated University Presses
440 Forsgate Drive
Cranbury, NJ 08512

Associated University Presses
25 Sicilian Avenue
London WC1A 2QH, England

Associated University Presses
2133 Royal Windsor Drive
Unit 1
Mississauga, Ontario
Canada L5J 1K5

The paper used in this publication meets the requirements
of the American National Standard for Permanence of Paper
for Printed Library Materials Z39.48-1984.

Library of Congress Cataloging-in-Publication Data

Van den Berg, Sara J.
  The action of Ben Jonson's poetry.

  Bibliography: p.
  Includes index.
  1. Jonson, Ben 1573?–1637—Poetic works.   I. Title.
PR2642.P63V36   1987   822'.3   86-40217
ISBN 0-87413-308-4 (alk. paper)

203843

Printed in the United States of America

Contents

Acknowledgments

Many people have assisted my work, and it is a privilege to thank them. Robert E. Moore, John Dennis Hurrell, and Jacob Levenson introduced me to the exacting pleasure of studying literature. My greatest debt is to Louis Martz, who supervised my dissertation on Jonson's poetry and continued to encourage this book in every stage of its growth. I have benefited from generous and challenging conversations with my colleagues and students at Fordham University, Fairfield University, Occidental College, The Ohio State University, and the University of Washington, and with Jonsonians at the Huntington Library and the Folger Shakespeare Library. The notes and bibliography reveal my debts to many scholars whose work has inspired my own. I have especially appreciated the encouragement of Eugene Waith, Roy Schafer, Bridget Lyons, Robert E. Knoll, Hugh Maclean, Jackson Cope, Lester Beaurline, Walter B. Davis, Mary Oates, Leah Marcus, Sydney Janet Kaplan, Hazard Adams, William Willeford, and Otto Reinert.

Richard Dunn and Donna Gerstenberger provided the personal and institutional support essential to academic work. Of those who read the manuscript of this book at various stages of its development, John Coldewey, Richard Dunn, Raimonda Modiano, and Kent van den Berg made especially helpful detailed comments. F. J. Levy and Alan Fisher offered astute suggestions. Finally, it is a pleasure to express my gratitude to D. Heyward Brock, who read the manuscript for the University of Delaware Press.

My work on this book has been generously supported by summer grants from the National Endowment for the Humanities, The Ohio State University Graduate School, and the University of Washington Graduate School Research Fund. I am grateful to the editors of *Studies in Philology, ELH*, and *Shakespeare Studies* for granting permission to reprint, in revised form, materials in Chapters 2, 3, and 6.

This book was written for my parents and is dedicated to my husband and son, Kent and David: "These I will honour, love, embrace, and serve, / And free it from all question to preserve."

The Action
of Ben Jonson's
Poetry

1

The Poem as Action

I must the true relation make.

(Und. 11)¹

Sense is wrought out of experience, the knowledge of humane life, and actions.

(Dis. 1887–89)²

Every Jonsonian poem can be described as a set of actions: the poet addresses a particular occasion, tests a particular literary form, affirms a particular social value. That Jonson thought of his poetry as a set of actions is evident in his list of the poet's achievements:

> his wisdome, in dividing: his subtilty, in arguing: with what strength hee doth inspire his Readers; with what sweetnesse hee strokes them: in inveighing, what sharpenesse; in Jest, what urbanity hee uses. How he doth raigne in mens affections; how invade, and breake in upon them; and makes their minds like the thing he writes. (*Dis.* 787–93)

His catalogue of the poet's actions refers to the effects as well as the content of art. Like Janus, the poet looks in two directions at once, toward his subject and toward his audience, and seeks a voice that can address them both.

"Voice" designates not the historical person who was Ben Jonson, not even the representation of the poet's consciousness in the text, but self in action, that capacity of Jonson which is occasioned by the specific circumstance he addresses in a particular poem.[3] In part, "voice" is a matter of rhythm and syntax: the strong sentence set against the strong iambic line; the recurrent pattern of initial negation, assertion, and qualification; the interplay of lavish catalogue and the one right word; the abrupt thrust that suddenly constricts narrative or dialogue to a single epigrammatic point.[4] Yet "voice" cannot be reduced to an abstract list of rhetorical schemes or tropes. It also involves the choice of a role appropriate to the occasion of a poem: father, friend, admirer, satirist, critic, professional writer. Manner and tone are even more important than role. In every role he plays, Jonson fashions for himself a stance of personal power and autonomy.[5] He presumes to stand outside of the occasion he addresses, so that his response to it can be shaped by his own moral and poetic standards, not dictated entirely by the demands of the occasion. "Voice" is both the consequence and the expression of the drama of Ben Jonson's poetry, the action of shaping a response to an occasion.

Jonson's poetry gains its distinctive realism from the energies of voice. The typical Jonsonian poem is written as an utterance addressing another person. The poet is responsive to, and often invites a response from, that person.[6] His poem thereby accommodates the circumstances that define that other person and prompt the poet's address. This accommodation is often achieved by describing a person or event, but it can also be achieved by a refusal (through deference or contempt) to speak further:

> My praise is plain, and wheresoe'er professed
>   Becomes none more than you, who need it least.
>
> (*Ep.* 103.13–14)

> You both are modest. So am I. Farewell.
>
> (*Und.* 16.86)

> Believe it, Guilty, if you lose your shame,
>   I'll lose my modesty, and tell your name.
>
> (*Ep.* 38.7–8)

> Playwright, I loathe to have thy manners known
>   In my chaste book: profess them in thine own.
>
> (*Ep.* 49.5–6)

Jonson achieves his distinctive poetic realism not by replicating the occasion within the poem but by dramatizing his response to the world outside the poem. Our sense of that world emerges more clearly from the drama of Jonson's responses to it than from the information provided through description. What kind of world is it? A social world populated by other selves, and therefore a world that needs to be addressed in a certain way and that may change its character in response to the manner in which it is addressed. Because the social world is not fully present in some neutral or objective sense, description of it ultimately requires description of one's response to it. Therefore, the hallmark of Jonsonian poetry is not its themes or images but the poet's voice.

In order to describe the complex effort and achievement of Jonson's art, this study will be grounded in the explication of single texts as acts of relationship. Whatever its occasion, literary form, or social assumption, a Jonsonian poem consists of two central actions: the poet describes the person he addresses and dramatizes his own response. The poem develops and defines the relationship between them. The first chapter of this study will explicate Jonsonian poems of satire, praise, friendship, and Petrarchan lament in order to illustrate this characteristic double action. Each set, an "exampled pair, and mirror of their kind" (*Und.* 75), has been chosen to illustrate the range of Jonson's poetic voice. The first poem in each pair documents Jonson's mastery of a received poetic method; the second goes beyond the norm.

In the actions of poetry Jonson sought to express "the life of man in fit measure, numbers, and harmony," and to write "things like the truth" (*Dis.* 2349–53). These are the goals of a Humanist poet, one who valued literary language as a tool to express human truth and address human history. Chapters 2 and 3 will examine two major contexts which contribute to the shaping of Jonson's poetic action: Humanism and history. Only one aspect of his Humanism, his engagement with classical literary texts, has been thoroughly explored.[7] Yet even in this case, critics either catalogue his Humanist assumptions approvingly, accepting his classicism as an unmediated engagement with Roman literature, or regard his imitation of classical texts as a kind of escape into art, a defense against the society that threatened to misjudge, corrupt, or ignore him. For Jonson, however, Humanism was more than a code word for an interest in classical poetry. As distinctive modes of thought, Petrarchan and Erasmian Humanism shaped his ideas of language and society. He finally rejected the Petrarchan mode, and shaped Erasmian prose into a new English poetry.[8] As a Humanist, he regarded the classical tradition as a place to stand from which he could address his world. The ideal of a timeless community of "the learned" and "the good" (*Dis.* 1943–44) implicit in his idea of poetic craft and imitation is enacted in his address to the real world of his patrons and friends. Although Jonson himself might have used the term "history" to mean only a chronicle or narrative of events, the Jacobeans were beginning to use the word to designate the subject matter or the materials interpreted by historians.[9] The circumstances Jonson made the subject of his art he defines and interprets according to Humanist tenets, but history to some degree resists his art and defines it. Community, then, is not only a Humanist ideal but also a network of actual human relationships, those which succeed and those which fail.

Jonson rarely generalizes about the nature of society, or history, or even his own character. Instead, he details particular moments, people, personal judgments. What generalizations can be made are possible because he gathered many of his best poems into two books, *Epigrammes* and *The Forrest*, published together in the 1616 Folio. A third collection, *Underwood*, was being prepared for publication at the time of his death and was completed by Sir Kenelm Digby. These collections trace the intersection of Jonson's poetry with literary history and historical circumstance, locating each Jonsonian poetic act within the shaping act that is the "book."

Every Jonsonian poem is embedded in significant contexts—extrinsic systems of literary tradition, belief, and social circumstance—but none of them can "explain" the origin or the impact of that poem. These contexts claim an explanatory force only insofar as they are replicated in the book of which the Jonsonian poem is a part. The relationship between poet and subject in a poem complements the relationship between poet and reader developed in the book. These two sets, moreover, are metonymic of the relationship between poetry and the world outside poetry. As an act implicated in all these textual and contextual systems, each poem is constitutive of the relationships that elicit and validate it.

The relationship between poem and book will be the subject of Chapters 4 and 5, which discuss *Epigrammes* and *The Forrest*.[10] Jonson carefully edited both books. By this editorial work, he virtually invented the idea that a book of short poems could have a coherence and order other than that suggested by genre or narrative sequence. Most readers encounter a Jonsonian poem in an anthology, and, because the poem is set before them as an autonomous text, never consider it as part of a carefully designed book of poetry. The anthologist assumes that each poem can stand on its own and that the poet can be thoroughly "known" through a selection of strong texts. The major alternative to this assumption has been thematic criticism, which extracts recurrent ideas from the poet's *oeuvre* without much regard to the integrity of an individual poem or book. The few critics who consider *Epigrammes* and *The Forrest* as unified books too often confine their argument to a catalogue of recurrent moral themes that can be abstracted from these collections.[11] This procedure disregards the complexity of the individual poem and of the collection. Each poem in *Epigrammes* and *The Forrest* stands alone, yet each contributes to the thematic and dramatic whole of the book and derives special meaning from its placement.

Ben Jonson organized *Epigrammes* and *The Forrest* according to an idea of poetry that emerges in the poems about poetry recurrent in both collections. That idea of poetry as a complex act of relationship is most fully developed in three major poems written at roughly the same time (1623–24): "To the

Memory of . . . William Shakespeare," "An Execration upon Vulcan," and "An Epistle Answering to One that Asked to be Sealed of the Tribe of Ben." These three poems constitute Jonson's most comprehensive meditation on his concept of poetry. The first poem is contingent on a book not his own, the folio edition of Shakespeare's plays, and argues for the triumph of art over its own occasion in time. The second confronts the harsh reality of devouring time and grounds all relationship in the fact of mutability and loss. The third works toward an acceptance of what art can and cannot be as the poet evaluates his own career, tracing a set of actions that constitute his being as a writer, his "character." These poems of praise, diatribe, and intimate conversation exemplify not only the three modes of voice most characteristic of Ben Jonson but also the ideals of craft, community, and autonomy that give purpose to his art.

The final chapter of this book briefly surveys *Under-wood*, Jonson's third collection of poetry. *Under-wood* ranges from religious devotional lyrics to acerbic epigrams, from Petrarchan love poetry to congenial epistles, from a sequence of baroque elegiac lyrics to lapidary translations of Horace and Martial. As a whole, Jonson's book defends poetry in all its variety as personal meditation, public statement, and literary continuity. In this collection, like *The Forrest* an apparent miscellany made coherent by the complex action of the poet, Jonson sets his defense of poetry in the context of his own diminished circumstances. Late in his life, he would test and accept the premise that his capacity to make an art of "true relation" was constrained, at least in part, by the conflicting relationships, true and false, that made him and occasioned his poetry. He still aspires to poetic "acts of grace" (*Und.* 1.1.28) and disdains "sordid flatteries, acts of strife" (*Und.* 70). Those people he admires "leave an echo in the sense" (*Und.* 84.4) that must be voiced in poetry, and he envisions for his poems a double audience, the specific subject and the general reader: "Being sent to one, they will be read of all" (*Und.* 78). Jonson not only juxtaposes different kinds of poems in his book, but juxtaposes the different actions of poetry. As literary act, each poem embodies "Newness of sense, antiquity of voice" (*Und.* 14). As historical act, each poem develops a "public voice" (*Und.* 61) specific to its occasion and an "eternal voice" (*Und.* 27) that can proclaim the meaning of that occasion to future readers. As personal act, Jonson's book dramatizes "the recovery of [his] voice" (*Und.* 15) made possible by the "true relation" that merits poetic speech despite the constraints of personal and political circumstance.

I

Jonson makes juxtaposition an organizing principle of his art. Within a single poem, he may set himself next to his subject, to other poets, to the general reader. Every reader has noticed that within a poetic collection Jonson often juxtaposes dissimilar poems, setting satire next to compliment, song next to epistle. I want to begin this discussion of Jonson's poetry by exploring another aspect of juxtaposition, his frequent pairing of poems about a similar occasion or to a single person. To illustrate the spectrum of Jonson's satiric method, I have paired two brief epigrams that take as their common subject a contemptible courtier, "On Something that Walks Somewhere" and "On Court-Worm." These poems are part of a group of attacks on courtiers placed early in *Epigrammes*. The first of these poems begins in personal encounter and narrows to an epigrammatic point. The second develops an impersonal narrative from an initial pointed name; the poet's self-dramatization consists of the judgment that emerges in the narrative.

Many of Jonson's finest satiric epigrams present the act of description as a dramatic encounter. The poet meets someone whom he then describes, often through simulated dialogue, and whom he finally dismisses with a curt comment. As Jonson remarks in an epistle to Edward Sackville, contemptible men "grow less and straitened, full of knot, / And last, go out in nothing" (*Und.* 13, 152–53). The final epigrammatic judgment places as much distance as possible between Jonson and his subject: "End fair enough." "Do what you come for, Captain; here's your meat." "Pay me quickly, or I'll pay you."

In Jonson's satiric poetry, the poet's acts of description and self-dramatization conflict and finally diverge. Typical is the riddling epigram, "On Something that Walks Somewhere." The divergence occurs when the poet recognizes that Something can be condemned by his own self-protective language. The poet, moreover, can make that language a vehicle of judgment without being implicated in its corruption:

> At court I met it, in clothes brave enough
>   To be a courtier, and looks grave enough
> To seem a statesman. As I near it came,
>   It made me a great face; I asked the name;
> A lord, it cried, buried in flesh and blood,
>   And such from whom let no man hope least good,
> For I will do none; and as little ill,
>   For I will dare none. Good lord, walk dead still.

> (*Ep.* 11)

By posing the question of Something's identity as a riddle, the poet establishes his own objectivity. His inquiry occasions the dramatic disclosure that Something is "a lord," but Jonson does not stop with this identification. He lets the lord's actions—or, rather, inactions—speak for him.

Jonson renders as speech what the lord's looks, face, gesture seem to say. Both poet and lord "say" what he is; the lord's action and the poet's act of description merge. Imputed speech is not, nor does it claim to be, a record of actual speech, but transposes into words the nonverbal signs—costume, gesture, demeanor—by which Something gives itself human substance. Using imputed speech, Jonson can present moral judgment as a dramatic encounter. He thereby makes his judgment more emphatic, and at the same time authenticates it by making it seem a confrontation with actual circumstance.

What seems a record, however, can more accurately be termed interpretation. The poet's own judgment is so inextricably bound to the act of description that initially it is hard to tell whether line 6, "And such from whom let no man hope least good," is spoken by the lord or by the poet. Line 7 ("For I will do none") resolves the question at that grammatical level: the lord is speaking. But the ambiguity remains at the level of signification. The poet has adopted an oblique satiric method whereby Something heaps damnation on himself.

Jonson adopts the satirist's conventional pose of naive observer to slow down and make explicit the process by which, even in brief encounter, he reads this man's signals and cracks his code.[12] Jonson gives voice not to the lord's authentic self but to his self-deception. He is a fraud not only to the world but to himself as well. "The New Motion," puffed up for no reason but the cut of his velvet cloak, is another such (*Ep.* 97); so also the Englishman bedecked in the latest continental fashion: "Would you believe, when you this monsieur see, / That his whole body should speak French, not he?" (*Ep.* 88). Imputed speech represents not only the significance of appearance but also the meaning of behavior. Don Surly is made to "say" what in real life would be communicated indirectly: "He speaks to men with a rhinocerot's nose" and "has tympanies of business in his face" (*Ep.* 28). By translating appearance and behavior into speech the poet makes people "say" more than they would want to reveal to others or to themselves. The most savage instance of such revelation is Jonson's epigram to Fine Lady Would-Be, who prefers life at court to motherhood at home. The poem, which consists of his questions and her putative answers, finally switches from speech to writing as its dominant mode. Jonson disgustedly gives over the act of writing to the lady herself: "Write, then, on thy womb: / Of the not born, yet buried, here's the tomb" (*Ep.* 62).

"On Something that Walks Somewhere" illustrates Jonson's capacity to create the sensation of dramatic encounter within the detached and self-sufficient activities of writing and reading poetry. Often such encounters are marked by the other person's reluctance (many of Jonson's targets are self-protective) or by the poet's own hesitation and diffidence. The action of encounter is highlighted by this resistance to it on the part of both poet and subject. The reason for resistance often turns out to be the real subject of the poem. In satiric epigrams, Jonson typically moves from an external description to an interpretation of what appearance and behavior signify. "Something that Walks Somewhere" abstains from all commitments that would arouse any expectations in others, but his body language reveals, paradoxically, his determination to avoid self-exposure.

The poet's own language rings changes on a court idiom that had been designed to protect people from the risk of communication. He transforms the flat formulas of courtly etiquette into a fictive, even fantastic mode that can unfold the metaphor of moral death-in-life implicit in the poem's realistic opening lines, as words that denote physical appearance (brave, grave) take on moral connotations. Only the lord's clothing is "brave"; he is incapable of either virtue or villainy. "Grave" initially means only "serious" or "sober," but "buried in flesh and blood" expands the figure to suggest what will be bluntly declared in the last line.

"Good lord, walk dead still." This mocking inversion of a standard courtly salute sums up the poet's moral judgment of the lord and ends their encounter. *Still:* motionless, nevertheless, always. Refusing to commit himself to any kind of action, this lord may walk but cannot move. Trying to protect his life, he dooms himself to death-in-life. The poet has moved from observation and analysis to a conclusive judgment that decisively encloses the imagined encounter in the permanence of verse. By couching the insult in the idiom of courtly exchange, Jonson not only returns to his initial language of realistic formula but merges it into the symbolic mode of metaphor. Address and judgment converge as poet and subject part.

The poet had spun out the riddle of "Something" through description and dialogue, moving from physical to moral description, from a language of fact to a language of symbol. The relationship between metaphor, fact, and judgment in the language of "Something that Walks Somewhere" is reversed in the epigram "On Court-Worm." This time there is no slow explication of a riddle. The title leads us to expect a satiric attack on a contemptible courtier, and that is what we get:

> All men are worms: but this no man. In silk
>   'Twas brought to court first wrapped, and white as milk;
> Where afterwards it grew a butterfly,
>   Which was a caterpillar. So 'twill die.
>
> (*Ep.* 15)

This concise biography of a court favorite exemplifies Jonson's exploitation of a single metaphor. The title names the courtier and judges him. The four lines that follow intensify that judgment in a metaphorical narrative that ranges through several kinds of signification: biblical, political, even entomological.

The narrative opens with an allusion to a text far removed from satire:

"But I am a worm and no man; a reproach of men, and despised of the people" (Psalm 22). Psalm 22 was read during Matins on Good Friday in order to commemorate the agony of the crucified Christ and to evoke contrition in the penitent Christian. Moreover, the metamorphosis of caterpillar into butterfly was a common emblem of Christ's resurrection and also of the Christian soul's emergence into eternal life. The usual meanings of the allusion are ironic in this satiric text; their inapplicability to the courtier's moral obtuseness emphasizes his triviality. The contrast between the self-abnegation of the psalm and the self-protection of the lord isolates and objectifies him as someone less than human: "no man." The courtier is all worm, reduced in the printed text to "it" and, in a climactic gesture of contempt, to " 't."

Jonson's allusion is political as well as religious. Wrapped in the silk generated by other worms, plaything of the great, Court-Worm becomes a butterfly by first becoming a particular kind of worm—a caterpillar. "Caterpillar of the commonwealth" was Jacobean political slang maligning men who fed fat on the kingdom, royal favorites whom James lavishly rewarded and quickly discarded. The last sentence of Jonson's epigram, "So 'twill die," prophesies Court-Worm's fate and judges his life. *So:* then, in this manner, therefore. Sequence, description, judgment.

The arrangement of the narrative intensifies the metaphor of the name but denies the metamorphosis it seems to promise. The courtier/worm is cocoon, then butterfly, then caterpillar. Placing what would ordinarily be the second stage last in the sequence reinforces Jonson's satiric message: this courtier was, is, and can be no more than a worm. Disruption of the narrative sequence creates the effect not of fragmentation but of looping back, to heighten the focus on one point: the nullity of Court-Worm's life.

These epigrams demonstrate the range of Jonson's satiric practice and the consistent patterns of his work. "On Something that Walks Somewhere" dramatizes a fictive encounter, its metaphorical dimension submerged beneath the surface of the dramatic event. "On Court-Worm" offers an impersonal narrative; the poet does not present an image of himself in the text. Its force depends entirely on the meanings that the reader can discover in the poet's metaphorical tale. Neither poem can be limited to a single actual target or a single occasion—Jonson claims to satirize types of men, not individuals (with the notable exception of several bitter and virulent attacks on Inigo Jones). However, these poems claim their truth not in the realm of literary imagination but in the actual world of London and the English Court. Jonson's satire is occasioned by that world and directed toward it.

In the first twenty epigrams, Jonson establishes the justice of moral authority and attacks as unjust, even unlawful, the success of unworthy courtiers. "On Something That Walks Somewhere" and "On Court-Worm" contribute to his group portrait of knaves and fools, their power inversely proportionate to their merit. Against their authority Jonson asserts his own moral force. Although a Jacobean reader might read these poems with reference to such notorious courtiers as Carlisle or Buckingham, the overt fictionality of the poetic occasion protects the poet and enlarges his argument. He does not direct his scorn to only one person.

II

The occasions of complimentary poetry require a different set of poetic actions. The acts of description and self-dramatization collaborate and converge in his complimentary poems as the poet imitates the behavior or the values of the person he describes. In these poems, Jonson's success often lies in a simultaneous act of dependence and independence, as poet and subject validate one another's worth. He often pairs complimentary epigrams to a patron or friend, using the second poem to comment on and amplify the first. Jonson's own formulation of that relationship is evident in the poems of praise and friendship that he himself chose to print together. Pairs of poems to Sir Henry Goodyere and Alphonso Ferrabosco typify Jonson's use of juxtaposition to enhance a compliment. The first poem in each pair documents his mastery of a received poetic method; the second goes beyond general praise to assert his distinctive voice and judgment and to enact intimate relationship.

Jonson's descriptions of his patrons and friends are of little value as portraits: we cannot picture from his text Sir Henry Goodyere or Alphonso Ferrabosco, nor does Jonson present them through imputed speech. He does not presume to encompass them or reduce them to a single trait or idiom. Instead, to shape the person he admires into an icon of virtue, Jonson often introduces mythical or historical allusion, using specific details only as a springboard for his generalizing praise. At the same time, he builds into each act of praise his own intentions, his limitations, his debt. The person he addresses challenges him to excellence. He meets that challenge in dramatic terms, replicating in himself the action of the person he praises. Emulation is the poet's truest act of praise and the necessary consequence of his understanding.

The pair of epigrams to Sir Henry Goodyere (*Ep.* 85 and 86) illustrates how Jonson shapes his own dramatic action to mirror that of the man he describes. The first of these poems centers on hawking, a sport Goodyere much enjoyed, and dramatizes Jonson's "discovery" of its value as an emblem of knowledge and of poetry:

> Goodyere, I'm glad and grateful to report
> Myself a witness of thy few days' sport.

Where I both learned why wise men hawking follow,
   And why that bird was sacred to Apollo:
She doth instruct men by her gallant flight
   That they to knowledge so should tower upright,
And never stoop but to strike ignorance;
   Which, if they miss, they yet should re-advance
To former height, and there in circle tarry
   Till they be sure to make the fool their quarry.
Now, in whose pleasures I have thus discerned,
   What would his serious actions me have learned?

                                                           (*Ep.* 85)

Goodyere's play occasions Jonson's playful compliment; both poet and sportsman take Apollo as their deity. What Jonson claims he could learn from the hawk might be pertinent to the life of Goodyere, who made his way in the labyrinth of Jacobean politics, spending some time away from London in the Netherlands, seeming to "miss" his quarry but in fact using that assignment to keep aloof from court intrigues until an interesting opportunity arose. Jonson, however, seems less concerned with politics than with his own and his society's tendency to moralize, like Duke Senior in Shakespeare's *As You Like It*, finding "tongues in trees, books in the running brooks, / Sermons in stones, and good in everything" (2.1.16–17). Jonson accepts sport as a moral emblem but takes care not to magnify it beyond its proper bounds. After drawing his moral message, he turns from his address to Goodyere to a private speculation: "Now, in whose pleasures I have this discerned, / What would his serious actions me have learned?"

    The second epigram to Goodyere answers that question. It almost seems that Jonson composed the first poem, with its moral commonplaces and playful tone, in order to set up the second, which can achieve a much closer connection between its two main actions, the description of Goodyere and the self-dramatization of the poet. Jonson describes Goodyere's love of learning and of friendship, and dramatizes his own effort to be adequate, to echo as well as address his subject:

When I would know thee, Goodyere, my thought looks
Upon thy well-made choice of friends, and books;
Then I do love thee, and behold thy ends,
In making thy friends books, and thy books friends:
Now I must give thy life, and deed, the voice
Attending such a study, such a choice.
Where though't be love, that to thy praise doth move,
It was a knowledge that begot that love.

                                                           (*Ep.* 86)

What had been a moral generalization about knowledge and ignorance in the first epigram is here charged with the force of intimacy. The "serious action" of Goodyere is his "well-made choice of friends, and books." He learns from his friends as though they were books, and cherishes books as his close friends. He is studious, his choices studied. As poet, Jonson enacts his understanding of the relationship between knowledge and love. And poetry: the causal chain articulated in the epigram argues that knowledge begets love that demands poetry. Jonson not only praises a friend who loves books but makes that friend part of his own book of epigrams. In the first epigram, Jonson portrayed himself as a "glad and grateful . . . witness," a bystander amused at his own easy moralizing on courtly pleasures. He is far more engaged and active in this second epigram; his action, like Goodyere's, can rightly be termed "serious." The carefully plotted rhetorical structure of the poem and the deliberate, almost plodding development of its key words give the poem a studied quality analogous to the studiousness of Sir Henry Goodyere.[13]

Jonson's way of addressing Goodyere embodies in language Goodyere's way of life—its methodical, balanced symmetry and wholeness. In the pivotal fourth line, as Jonson seeks to understand Goodyere's purpose "In making thy friends books, and thy books friends," the same verb governs two different phrases, and these phrases mirror each other. This rhetorical *concordia discors* replicates Goodyere's own act of distinguishing learning and friendship and then using each to enhance the other. There is yet a third rhetorical scheme, *traductio*, that structures this poem. This scheme, termed the "tranlacer" by Puttenham, "is when ye turne and tranlace a word into many sundry shapes as the Tailor doth his garment."[14] Jonson uses this device to emphasize the completeness of his own act. Jonson's act blends knowing and loving Goodyere; by the end of the poem, Jonson has 'read' him, has come to know him by studying him. The verbs "know" and "love" that begin the poem are "tranlaced" by the end into the more enduring nouns "knowledge" and "love." In this poem, Jonson holds the two categories of knowledge and love apart even as he brings them together. Thinking, he understands thought; loving, he understands love; most important, by following the example of Goodyere's "well-made choice," he can show how thought and love complement one another. It is even tempting to see "though't" (in the phrase "though't be love") as a typographical pun on "though it" and "thought." As a "tranlacer" of "thought," such a pun would equate "thought" and "love."

Jonson works out the relationship between knowing and loving not only in rhetoric and syntax but also in the narrative structure of the poem. "When" and "Then" in the opening lines seem to be terms of a logical syllogism, terms of thinking and knowing. They recover their common temporal meaning as terms of experience only in context of the "Now" that begins the third couplet: "Now I must give thy life, and deed, the voice / Attending such a study, such a choice." "Now" and "must" are words of immediacy, of the 'moment' that means both time and significance. To end his poem, Jonson shifts to "Where," a term at once logical and temporal, designating a point of thought and of time, of interpretation and experience. "Where" also has a third common function: it designates place—the place that is the poem, in which thought and feeling come together. Even the shifting tenses of the verbs—from conditional ("When I would know thee") to present ("Then do I love thee" and "Now, I must give thy life, and deed, the voice") to reflective past ("It was a knowledge that begot that love")— enhance the illusion of the poem's range and wholeness. After ranging through past and future, the poet comes to rest in the "Now" that occasions his commitment to Goodyere.

The meaning of the poem, the "Now" and "Where" of it, is actualized in the poet's "voice" celebrating Goodyere. Jonson's action—studying Good- yere studying—replicates Goodyere's own deed. The metaphorical account of Goodyere's "deed" literally describes what Jonson does: the poet is in fact "making [his] friends books," transcribing them into texts. Seen from an- other angle, Jonson's action is the metaphorical equivalent of Goodyere's. Syntactically, the phrase "such a study, such a choice" can apply equally to both men. Jonson admires Goodyere for choosing books and friends wisely; that choice demands a poem. Jonson has chosen to study Goodyere; that choice also demands a poem. The epigram balances not only Goodyere's love of books and friends, not only Jonson's knowledge and love, but also two men and their complementary choices. Jonson's address to Goodyere mirrors Goodyere's address to the world. This coalescence of reference (Goodyere's action) and utterance (Jonson's action) is the core of the epi- gram's persuasive force.

In his satiric epigrams on lords and ladies, poetasters and plagiarists, hucksters and hypocrites, Jonson often attacks their way of being in the world by inverting or exploding their own language. After decoding their language he condemns them to the self-centered, confining idiom they themselves have chosen. Jonson's complimentary poems, exemplified by the epigrams to Sir Henry Goodyere, proceed toward a quite different end: community. On such occasions, the poet would never attempt to alter his subject. Tact and self-interest, if nothing else, would preclude any attempt to do more than praise his subject for already being exemplary. What prevents such poetry from being repetitive and hollow is the poet's representation of his own response to his subjects' particular virtues. Jonson is inspired to emulate their language of being in his language of art. Emulation is central to the poems Jonson writes to his social superiors: without deferring his authority as poet, he gives them moral counsel by depicting himself as their student, guided by them. He pays them the tribute of showing them their impact on his own life.

Compliments to his friends and fellow artists require tact of another sort, mutual respect based on their common bond as artists. This common bond underlies the pair of epigrams to Alphonso Ferrabosco, who composed settings for many of Jonson's masques and songs.[15] Here again, as in the poems to Goodyere, the first epigram sets the stage for the second. The first epigram (*Ep.* 130) summarizes the Humanist theory of music that Ferrabosco helped introduce into England, and then moves beyond description to enact the attitude that underlies the theory:

> To urge, my loved Alphonso, that bold fame
>   Of building towns, and making wild beasts tame,
> Which music had; or speak her known effects:
>   That she removeth cares, sadness ejects,
> Declineth anger, persuades clemency,
>   Doth sweeten mirth and heighten piety,
> And is to a body, often ill-inclined,
>   No less a sovereign cure than to the mind;
> To allege that greatest men were not ashamed
>   Of old, even by her practice to be famed;
> To say indeed she were the soul of heaven,
>   That the eighth sphere, no less than planets seven,
> Moved by her order, and the ninth more high,
>   Including all, were thence called harmony:
> I yet had uttered nothing on thy part,
>   When these were but the praises of the art.
> But when I have said, The proofs of all these be
>   Shed in thy songs, 'tis true: but short of thee.
>
> (*Ep.* 130)

The poet argues that merely to repeat the Humanist praise of music falls short of praising Ferrabosco, even if it were added that his music exemplifies the virtues that the theory claims for music. However, the poem goes exactly contrary to its disclaimer and does praise Ferrabosco by praising music. Jonson compliments Ferrabosco not merely by general association (Ferrabosco, as a musician, participates in music's virtue) but also by implied references to Ferrabosco's particular contribution. He helped introduce the Humanist theory of music into England, just as Jonson brings the theory into *Epigrammes* by summarizing Humanist ideas in the body of the poem. The theory (personified in the figures of Orpheus, whose music subdued wild beasts, and Amphion, whose music built Thebes) asserts the power of music to subdue passions and sustain civilizations. This theory, which urges music's bold fame, speaks its effects, alleges its acceptance by the great, and asserts its supreme place in the order of things (the music of the spheres), requires musicians whose work can forward those goals. As a praiser of music, Ferrabosco (like Amphion) brings forth what he celebrates—and Jonson celebrates him for doing so.

Jonson's disclaimer has the familiar rhetorical effect of amplification: "You are even better than the best I can say." Yet in the context of Jonson's other poetry, the conclusion here—" 'Tis true, but short of thee"—may be heard to echo his frequent skepticism about the power of praise to equal, let alone improve upon, its human subject. The most he can do as a praiser of persons is to make his subject (and the reader) aware of a virtue already possessed, an achievement already earned, in hopes that such awareness will fortify moral autonomy. What matters is the awareness of self-sufficiency; insofar as praise objectifies a person's virtue in any external attribute or accomplishment, it inevitably falls short.

How far the praise of music falls short of Ferrabosco becomes the subject of the second, and finer, poem of this pair. Here, as in the poems to Goodyere, Jonson uses a conventional poem of praise to introduce a more intimate encounter in which praise expresses friendship:

> When we do give, Alphonso, to the light
>   A work of ours, we part with our own right;
> For then all mouths will judge, and their own way:
>   The learn'd have no more privilege than the lay.
> And though we could all men, all censures hear,
>   We ought not give them taste we had an ear.
> For, if the humorous world will talk at large,
>   They should be fools, for me, at their own charge.
> Say this or that man they to thee prefer;
>   Even those for whom they do this know they err:
> And would, being asked the truth, ashamed say
>   They were not to be named on the same day.
> Then stand unto thyself, not seek without
>   For fame, with breath soon kindled, soon blown out.
>
>   (*Ep.* 131)

This poem begins with the truism that even the well-known artist loses control of his work when he surrenders it to public judgment. Yet Jonson urges Ferrabosco to deny any knowledge of that judgment and proposes that even the musicians the crowd prefers would admit Ferrabosco's superiority. Admonishing his friend to stand alone, secure in his own knowledge of his work, the poet defends the authority of the artist. It seems to be the task of the poem, therefore, to admit and then to deny the authority of the audience.

The competition between the authority of the audience and the authority of the artist is expressed in a language of saying, talking, naming: a contest of voices. To dramatize the reception of a work of art and to claim final authority for the artist, Jonson develops a single metonymic image: the mouth of the audience. The mouth speaks ("For then all mouths will speak"), although it has no taste. Jonson makes the obvious pun on taste as sensation and judgment, but also uses the word to designate a tiny amount: "We would not give them taste we had an ear." The disjunction between sensation ("taste") and the organ of perception ("ear") is at once a joke and a guide to the reader's discrimination. Redefining "taste" as "a tiny amount," we choose the interpretative mode of the poet over that of the boorish crowd. Jonson will not ascribe taste to the crowd; he will not admit that he has heard even a small amount of their criticism. The mouth of the audience finally has only the power to breathe.

Opposed to this satiric fantasy of the audience as giant mouth is a meditation on fame, with light as its dominant metaphor. Artists give their work "to the light"—to public view, to the daylight. Jonson contrasts this appropriate, natural realm of judgment to the artificiality and ephemerality of popular judgment, a flickering candle "with breath soon kindled, soon blown out." The two tropes of this epigram to Ferrabosco—the metonymic image of the mouth and the metaphor of fame's flickering light—combine in the final line.

Ben Jonson, giving "his opinion of Verses," told William Drummond "that he wrott all his first in prose, for so his master Cambden had Learned him" (*Conv. Dr.* 377–78). In this poem for Ferrabosco Jonson sets the experience of the artist against the norm of a literary proverb, the familiar saying of an unfamiliar Roman writer: "Pro captu lectoris habent sua fata libelli" (Books entrust their fate to the hands of readers—Terentius Maurus, *De Literis, Syllabis, et Metris Horatii*). The more immediate source of the poem, however, is Jonson's own preface to *Catiline.* When his address "To the Reader in Ordinarie" is juxtaposed to this epigram, it is possible to see Jonson's method of revising prose into poetry. Distinctive ideas and phrases from the prose epistle recur in the epigram. Jonson admits that he "departed with [his] own right" by allowing the play to be performed. He sardonically permits his audience to "Be anything you will be, at your owne charge."[16] To shape these ideas into an epigram, Jonson introduces and exploits the metaphors of mouth and light. These images enunciate the argument and the drama of the poem. Jonsonian craft involves far more than adapting prose to the dictates of meter and rhyme. From a basic idea or image, Jonson shapes a poetic act that can define and mediate the claims of tradition and originality, poetry and history, audience and artist.

The poem begins in intimacy and collegiality: these men have worked together and have endured the anxiety of giving their work to the public. Addressing his friend as Alphonso, his first name, Jonson distinguishes between their friendship and the public fame that earns the artist a "name." The poet imagines a set of circumstances and possible responses ("Say . . ."). The imagined drama is not that of Jonson responding to his friend, but rather of the audience and other musicians responding to Ferrabosco's work. In the final admonitory lines of the epigram, Jonson declares that confidence and self-esteem, even more than the affection of friends or the respect of rivals, can sustain an artist. Jonson's epigram addresses not Ferrabosco's achievement but the circumstances the two men share as artists: Amphion and Orpheus are models for the poet as well as the musician. The counsel he offers his friend he often tried and failed to give to himself. His poems raging against unsympathetic audiences and inept or unscrupulous rivals suggest how much he longed for the autonomy he urges on Ferrabosco.

III

If, as Stephen Greenblatt argues, the English Renaissance was an era of extravagant self-fashioning, it may have been in part because London, the largest and fastest growing city of Renaissance Europe, required each person to claim a role there through personal action.[17] A person could join the impersonal city only by using gestures, language, clothing, and other accoutrements to create a "public self."[18] Yet the ontological crisis of early modern Europe described by John Donne suggests that an interior self-fashioning was required as well:

> 'Tis all in pieces, all cohaerence gone;
> All just supply, and all Relation:
> Prince, Subject, Father, Sonne, are things forgot,
> For every man alone thinks he hath got
> To be a Phoenix, and that there can be
> None of that kinde, of which he is, but hee.
> ("An Anatomie of the World," 213–18)[19]

Jonson's poetic self-fashioning seeks to restore relation. In his social epigrams of praise and blame, he documents his own feelings of sympathy and antipathy, and thereby fashions his own identity through voice. This self-presentation as fulcrum of praise and blame is best described by Michel Foucault in *The Order of Things:* "The identity of things, the fact that they can resemble others and be drawn to them, though without being swallowed up or losing their singularity—this is what is assured by the constant counterbalancing of sympathy and antipathy."[20] Foucault is describing "The Prose of the World," the patterns of order assumed by Europeans in the sixteenth century. Jonson, writing a poetry that tried to affirm those patterns, translates them into the created relationships of his society: friendship, patronage, collegiality, and class. Through repeated acts of praise and blame, sympathy and antipathy, Jonson maintains a voice distinctively his own. What seems lost, perhaps inevitably, is the innocence of assumed relation that we associate with children: Jonson's only poems for children are epitaphs. As urban man, Jonson attends to the relationships that can be chosen: friendship and love. He is the first English poet to make friendship a major theme of art, and friendship (including its dissolution) occasions many of his finest poems. His few love poems seem more problematic, even anomalous, at odds with the genre or with the poet. By juxtaposing conventional and unconventional Petrarchan love poems, in correspondence with William Drummond and in *Under-wood*, Jonson documents both his engagement with and his rejection of a dominant mode of Renaissance self-fashioning.

Jonson's love poems can be classified as impersonal songs or personal narratives of comic self-mockery. Many of his songs serve the action of a play—summing up a moment in the plot, forwarding or commenting on the action—and do not necessarily have as their primary or even possible meaning a true expression of the poet's "self." They voice the capacity of language itself to "keep time" (*C.R.* 1.2.65), and to be perfectly, neatly "dressed" (*Epicoene* 1.1.91). Petrarchan love poetry conventionally depicts a fragile and frustrated relationship valuable because the poet's desire occasions introspection and self-discovery. Jonson sets the usual plot of desire in a language of fierce realism and comic self-awareness. His must be a courtship devoid of courtiership.

Among the most popular of Jonson's songs, to judge from its frequent inclusion in commonplace books, is "The Hour-Glass," which was not composed as part of a play. Jonson paired it with a poem of self-mockery, "My Picture Left in Scotland," and sent them to William Drummond in gratitude for his hospitality during the poet's visit to Edinburgh. Each of these poems takes as its subject the poet-lover's frustrated desire. "The Hour-Glass" (Und. 8) is a polished exercise of wit, squarely within the Petrarchan tradition. "My Picture Left in Scotland" (*Und.* 9) turns that tradition inside out. Drummond was a Petrarchist, and we know from his record of their conversations that Jonson belittled Petrarchan poetry and slighted Drummond's own work as old-fashioned. By sending these two Petrarchan poems to Drummond, Jonson may have wanted to demonstrate at once his mastery and his rejection of the courtly stance.[21] Digby, probably following Jonson's own plan, paired these poems in *Under-wood* and grouped them with other examples of Jonson's Petrarchan poetry (*Und.* 2–11).

In "The Hour-Glass," the poet holds before us as a *memento mori* an hourglass that uses the ashes of a lover to measure the passing of time. Or so the poet claims, challenging us to take as fact what we would ordinarily accept only as poignant metaphor. His wit makes the audience the counterpart of his lady; as her glance turned him to cinders, so our glance transforms cinders into the poet-lover. The lover, slain by the glance of a fair cruel she, finds no rest even in death: the emblem of the hourglass, and the poem itself, have not "expressed" the full truth of his love. The poem ends with a claim that it is disproportionate to the feelings of the poet-lover and thereby comments on itself as well as on the singer and the audience.

"My Picture Left in Scotland," a more complex and personal poem that Jonson may have composed especially for Drummond, also depends on our interpretation of the visible, the audible, and the relationship between what is seen and what is heard:

> I now think Love is rather deaf than blind,
>   For else it could not be
>   That she
> Whom I adore so much should so slight me
>   And cast my love behind;
> I'm sure my language to her was as sweet
>   And every close did meet
>   In sentence of as subtle feet,
>   As hath the youngest he
> That sits in shadow of Apollo's tree.
>   Oh, but my conscious fears
>   That fly my thoughts between,
>   Tell me that she hath seen
>   My hundred of grey hairs,
>   Told seven-and-forty years,
>   Read so much waste, as she cannot embrace
>   My mountain belly, and my rocky face;
> And all these through her eyes have stopped her ears.

$$(Und. 9)$$

The intricate form of the poem, the idealization of sweet language, the cruelty of the lady, the indifference of Love, and the melancholy pose of the rejected lover all place this poem in the Petrarchan tradition. Jonson's rejection of that tradition can be located in the new relationship of self and language, grounded in prosaic realism, that emerges in the second stanza. His personal poems are almost always contingent on his idea of himself and its measure in actuality. He often sees himself as "a tardy, cold, / Unprofitable chattle, fat and old, / Laden with belly" (Und. 56), forced willy-nilly to trust to good verses. In such poetry, his self-dramatization enacts the tension between Jonson the man and Jonson the poet. The tension in this poem resides not only in the disparity between Jonson the lover and Jonson the poet but also in the conflict between Petrarchism and the realism that finally displaces it.

Drummond may not have appreciated Jonson's poetic skill, but he certainly shared the judgment of the lady in Jonson's poem. His only direct comment about the poem—that Jonson's picture was "as he said"—obliquely indicates that he shared the poet's estimation of his "mountain belly" and "rocky face."[22] After recording the texts of the two poems, Drummond paints his own portrait of Ben Jonson:

> He is a great lover and praiser of himself, a contemner and Scorner of others, given rather to losse a friend, than a Jest, jealous of every work and action of those about him (especially after drink, which is one of the Elements in which he liveth) a dissembler of ill parts which raigne in him, a bragger of some good that he wanteth, thinketh nothing well bot what either he himself, or some of his friends and Countrymen hath said or done. He is passionately kynde and angry, carelesse either to gaine or keep, Vindicative, but if he be well answered, at himself.[23]

Although most of what Drummond writes seems the result of astute observation, especially the comment that Jonson "is passionately kynde and angry," at least one of these astringent comments—that Jonson was "given rather to losse a friend, than a Jest"—probably echoes something the poet had said of himself, for the line occurs in a Jonsonian play.[24] A reader of the *Conversations with Drummond* cannot help detecting the poet's self-dramatization even without taking into account Drummond's editorial rearrangements. The madrigal and "My Picture Left in Scotland" can to some extent be read as Jonson's final impertinent acts of poetic self-dramatization for Drummond.

In "My Picture Left in Scotland," Jonson exploits Petrarchan convention and then turns against it. Each stanza of this poem offers a different reversal of the old proverb that "Love is blind." As the comedy of that reversal is worked out—that Love must be deaf, that Love (or the lady) sees all too well—other values and assumptions are turned topsy-turvy as well. The first version of the proverb neglects the meaning behind the original version, that Love does not judge by appearances alone, that for inexplicable reasons an unattractive person may be loved and cherished. Jonson began his suit refusing to believe that Love could be blind, and trusted to words because he detested his appearance. The second stanza offers another challenge to the original proverb. Love, far from being blind, sees only his mountain belly and his rocky face. Or, rather, whatever Love might see, his lady (and she is more important) sees only those. To paraphrase the poem: Love is not blind, nor is the lady. Love is deaf, and so is the lady, because what she sees determines what she will hear. The poem ends by affirming the opening line, but in a new and unexpected way. The poet's situation, of course, remains unchanged: he was rejected before the poem began, and he is rejected when it ends. What seemed to be a reversal instead clarifies and reinforces the poet's original perception. What has changed is the framework of images he uses to describe his predicament.

Jonson revises the conventional drama of Petrarchan love poetry, reversing the customary relationship between poet and lady. Although he describes a lady's response to him, he does not address her. Instead of cataloguing her ivory complexion, golden hair, and perfect form, Jonson describes his own pock-marked face, gray hair, and paunch. Moreover, instead of starting with that description and showing how Petrarchan language might permit him some mastery of his romantic frustration, Jonson bewails the uselessness of that language. The poet's most intense feeling concerns not the lady's dislike of his physical presence but her indifference to his poetry. The first stanza exemplifies the sweet, subtle poetics of Petrarchan love poetry, and Jonson proudly ranks his work with that of "the youngest he / That sits in shadow of Apollo's tree." Poets (like Drummond), not handsome youths, are his rivals. As the poet-lover who speaks the poem, he is shocked when his "sweet" and "subtle" poetic language fails him: "it could not be," "I'm sure." Yet he must admit, in terms just as certain, the power of his appearance to determine his fate: "she cannot embrace / My mountain belly and my rocky face."

The language in this poem shifts to reflect Jonson's comic recognition of the varieties of language, the ways of "telling" and "reading" that make us knowable to each other. At first, he gives priority to speech: his suit will be heard or not heard by the lady, in his elegant measures of sweet, polished song. From the speaking or telling of love, of speech and song unheard, the rueful poet considers another kind of telling, the damning enumeration of his "hundred of grey hairs," his "seven-and-forty years." These all too real numbers count for more than the conventional Petrarchan mathematics of all, one, two, and none. He turns from the failure of his song to her success at reading him like a book. She has, unfortunately, "read" only his "waste" (waist): the pun names both his physique and his disparagement of it. In the last line of the poem, the spoken and written modes of language clash, and the written language of the poet's body triumphs over the finest words he can speak. What she sees is so powerful that it has "stopped her ears."

Although Jonson sets realism against Petrarchan conventions about the power of poetry, there is an important sense in which fact does not triumph over language. What begins as a comic contrast between his self-image as poet and his self-image as man ends in the affirmation, if not convergence, of both. When he turns from the conventional loftiness of "Love" and "Apollo" to face his own particular situation, he shifts to another mode of poetry: regular, neat, plain, even harsh and prosiac. Regular lines and plain language permit him to confront the picture of himself he left in his lady's eye. That language, however, is no longer shackled by the Petrarchan "subtle feet" that govern the first stanza. By writing with vigor and plain honesty, shifting from conventional poetic fantasies to the facts of his own face, Jonson affirms the power of poetry more powerfully than would have been possible in his initial "poetic" idiom. His vivid language, unlike the lady, can embrace everything about him. That he can write the second stanza implies that he might not want to change places with "even the youngest he" after all. Jonson redeems language from the ineffectuality he considered the hallmark of the exhausted Petrarchan tradition. As the poet grows—rejecting a poetic pose not his own, acknowledging the picture he left in the lady's memory, crafting that picture in his own blunt words—he masters the experience he describes. By finding a new language to write himself, he triumphs over the book of self "read" by his lady. He finally affirms himself, *ut pictura poesis:* the picture he leaves in Scotland is, and he wants it to be, this poem.

IV

Thus far, the double action of the Jonsonian poem has been construed in terms of its dramatic referents, the subject and the poet. Although this relationship is complicated when the poet becomes his own subject, the poem is still organized to clarify this dyad. In many of his poems, however, Jonson's self-presentation depends on the double action of his own utterance as speech and as writing. In the act of speech, the poet confronts and participates in the occasion. As collected or recollected writing, his poetry establishes itself outside the confines of circumstance and participates in the "golden world" of art. As an act of speech, the poem is an event in history. As an act of writing, the poem becomes an aesthetic moment shared with a larger audience.

The dualities of speech and writing are more than aesthetic markers in Jonson's art: they are major components of voice. The two satiric epigrams on "Something That Walks Somewhere" and "Court-Worm" illustrate one way speech and writing converge in a Jonsonian text. Both privilege the poet as writer: he is not an overt subject of either poem. In his encounter with "Something," we may wonder why he bothered to notice the lord and why the lord is so testy about their meeting, but those questions are precluded by the encounter as Jonson writes it and the ending as Jonson speaks it. His sole concern is to condemn the lord as a pompous coward; we are not permitted to speculate about the poet's motives. His speech is defined and bounded by the written narrative it adumbrates. When Jonson alludes to other texts, their writing adumbrates his speech. The idiom of Psalm 22, for example, in the satiric epigram on "Court-Worm," isolates the lord and heightens Jonson's attack when, in the last line, he delivers his satiric verdict in his own unmediated voice.

Speech and writing become metaphors that define friendship in the two poems to Goodyere. The true craft of art becomes a metaphor of true community. This use of speech and writing as interlocking metaphors marks Jonson as a Humanist, one who reads his friends like a book and whose book speaks their virtues. His art must give "voice" to Goodyere's "life, and deed." The deed for which he praises Goodyere, moreover, is a double act of reading, "making thy friends books, and thy books friends." Jonson's metaphor reenacts in poetry Goodyere's act in life.

Speech and writing become the actual subject of poetry in the epigrams to Alphonso Ferrabosco. In the first poem Jonson writes what he would say, only to declare "I yet had uttered nothing on thy part." His writing is held apart from what he has said and what he would say. The second epigram affirms the written permanence of a "work" even as Jonson admits its vulnerability to whatever "the hum'rous world" decides to say. Their speech is set against the art of musician and poet: "all mouths will judge, and their own way." The poet, however, insists on his autonomy, and urges Ferrabosco to insist on the same: "stand unto thyself."

Jonson exploits the duality of speech and writing in order to acknowledge the complexity of the occasion that evokes each poem and to shape our understanding of his poetic book. As his own editor, he creates a new aesthetic context, the "golden world" of the collection, for his occasional texts. Because he could not presume to know the readers of his book as he knew the people for whom he wrote each particular poem, he requires his readers to "study" and "understand" each poem as part of a collection, or as the preface to another book, or as part of his entire canon. The dualities of speech and writing, of poem as historical and as aesthetic event, adumbrate the double action of description and self-dramatization within each poem.

In the satiric poems that dominate the first half of *Epigrammes,* Jonson presents his vitriolic attack on false authority, whether political or literary (realms that inevitably overlap in the Jacobean system of literary patronage). The complimentary poems later in *Epigrammes* celebrate the true, mutual authority of the poet and his subjects. The last group of poems in the collection, including the epigrams to Ferrabosco, transfer the burden of authority to the audience. No single poem can fully epitomize the action of the book as a whole; together, all the poems in the collection provide a complex act of shared authority. Jonson's epigrams can be read as autonomous texts, but when they are set in place in *Epigrammes,* they can take on additional meaning as components of a larger act of writing. The book serves as a kind of megaphone to enhance the poet's voice in every text.

Although "The Hour-Glass" and "My Picture Left in Scotland" were later included in *Under-wood,* when Jonson originally sent them to Drummond there was no book to mediate between the historical occasion of the poems and the ahistorical aesthetic event of reading them. Even so, Jonson uses the act of writing to comment on speech. It is only by an accident of good fortune that Drummond chose to record his conversations with Jonson and to append the texts of these poems to his notes. Whether or not Jonson composed these poems especially for Drummond, they were sent to him as a kind of gloss on the conversation of two poets radically different in their ideas about writing poetry. The song equates art with life, as ideals never quite "expressed" in any single text. "My Picture Left in Scotland" sets eye against ear, writing against speech, as the poet laments that no act of reading a poem can overcome the lady's initial reading of his waist, his belly, and his rocky face. Writing, however, can address and supersede her reading by recording the harsh event. A second reader can sympathize with the poet's rueful self-recognition and can value the interplay of poetic voices in the text.

Speech and writing form the matrices by which we can graph Jonson's poetic voice in the three poems discussed in the sixth chapter of this book. "To the Memory of . . . William Shakespeare" (*U. V.* 26) pays tribute to a rival playwright's book; "An Execration upon Vulcan" (*Und.* 43) details Jonson's loss of his own library and manuscripts. Both poems are organized on the rhetorical pattern of the epideictic oration. Praising Shakespeare, Jonson speaks directly to him, and through him to the readers of the First Folio. Cursing Vulcan, Jonson incorporates the subsidiary imagined voices of the Puritan Brethren, a London crowd, Record Office clerks, even Vulcan himself. Jonson composed the third poem, "An Epistle Answering to One that Asked to be Sealed of the Tribe of Ben" (*Und.* 47) as intimate, non-rhetorical speech, close to the free play of conversation and introspection. The Tribe of Ben epistle can be read as a performative speech act: the last line, and by extension the entire poem, initiates the new friend into Jonson's friendship.[25]

All three poems share not only the illusion of the speaking voice but also a single pattern of figuration, the act of writing. Jonson praises Shakespeare's work in its dual character as performance and as written book, the "issue" of his mind. *Corpus*, a term that can mean both a body and a body of texts, is the governing trope of the "Execration." The dominant term in the Tribe of Ben epistle is "character," writing as a system of signs and a signifying of oneself. Although each of these poems conveys a strong sense of the poet's own feelings and beliefs, only the Tribe of Ben epistle, through its pun on "character," invites us to equate the poet's writing and the poet's "self." Only here, moreover, does the poet suggest an equation between the act of writing and the act of reading. Jonson vows to accept his new friend "As you have writ yourself" (77). Responding to the poem as it has unfolded, the friend reveals—writes—himself.

In the idiom of Derridean literary theory, "presence"—or the presentation

of self in art—is a trace of the deferring and differing alterity that *is* self.[26]
Something there is that does not love a word. In presenting himself con-
tingently—his voice occasioned by a courtier's rudeness, a friend's achievement, a lady's rejection, a publication, a fire, an initiation—Jonson retains
the capacity to remain significantly undefined and unreadable. Something of
Jonson is not, and cannot be, made wholly present in any occasion or in any
act of writing. Those who accept his poetic self-portrait as a total representation of self miss the crucial gap in his work. He himself will only claim to
"know myself / A little." Like Cupid, who cannot be caught in Jonson's
poetic net (*For.* 1), Ben Jonson slips through whatever hermeneutic net we
can devise. This study of his poetry, therefore, will attempt not to capture
the poet but to describe the different threads he weaves into his own net of
poetry and to discover what he can capture there. In other words, the
subject of this book is not Ben Jonson, but the action of his poetry as we can
replicate it in our own act of reading. Together, these actions constitute the
text.

Throughout his career, Jonson dislocates and relocates authority, so that it
resides not in the subject he addresses, not in the literary history he brings to
bear upon an occasion, and not even in his own voice within the text, but in
the relationships he inscribes among all these and with the reader. What
finally matters is the authority of relationships. These ground the wit of
Jonsonian art in community. There is no isolated play of mind in Jonson, no
introspective eccentricity or rhetorical indulgence in language for its own
sake. "Pure and neat Language I love, yet plaine and customary," he declares. "Metaphors far-fet hinder to be understood" (*Dis.* 1870–71, 1905–6).
Understanding can shape occasions into history, poems into books, people
into community. Understanding recognizes the value of autonomy as well,
the discrete text and occasion honoring the individual person. Wit negotiates
the competing claims of occasion and history, text and tradition, poem and
book, individual and community, poet and reader.

2

"Fair Acceptance": Jonson's Poetry of Love and Friendship

> The delivery of the most important things, may be carried with such a grace, as that it may yeeld a pleasure to the conceit of the Reader.
>
> (*Dis.* 2266–68)

William Camden trained Ben Jonson in the Humanist tradition, and Jonson's occasional poetry is informed by the continental ideas of Camden and other English Humanists. They construct and mediate his classicism and his ethical values.[1] The Humanist contexts of Jonsonian poetry provide a framework of ideas that are realized in the action of the particular text. Each poem, in its double participation in literary tradition and social discourse, reflects the tension in Humanism between detachment and engagement, between acts of private and public language.

Jonson defines his place in the Humanist tradition by exploring in self-dramatizing poetry two great themes of Renaissance literature: love and friendship. Petrarch served as his model for love poetry, Erasmus for his poetry of friendship. If, as Daniel Javitch argues, the poet replaced the courtier as the embodiment of Petrarchan ideals, in Jonson's work the poet replaces the orator and conversationalist as the embodiment of Erasmian ideals.[2] This replacement is formally inscribed in his procedure of converting prose drafts to poetic texts and in his incorporation of Erasmian language into his poems.

"A Celebration of Charis" represents Jonson's most complex work in the Petrarchan mode; "On Inviting a Friend to Supper" is paradigmatic of his Erasmian poetry. Despite their thematic differences, the lyric sequence and brief epistle share traits prominent in all his poetry: his often rueful self-

36

awareness; his insistence, nevertheless, on lofty poetic and social ideals; and his delight in language. In both poems he adopts a tone that mingles seriousness and play, and in that tone enacts the fundamental Humanist ideal of *libertas*.[3]

I

Whatever their differences, most of the writers who are usually labeled Renaissance Humanists construe the place and nature of the individual person as a major issue in their work. In this passage from *Discoveries*, Jonson describes a man quite like himself who ponders the problem of self as it affects his work. The nominal issue is the relationship between leisure and labor:

> I have knowne a man vehement on both sides; that knew no meane, either to intermit his studies, or call upon them againe. When hee hath set himselfe to writing, hee would joyne night to day; presse upon himselfe without release, not minding it, till he fainted: and when hee left off, resolve himselfe into all sports, and loosenesse againe; that it was almost a despaire to draw him to his booke: But once got to it, hee grew stronger, and more earnest by the ease. His whole Powers were renew'd: he would worke out of himselfe, what hee desired; but with such excesse, as his study could not bee rul'd: hee knew not how to dispose his owne Abilities, or husband them, hee was of that immoderate power against himselfe. (*Dis.* 824–36)

Not just two attitudes toward work but two theories of self are set against each other in this portrait. They correspond to two concepts of "self" that Richard Lanham describes as constant rivals for supremacy in the West: *homo rhetoricus* and *homo seriosus*.[4] Rhetorical man has no constant, central "self," but becomes whatever role he plays. *Homo seriosus* assumes a constant self underlies all role-playing and tests its validity; such a man can husband his abilities and "worke out of himselfe, what hee desired." For rhetorical man, language is the means of becoming; for *homo seriosus*, language ideally is transparent, revealing the essential self beneath the surface of style. Although Jonson privileges *homo seriosus* over *homo rhetoricus*, the comments on language that conclude this (self?) portrait admit the power of both attitudes toward language:

> Nor was hee only a strong, but an absolute *Speaker*, and *Writer*: but his subtilty did not shew it selfe; his judgement thought that a vice. For the ambush hurts more that is hid. Hee never forc'd his language, nor went out of the high-way of *speaking*; but for some great necessity, or apparent

profit. For hee denied *Figures* to be invented for ornament, but for ayde; and still thought it an extreme madnesse to bend, or wrest that which ought to be right. (*Dis.* 837–45)

The metaphors of force, divergence, ambush, and madness argue the dangerous power not of Euphuistic "subtilty" but of thought and language that are not under absolute control. These metaphors figure forth actions *homo rhetoricus* could regard as generative self-discoveries and *homo seriosus* would condemn as vice. "The best education," Lanham insists, "has always put the two views of life into profound and fruitful collision."[5] In the Humanist formulation of this conflict, Petrarch and Erasmus stand at opposite extremes.[6]

Petrarch, whose monumental discovery of self Thomas Greene has called "an event in European intellectual history," was irresistibly drawn to many roles: secular recluse, lover, scholarly philologist and bibliophile, poet laureate, public counselor, friend, perpetual wanderer. Describing how Petrarch cast these familiar roles into new and unprecedented shapes, Greene declares that Petrarch "achieved, simply by living as fully as he did, a freedom which to him was terrible in its confusing and distracting disorder, but a freedom which remained and still remains to us a token of his greatness."[7] At times, he despaired of ever reconciling or integrating his various roles into "the one, the good, the true, the secure, the abiding."[8] As *homo rhetoricus*, he longs for the security of *homo seriosus*, yet the compelling attractiveness of the many different roles he played seemed always at odds with his search for a unitary self. The collision was entirely personal; Petrarch was not an educator, and took no particular interest in guiding others in their search for self-definition.

Erasmus was as various in his role-playing as Petrarch, but in place of Petrarch's profound ontological doubts he adopted a cool, ironic skepticism toward the power of any individual apart from the structures of a linguistic, moral, or social discipline (with the exception of his sardonic refusal to obey the ecclesiastical regulations mandating the consumption of fish). As *homo seriosus*, he took great pleasure in studying the intricacies of those structures, and by muting his own presence seemed to play the part of *homo rhetoricus*. As educators, moreover, Erasmus and his northern colleagues systematically explored ways to reconcile the different roles they played and the modes of thought they entertained. Self-dramatization for Erasmus did not occasion anguish but served as a focal point for the dramatization of ideas about ethical action—that is, about the ideal relationship between self and society.

When Jonson defines himself as a Humanist, he does so by stressing ethical judgment in the manner of Erasmus. In the preface to *Epigrammes*, Jonson derides "ignorant and guilty mouths" who fear his astute moral judgment and who "hold their dear mountebank or jester in far better condition, then all the study or studiers of humanity." The phrase "study or studiers of humanity" translates the Humanist term *studia humanitatis*, and it is as a Humanist that Jonson refers to his collection as "the ripest of my studies." He does not commit himself to a programmatic exercise in Humanist theory; each poem records a specific moment and has its own specific dramatic requirements. However, his poems enact, in all their variety and vigor, his Humanist commitment to poetry as ethical action. His other Humanist principles radiate from that commitment.

Jonson's position as a professional poet makes him unusual among English Humanists. He could have been a professional educator; such a choice might have been predicted for a young scholar who had neither wealth nor title. *Discoveries* may contain Jonson's notes for a course in rhetoric he planned to teach at Gresham College (although this argument is highly speculative), and it explicitly records advice Jonson offered a nobleman concerning the proper education of his sons (1636 ff.). In line with the Humanist education Jonson himself had received, he urges that the boys be sent to school rather than tutored at home, recommends the reading of classical poets, historians, and philosophers, and sets forth a method of composition based on the imitation of their texts. Jonson's advice is itself an example of such imitation: much of it is based on Quintilian's *De Institutio Oratoria*. But Jonson preferred none of the careers common to Humanists: he was neither teacher nor scholar, clergyman nor government official. These careers may have been denied him because he had no university degree, but he came to stand foremost among the young men who moved out from the schools to pursue careers as professional writers.

As a man whose own formal education stopped short of university training, Jonson seems on the one hand to out-Humanist the Humanists in his emphasis on learning, and on the other hand to defend poetry against the rigidity of scholars. In *Discoveries,* Jonson compares the poet to the orator, doubtless mindful that the first Humanists were rhetoricians who centered their attention on the spoken word rather than on written texts: "The *Poet* is the neerest Borderer upon the Orator, and expresseth all his vertues, though he be tyed more to numbers; is his equall in ornament, and above him in his strengths" (2528–31). Jonson is quoting Cicero's *De Oratore* (1.16.70), which declares poetry limited by "numbers" but freer in other uses of language. A few lines later, Jonson returns to the issue of the poet's freedom: "I am not of that opinion to conclude a *Poets* liberty within the narrowe limits of lawes, which either the *Grammarians*, or *Philosophers* prescribe. For, before they found out those Lawes, there were many excellent Poets, that fulfill'd them" (2555–59). He takes pains to declare that the poet's ethical role is not precluded by other Humanist-dominated professions:

> I could never thinke the study of *Wisdome* confin'd only to the *Philosopher:* or of *Piety* to the *Divine:* or of *State* to the *Politicke.* But that he which can faine a *Common-wealth* (which is the *Poet*) can governe it with *Counsels,* strengthen it with *Lawes,* correct it with *Iudgements,* informe it with *Religion,* and *Morals:* is all these. Wee doe not require in him meere *Elocution;* or an excellent faculty in verse; but the exact knowledge of all vertues, and their contraries; with the ability to render the one lov'd, the other hated, by his proper embattaling them. (*Dis.* 1032–41)

As Jonson's Oxford editors note, the poet has once again turned to Quintilian.[9] He may also have had in mind a passage from Sidney's *Apology for Poetry* commenting on philosophy, poetry, and Thomas More. Sidney, himself alluding in a general way to Quintilian, argues that the poet is a moral guide superior to all others:

> But even in the most excellent determination of goodness, what philosopher's counsel can so readily direct a prince as the feigned *Cyrus* in *Xenophon,* or a virtuous man in all fortunes, as *Aeneas* in *Virgil,* or a whole commonwealth, as the way of Sir Thomas More's *Utopia?* I say the way, because where Sir Thomas More erred, it was the fault of the man and not of the poet, for that way of patterning a commonwealth was most absolute, though he perchance hath not so absolutely performed it.[10]

It was the obligation of the Humanist to secure a place as moral spokesman for society, but that obligation posed special problems for a professional poet not born to wealth or power. We cannot know if Jonson shared Sidney's opinion of *Utopia;* we have only the statment in *Discoveries* that More was among those "for their times admirable: and the more, because they began Eloquence with us" (904). Certainly Jonson did not follow More in creating an entirely fictive commonwealth, the achievement for which Sidney praises him. More, as a public official, may have found it effective and discreet to write in a fictive mode. Jonson, born an outsider, may have found it advantageous to form his commonwealth of actual men and women, and thereby to secure for himself a place in a community he valued.[11]

Thus far, both Jonson and Humanism would seem to be entirely serious. However, an ethical poetics does not preclude play. Rather, both poet and reader must know when to play and how. Not for Jonson the verbal pyrotechnics and highjinks, the enticing but empty rhetoric, the deceitful, self-serving role-playing of his own great mountebank, Volpone. Jonson offers his audience not snake oil but freedom—the *libertas* that is the most fundamental Humanist ideal. *Libertas* allows for—in fact is characterized by—wit. When one thinks of Erasmus and More, the founders of English Humanism, one is as apt to cherish their wit as admire their moral grandeur. So also Ben Jonson.[12] His defense of poetry in *Discoveries* suggests that he values poetry for the pleasure it gives as well as for the efficacy of its moral teaching—and, true to the Horatian paradigm of this theory, the pleasure and teaching of poetry are inseparable:

> The Study of it (if wee will trust *Aristotle*) offers to mankinde a certaine rule and Patterne of living well, and happily; disposing us to all Civil offices of Society. If wee will believe *Tully*, it nourisheth, and instructeth our Youth; delights our Age, adornes our prosperity; comforts our Adversity; entertaines us at home; keepes us company abroad, travailes with us; watches; divides the times of our earnest, and sports; shares in our Country recesses, and recreations; . . . And, wheras, they entitle *Philosophy* to bee a rigid, and austere *Poesie:* they have (on the other hand) stiled *Poesy* a dulcet and gentle *Philosophy,* which leades on, and guides us by the hand to Action, with a ravishing delight, and incredible Sweetnes. (*Dis.* 2386–2400)

Like so many passages in *Discoveries,* these lines blend general allusion (to Aristotle) with close literal translation (of Cicero's *Pro Archia* and Strabo's *Geographia*). Jonson has also added one relevant phrase of his own, reminiscent of Chaucer's idea that poetry exists "twixt ernest and game." Poetry, Jonson declares, "divides the times of our earnest, and sports," It is the poet's function to lead his readers toward play as well as seriousness; some poems serve "the times of our earnest," others our "sports."

Because Jonson sets a moral framework for his poetry, he has the freedom to play. Play is essential to *libertas:* to be free is to be able to play, securely, frankly, and without guile. But if liberty, honesty, and simplicity are to be more than license, crudeness, and simple-mindedness, play requires the daring of a Petrarch and the emotional and intellectual poise of an Erasmus. It is the Humanists who instructed Jonson in play as well as in ethics. The result can be seen in his comedies: not moralistic exposure of vice but magnificent contraptions of plot, language, and even physical objects (Volpone's schemes, the alchemist's furnace, the whole system of Bartholomew Fair) enthrall the audience, contraptions that please us in their construction and final collapse alike.[13]

The poems are more subtle, more limited in scope, and more overtly personal than the plays. Both "A Celebration of Charis" and "On Inviting a Friend to Supper" combine the serious and the playful. The sequence of lyrics proceeds from the serious to the playful, the invitational epigram from the playful to the serious. In Charis's portrait of her ideal man and in the final crude joke of an unnamed lady bystander, the "Celebration" mocks the serious desire that motivated the poet's game. "On Inviting a Friend to Supper" begins by mocking the poet's own fantasy of promised bounty but ends with a serious vow of trust and intimate good will. Far from indicating the poet's paradoxical, contradictory, or confused nature, this poetry reveals his understanding of the range of feelings and tones possible in love and friendship. Jonson shares the Humanist desire to address our entire experience—"the times of our earnest, and sports." In each of these poems, he creates a privileged sphere of play, grounded in his tact and care. He seeks from Charis and from his unnamed guest a "fair acceptance" that he cannot assume as each poem begins. He sets up a special relationship with the lady and with his guest, which he protects from the crudeness or violence of the unworthy as each poem ends. Intimate and urbane, these poems present Jonson's poised mastery of Humanist possibilities. His distinctive poetic tone can encompass the apparent opposition of seriousness and play.

II

Jonson's own comments on Petrarch suggest that he reacted strongly to the poetry others had written imitating Petrarchan forms. Jonson includes Petrarch and Laura in the list of famous poetic lovers in "An Ode" (*Und.* 28), but his comments elsewhere betray a hostility to the kind of love poetry that had proliferated in imitation of Petrarch's sonnets. Jonson, writes Drummond, "cursed petrarch for redacting Verses to Sonnets, which he said were like that Tirrants bed, wher some who were too short were racked, others too long cut short." The comment is reminiscent of Jonson's "Fit of Rhyme Against Rhyme," in which the poet, despite his own exploitation of rhyme, attacks it as "the rack of finest wits" (*Und.* 29). Lady Would-Be, an Englishwoman on the loose in Volpone's Venice, predictably disregards such matters of poetic craft and judges Petrarch "passionate" in her comic summary of Italian literature (*Volpone*, 3.5.93). Herford and the Simpsons conclude that the rigidity, not the intimacy, of the sonnet from offended Jonson, and that Petrarch was less at fault than his extravagant imitators.[14]

Jonson's great debt would have been to Petrarch's idea of self and to the ideas about language, literature, and community which complemented that new sense of individuality. It was the governing principle of Petrarchan Humanism that one could learn from oneself by examining and describing all the nuances of human feeling, memory, and image making evoked in a specific moment of experience. Eloquence and verbal artifice were directed toward that expression. Petrarch used love poetry as a way to explore his experience and to investigate how close to adequate language might be, but Petrarch's imitators had become formulaic and brittle in their witty passion. Jonson's protest against their rigid formalism and inflated style can best be understood as a protest against any use of language that constrains the very expressiveness it should facilitate.[15]

Petrarch's ideas about literature and community are clearly dramatized in his familiar letters, which are modeled on those of Cicero.[16] These letters reclaim for the Renaissance the classical ideal of friendship, but it is lifted to the realm of personal fantasy in the fourth book when the "friends" to whom Petrarch writes include Horace and Virgil. Fundamental to this fantastic play is the serious ideal of timeless community that Jonson shares with Petrarch. This ideal can be realized only in the work of the living, a work of self-definition in accord with the remembered virtue of the dead. Petrarch's letters construe friendship, whether with the living or with the dead, as an occasion for self-definition.

Love, even more than friendship, presented Petrarch with an occasion for knowing himself. As Neoplatonist, he sought to go beyond his lady, and even beyond self-knowledge, in order to contemplate Divine Beauty, Goodness, and Love. Yet Petrarch's attention remained centered on himself, the self that was so puzzling a mixture of limitation and possibility. As he writes in the *Secretum:* "I do not think to become as God, or to inhabit eternity, or to embrace heaven and earth. Such glory as belongs to men is enough for me. That is all I sigh after. Mortal myself, it is but mortal blessings I desire."[17]

The dilemmas of possibility and limitation inherent in Petrarch's model of love poetry and epistemology were explored with varying degrees of sophistication by the sonneteers who imitated him. The conflict between action and contemplation, between experience and transcendence, between mortality and idea, became the major concern of continental poets. Among English poets, the claims of experience, action, and mortality seem especially strong. Typical, if atypically vivid, is the frustration of Sidney's Astrophil, who clambers up the Neoplatonic ladder of love only to admit that "Desire still cries, 'Give me some food.' "[18]

Jonson's Petrarchan poems to ladies reflect the English emphasis. Both he and the ladies he compliments remain firmly in the actual world. He uses Petrarchan motifs to define his ideal relationship to them, often with a rueful awareness of his own shortcomings: his age, his mountain belly, his rocky face. For his ladies, on the other hand, actuality measures not their limitations but their excellence. Anne Ferry has noted that Jonson praises the Countess of Bedford as 'Bedford' rather than the more easily metaphorized 'Lucy' and that "to celebrate 'Bedford' is to insist on her actuality outside the mythological world created by the language of the poem."[19] In another poem, Jonson does praise her as "Lucy, you brightness of our sphere," at once day-star and evening star to poets (*Ep.* 94). The point of the poem is the inadequacy of even that extravagant metaphor, much as, in a compliment to Lady Mary Wroth, all mythic figures are judged inferior to her actuality (*Ep.* 105). Anne Ferry, contrasting Sidney's sonnets and Jonson's compliment to Lady Cary (*Ep.* 126), notes that "The mythological world of Jonson's narrative is placed in relation to the actual geographical and social world evoked by 'Hampton' and 'Cary.' "[20] Even Jonson's amorous songs, polished redactions of Catullan lyric, often measure the world of love in terms of the actual English world: the poet seeks kisses that equal in number "All the grass that Romney yields, / Or the sands in Chelsea fields, / Or the drops in silver Thames" (*For.* 6).

Jonson's own Petrarchan imitations use actuality to test or to transform the Petrarchan situation. These poems include songs, monologues, and narratives (*Und.* 2–11). Several, including "A Celebration of Charis," give voice to the lady. "The Musical Strife" is a "pastoral dialogue" for "He" and "She" (*Und.* 3); two songs defending woman's inconstancy (ideal replies to Donne's witty exercise on that theme) and a third tracing the comic torment of "A Nymph's Passion" (*Und.* 5–7) are written for a woman's voice. Two songs in the voice of a male poet-lover acknowledge the frustrations and complex feelings each glance of his lady can evoke ("Oh, do not wanton with those eyes"—*Und.* 4) and prove that a lover can find an emblem of his own desires and fears even in an hourglass (*Und.* 8). The last three poems in this group are comic self-portraits: "My Picture Left in Scotland," "Against Jealousy," and "The Dream." In each of them, the poet laughs at his own experience, setting his strength as poet against his frailty as lover. Although "My Picture Left in Scotland" is the most complex and rewarding of these comic poems, the epigrammatic ending of "Against Jealousy" ("I ne'er will owe my health to a disease") and the clever narrative turns of "The Dream" deserve to be better known. These poems give a comic cast to the Petrarchan situation, either because they are spoken by "realistic" women, or because they insist on "reality testing"—measuring either love or the love-poet against quotidian fact.

"A Celebration of Charis," Jonson's most extensive attempt to write in the Petrarchan mode, adds to the complex self-dramatization of the poet the additional complexity of narrative action.[21] In "A Celebration of Charis," Jonson creates a narrative for "Love's world," the poet's wit and play poised against the court world of callous manipulation and hapless isolation. Jonson begins with a self-conscious announcement that he is trying something new, no less surprising to his readers than to him: "Let it not your wonder move, / Less your laughter, that I love," he pleads (*Und.* 2.1.1–2). His sequence plays our initial laughter at him against our pleasure in his poetry.

Jonson's sequence begins with descriptions of his own frailty and the lady's beauty, proceeds through various contests of wit and wordplay, and ends with an unnamed lady's coarse sexual joke. This kind of sequence, featuring three speaking characters, required a style larger in scope than the moral praise or moral censure prominent in so many of his poems. Jonson found such a style in a classical treatise by Demetrius, *On Style*, which was widely reprinted during the Renaissance and presumably was known to Jonson. Demetrius postulates four categories of style: the eloquent, the forceful, the plain, and the elegant. Much of Jonson's poetry, Wesley Trimpi argues, is written in the "plain style," and he repeatedly cites Demetrius as an influence on Renaissance understanding of plainness.[22] But Demetrius' concept of elegance is of interest here. The main characteristic of elegant writing, according to Demetrius, is *charis,* or grace. Ben Jonson celebrates his lady in the style that bore her name.

"Charis," a mixed style of elegant wit, could draw on plainness and ornateness at will, could play when other styles could not. "Elegance of expression," writes Demetrius, "includes graceful pleasantries and gay, genial speech. Some pleasantries—those of the poets—are loftier and more dignified, while others are more commonplace and jocular, resembling gibes" (128).[23] His most recent translator, G. M. A. Grube, protests that any classification which presumes to encompass the description of Nausicaa and the jokes of the Cyclops is so vague as to be "faulty" and useless.[24] Jonson's "Celebration of Charis" can be cited in reply, for the narrative covers just such a range. The sequence dramatizes Jonson's perception of Charis, of himself, of wit and love, using the ever-shifting relationship of the elegant and the comic. He exploits "charis" as a style of "ilaros logos"—"a certain bright playfulness of expression," according to Demetrius.[25] As the sequence begins, Ben has a proper object for his poetry; he seeks the proper style. He finds it by using all the resources Demetrius includes under the rubric of "charis." Such a style, marked by humor, urbanity, and evanescent surface, suits a mature would-be lover and his kind of compliment.

Such a style also suits a Humanist eager to explore the possibilities of language and the connections between desire and control mediated by play. The "Celebration of Charis" is a game, and reveals its playful character in the several games it contains. Ben debates Cupid, implicitly competes with the court for Charis's favor, and uses witty repartee to win a kiss—and then another—from her. There are even allusions to games, from billiards to the Judgment of Paris.

Ben begins as an obviously unfit player in the game of love: he is too old and too fat, his only assets "the language, and the truth." The syntax and vocabulary of the first lyric are formal, serious, and earnest, but its trochaic tetrameter, conventionally a comic form, would have predisposed anyone reading "let it not your wonder move. / Less your laughter, that I love" at least to smile. In the mingled formality and comedy of the first poem the double tone of earnest and sport that makes the play of the sequence possible is already present.[26] The joke is reversed in his first description of Charis:

> . . . this is she,
> Of whose beauty it was sung,
> She shall make the old man young,
> Keep the middle age at stay,

> And let nothing high decay,
> Till she be the reason why
> All the world for love may die.
>
>   (1.18–24)

The wit of these elegant lines depends on our knowledge of Ben, the wistful lover, with his gray hairs and fifty years, who invests these clichés with a wish for magic as well as love.

If Ben is to be more than a mock-heroic buffoon, aping Cupid but all too much resembling oafish Hercules, he must work the transformation through wit. "Her Triumph," his song, works that transformation—at once dramatizing the poet at his best, without self-mockery, and describing the idealized lady in images of unparalleled delicacy. The lady's triumphant progress through "Love's world" is mirrored in the poetry. Just as she reconciles the "elements' strife," so the poet's language reconciles a variety of literary traditions and even competing metrical norms to create an effect of unobtrusive, perfect simplicity.[27] The song is Ben's triumph as well as hers, his display of "the language and the truth" that can transform him, at least for a moment, into a worthy suitor. Appropriating Ovid, Martial, Ficino, Spenser, native ballads, even his own masques and plays, Jonson creates a mythic portrait of a lady whose beauty exceeds even those "words that soothe her" (4.16):[28]

> Have you seen but a bright lily grow,
>   Before rude hands have touched it?
> Have you marked but the fall o' the snow,
>   Before the soil hath smutched it?
> Have you felt the wool o' the beaver?
>   Or swan's down ever?
> Or have smelled o' the bud o' the briar?
>   Or the nard i' the fire?
>   Or have tasted the bag o' the bee?
> O so white! O so soft! O so sweet is she!
>
>   (4.21–30)

The lyric, which begins as masque mythology and ends as pastoral, draws on allusion, anaphora, metaphor, simile, parallelism, hyperbole, and subtle rhythmic variation, all included by Demetrius under the stylistic category of "charis" (142–80). These disparate elements, each common enough in poetry, coalesce to celebrate Charis. The song praises what it is; poetic style and poetic subject are one. William Spanos and Roger Sale have noticed how purely fictive Charis is made to seem; Jonson's analogies envision an experience never attained but only imaginable.[29] The more perfected such play, the more fragile and cherished.[30]

The seventh poem marks the climax of Ben's success. He has played the game of love and language well, celebrating Charis with the public rites of poetry and the private indulgence of deliberate parody. He has teased and trapped her into a pleased response: she has kissed him. Now in the eighth lyric, he gives her a chance to be an actor in the game, gives her the autonomy and freedom he has enjoyed. Instead of portraying her only as the object of desire, he urges her to take her part as a desiring character, to "tell / What a man she could love well" (8.3–4).

In both the seventh and eighth lyrics, the word "lightly" is the key to the poet's tone. Charis has "Lightly promised" to describe her ideal man, and Ben impatiently anticipates her "work," only to find it just a web of excuses as she plays a teasing game of her own. Her delay provokes an equally teasing threat from Ben: he will harass her until she can neither eat nor sleep, primp nor gaze out her window at handsome passersby. The eighth lyric is an appropriately playful threat, made as "lightly" as was her promise. The punishments are those suited to the sophisticated ease of a game: other pastimes (toying with new makeup and new men) will be denied her on the comic Day of Judgment.

The undertone of seriousness in both lyrics stems from the force of desire. "A Celebration of Charis" depends on the tension between serious desire and play, as the stakes in the game inevitably rise from one kiss to many to "love." But even as Ben's demands grow, he reasserts the controlling framework of play. Desire lends special power to the fourth and seventh songs, but the immediate reversion in each case to public rather than private contest—after the fourth song a debate with Cupid, after the seventh a court discussion of love—shifts the tone and the perspective away from possibly dangerous feelings. Desire, which motivates Ben to engage in the game, is controlled by it. Destruction of the play-world will not come from him.

Nor will it come from Charis, who values the control she can exert in game. Her reply to Ben shows that she is fully aware of the game's requirements and values. She responds to him with a "dictamen" that catches up all his previous strategies and foibles. This playful reversal is not an unwitting self-indictment, nor is it a satire on Jacobean values. A charming woman mocks her suitor's pretensions, using humor to make us aware that she is not to be taken seriously. She is not to be taken at all. Following Ben's lead, she too plays at love's school, and her description of the ideal conveys her indirect refusal to move outside the world of game. She teasingly describes a man who could be almost anyone *except* Ben. The "fashion" she wants is French, and she never alludes to the "language" he so hopefully listed as his best asset and so memorably used to describe "Her Triumph." Her ideal lover has other qualities: "crisped hair" touched with gold, and a "cheek (withal) / Smooth as is the billiard ball" (9.19–20). She wants a lover virtuous and young, ardent yet temperate, gentle in manner as well as in rank, free from any baseness or powerful emotion. In a word, someone controllable: "his lips should kissing teach, / Till he cherished too much beard, / And make Love or me afeared" (9.22–24). Her catalogue deliberately echoes Ben's praise of her beauty in the fourth song. She alludes, as he had, to the softness of down, to the untouched whiteness of snow, to arched brows and "what we harmony do call" (9.34), turning Ben's own words against him. These echoes emphasize the reversal of roles implicit when she takes the initiative and describes a man in the reductive terms that are inevitable whenever a person functions as an object or objectification of desire. Only in the last few lines (9.41–52) does she allude to the "truth" Ben had relied upon so confidently. Even then, she paints a portrait of honesty and integrity more notable for its negative qualities than for any positive ideal. In her witty "dictamen," Jonson indirectly acknowledges the limits of love and poetry as he playfully, but pointedly, dramatizes Ben's dim prospects for success.

Charis's statement, "Lightly promised" and lightly given, concludes with a declaration that she is independent of the claims of love:

> Such a man, with every part,
> I could give my very heart;
> But of one, if short he came,
> I can rest me where I am.
>
> (9.53–56)

We see in Charis a woman of attractive self-sufficiency.[31] If her suitor lacks any of the traits she mentioned, she will offhandedly dismiss him. She may, of course, almost mean that she will continue to receive Ben's suit until the perfect man appears, an event which may never occur. Charis can tease, can play, can pun with assurance. She has spoken, she says, "Of your trouble, Ben to ease *me*" (9.1, emphasis added). She is withdrawing from her role as Ben's ideal while at the same time cementing her status as an unattainable woman—but on her terms rather than his.

"Another lady" present at this "hearing" has none of this grace or poise. Lacking Charis's humor and ability to pun, the unnamed lady sees in Charis's last remark only the most vulgar possibility: "What you please you parts may call, / 'Tis one good part I'd lie withal" (10.7–8). Her gibe ends the sequence, which has moved from Ben's "excuse for loving" to his "example" (3.26) of love to this abrupt "exception." The critical discomfort at Jonson's decision to end "A Celebration of Charis" with this joke may result from a lingering remnant of Victorian propriety, a standard not to be confused with the decorum Jonson valued. The comic lady-in-waiting is, after all, a perennial character, giving her practical, earthy advice to Phaedra, to Juliet, to Desdemona. Such a character provides basic vitality in idealistic, romantic tragedy, but in no way diminishes the stature or virtue of the heroine. Here, too, the contrast between Charis and her uncouth companion serves to enhance Charis rather than to detract from her grace. Charis could not have been so coarse.

The conventional presentation of a foil can hardly justify Jonson's decision to end "A Celebration of Charis" with this poem. An explanation can be better sought in the nature of game itself. The world of play is fragile, easily shattered by external events or by changes in the players themselves. To quote Johan Huizinga:

> At any moment "ordinary life" may reassert its rights, either by an impact from without which interrupts the game, or by an offence against the rules, or else from within, by a collapse of the play spirit, a sobering, a disenchantment.[32]

We might speculate that the tenth poem presents a sudden intrusion of reality into the world of game. "Reality," though, has been present as an alternative world throughout the "Celebration," in the social banter, in the seductive seventh lyric, even in the sublimated court and pastoral metaphors of the fourth song. The poet's imagination, dismissed as an inconsequential "toy" by the unnamed lady, has played a game of love which increasingly is set in tension against the play of passion.

The last poem is the end of the game, a necessary comic ending similar in function to "On the Famous Voyage" that ends Jonson's *Epigrammes*. It is the best way—perhaps the only way—to finish a game which, from this point on, could only be tiresome. The last speaker's phallic humor comments reductively on Charis's ideal man, and indeed on the whole act of courtship, and once play has become subject to this kind of joke, the game is over. Charis's *double entendre*, to be possible at all, requires a perfect balance of plausible meanings. The last poem, which sweeps away every alternative but one, ends the sequence at the necessary and convenient point, without doing violence to the characters of Ben and Charis. They may not have suffered "a collapse of the play spirit, a sobering, a disenchantment," but the other lady's comment has certainly violated the rules of the game.

To see the last poem as a comic necessity suits the play-quality of the "Celebration." Play, like comedy, contains within itself all possible amplification and all possible reduction. We delight in that coherent, completed "sphere of activity with a disposition all of its own."[33] The comic ending of this game shelters Ben from the pain of defeat and preserves both the game and its players from disillusionment. A game, even a romantic one, does not require the kind of narrative satisfaction we derive from a happy ending (as in Spenser's *Amoretti* and *Epithalamion*) or a sad one (as in Sidney's *Astrophil and Stella*). We delight simply in playing the game to the full. Amplification, which we see in "Her Triumph" and "On Begging Another Kiss," and reduction, which we see in the final lyric, are complementary developments in the realm of bright word play. The game is played to its limits, and then is put aside.[34]

Jonson's "Celebration" emphasizes the play of wit and love, not satiric disaffection or deep psychic anxiety. The sequence traces a game played by two sophisticated people at court. To win the confident, clever Charis requires from Jonson a blend of admiration and assured wit—the latter at his own expense. Satire is present in the "Celebration," coloring the portrayal of the court, of Ben, of courtship and human longings. He is ill at ease in the role of lover, and the satiric tinge of the sequence indicates that any sane man would do well to share his distrust. But to interpret the lyrics as entirely satiric neglects the playful self-dramatization of the poet, his delighted mastery of his own role, the rich allusiveness and formal variety of the verse, and the teasing ambivalence of the courtship itself. He learned from Petrarch how to locate himself 'twixt earnest and sport. That is not to say Jonson was torn between one and the other. As he remarks in *Discoveries,* quoting Seneca, "There cannot be one colour of the mind; an other of the wit. If the mind be staid, grave, and compos'd, the wit is so; that vitiated, the other is blowne, and deflower'd" (948–50). This sequence sets the vitiated wit of the unnamed lady against the composed wit of Charis and her poet.

III

Petrarchan love poetry had been the vehicle for expressing ideas and values central to the Italian Renaissance, but for Jonson the mode of Erasmian Humanism proved more congenial. The Northern Humanists took community as their dominant value. Underlying all their work is the assumption that one person can learn from another person's thought. They sought and formed community through correspondence and conversation, through translation, imitation, and exegesis. The search for community influenced their choice of professional activities: they were educators, translators, scholarly editors and commentators. Their educational program and their Christian philosophy centered on ethics, on human conduct in society; even the contemplation of God often yielded to the more immediate goal of proper Christian action. Friendship, not erotic love, provided them with a literary motif suitable to their search for self-knowledge and for the ideal community. The enclosed garden became the setting not for courtship but for the conversation of close friends.

Despite the neat contrast suggested in the preceding paragraph, the relationship between Petrarchan and Erasmian Humanism is not easy to untangle. Both attempt to reconcile Christianity and classicism; both value language as word in the service of the Word; both set as the first rule of

Christian life a classical precept, *nosce teipsum*. Erasmus believed that his work constituted an advance over Petrarch's: "I brought it about that humanism, which savored of nothing but Paganism, began nobly to celebrate Christ."[35] Yet Erasmus's great contemporary and adversary, Martin Luther, is known to have "felt (as some modern scholars feel) that what Erasmus effected was the very reverse of this program."[36] The intricacies of the controversy need not be rehearsed or resolved in a study of Ben Jonson's poetry. What is relevant is the simple but fundamental difference in the formulation of the central Humanist experience as private introspection emblemized by the contemplation of human and divine love, or as shared friendship emblemized by feast and dialogue. After writing a series of comic Petrarchan poems, Jonson rejected the Petrarchan model of introspective poetry. He finally chose as his major task the poetic enactment of Erasmian friendship. Such friendship is also marked by the free play of mind between the extremes of earnest and sport, the *lusus* valued by the cool, controlled Erasmus and the hot, impassioned Jonson.[37]

Jonson's most characteristic poems, and many of his finest, describe and dramatize friendship. Variations of the words "friend" and "friendship" resound through his poems, occurring 124 times.[38] Jonson celebrates friendships—of Henry Morison and Lucius Cary, of John Selden and Edward Hayward—and praises men who fulfill the offices of a friend. Sir Benjamin Rudyerd's affection for the Earl of Pembroke, for example, "proves" that "holiest friendship" exists in the real world and can be preserved in art (*Ep.* 122). The poet may place himself in the role of admirer, almost intruder on other men's friendships, but more often he celebrates his own friendships with such men as Alphonso Ferrabosco, Francis Beaumont, Sir John Roe, John Donne. Even his poems to women bespeak an intimacy better described as friendship than flirtation. Writing to the Countess of Bedford, for example, Jonson offers friendship as a model for the ideal relationship between poet and reader: "Rare poems ask rare friends" (*Ep.* 94). Most of his poems, however, are addressed to men, and take as occasion and subject matter Jonson's experience of friendship.

Jonson's ideas about friendship are entirely congruent with the moral ideals set forth in Aristotle's *Nichomachean Ethics*, which had been translated into an English school text by John Wylkynson in 1547.[39] The philosophy of friendship that Jonson could have learned at school became a practical tool as he pursued his literary career. A man without father or brothers, making his way in London with only wit and talent to help him, Jonson turned to friendship not as a moral platitude or a solace but as a necessity. In the anonymous city, each person had to create a community of friends, chosen because of shared interests, values, personal affinity, or at least temporary usefulness. Jonson made a virtue of that necessity and recognized in the occasion of need the reason for the ideals he espoused. His poems of friendship, therefore, anchor his Humanist ideals in harsh reality and in the actual experience of friendship that helped make that harshness bearable.

Paradigmatic among his poems of friendship is the long epigram, really a brief epistle, "On Inviting a Friend to Supper" (*Ep.* 101). The poet describes the promised evening, trying to whet his guest's appetite for good food, good talk, and good company. The invitation enacts what it promises: the poet plans the menu (including the shopping trip to procure special items), outlines the entertainment, turns with special pleasure to the thought of good talk over good wine, and even envisions the fond memories the morning after will bring. This narrative line gives continuity and unity to a poetic feast of language that brings together learned allusion and homely proverb, poetry and pastry, fact and wish. Like the friendship it promises and seeks, the poem defines, balances, and ultimately affirms a range of ideas and images.

"Tonight, grave sir, both my poor house and I / Do equally desire your company" (1–2). The poet not only describes the promised evening, but dramatizes his effort to make the resources of his "poor house" equal to his desire and to his guest's "worth." The account of the menu marks the first step in the drama. It begins straightforwardly enough, but the orderly presentation of dishes falls into disarray as the poet piles up more and more courses, ending with a catalogue of virtually indistinguishable gamebirds: "partridge, pheasant, woodcock . . . godwit . . . Knat, rail and ruff, too" (18–20). Qualifications, however, intrude on his extravagant imaginings: "[You shall have] a short-legged hen, / If we can get her" (11–12); "a coney / Is not to be despaired of, for our money" (13–14); "And though fowl now be scarce . . . we may have larks" (15–16). Jonson finally takes three steps back from his promise of such lavish bounty: ". . . some / May yet be there . . . if we can" (18–19). His vision testifies less to his provender than to his desire: "I'll tell you of more, and lie, so you will come" (17).

Throughout his description of the supper, the poet contrives to be at once excessive and understated. The gap between extravagance and modesty is marked by good humor, not discomfort, as the intricate interplay of promise and qualification, certainty and doubt, becomes an expression of Jonson's eager attempt to secure the "fair acceptance" of his friend. On that acceptance everything else depends. The fourth couplet is the key to the poem: "It is the fair acceptance, sir, creates / The entertainment perfect, not the cates" (7–8). In pairing "entertainment" and "cates," Jonson precisely balances words which are in one sense synonymous but which also have quite different meanings. Both words can mean "a meal," but "cates" has an older, more limited meaning: it designates food that is purchased rather than homegrown. Jonson, as a city dweller, admits that his menu is contingent on what he can find at the food stalls. He will do the best that his budget and their supplies allow, but the food matters less to him than "the entertainment"—the reception and welcome he will offer his guest, and the entire evening's activity. At this point in the poem, "fair acceptance" refers to the guest's decision to attend the supper. Yet to secure that acceptance, the poet proceeds to act as if only "the cates" could persuade his guest to attend. In case his guest feels that he is somehow expected to be "the entertainment perfect," Jonson hastens to promise a lavish array of salad, mutton, rabbit, poultry, and gamebirds. But as he describes the other elements of the evening—good conversation and good company—we slowly come to realize that "fair acceptance," not food and drink, is the one gift the host can truly deliver. The poet's acceptance of his guest, and his guest of him, will enable them both to "enjoy" the "liberty" (42) of the festive occasion. Mutual acceptance marks the supper and the friendship it emblemizes.

"On Inviting a Friend to Supper" describes an idyll barely constrained by the conditions of city life. Urban fact, moreover, heightens the appeal of the poet's fantasy. The pleasure of anticipation—describing the special foods to be sought out, the scarcities to be overcome, the recipes to be tried—becomes part of the event. The poet does not escape or deny the city but enjoys it by turning its resources to his own use insofar as he can. In a sense this poem of anticipation prolongs the event, giving the poet and his guest a way to savor it more fully. The pleasure of the poem ranges from choosing the particular foods to indulging extravagant claims for the wine to vowing that the participants will "sup free, but moderately" (35). The immoderate imagining of the menu is pleasantly tempered by that final promise of restraint. It can even be said that the invitation, more directly than the meal itself, makes the meal expressive of something greater than the mere act of eating. Itemizing the menu, resolving to select only the choicest items from the foodmongers, declaring that Canary wine can make those who drink it immortal, finding pleasure in both indulgence and restraint—these acts bespeak Jonson's desire to honor his guest and "dignify" their "feast" (4).

This poem seems less occasional than mythic, in part because the poet includes so many evocative images of the perfect supper, in part because Jonson does not name his guest. This decision seems all the more surprising because the act of naming is so central elsewhere in *Epigrammes*. Yet perhaps the main reason for the poem's mythic quality is its allusiveness. To dramatize an idyllic moment of virtue reconciled to pleasure, Jonson brings the weight of classical tradition, notably the invitational poems of Horace and Martial, lightly to bear on this intimate occasion.

Horace provided Jonson an archetypal poetry of invitation. Inviting Torquatus to supper, for example, Horace promises comfortable surroundings, congenial companions, an ample supply of wine, and security: "Ne fidos inter amicos sit qui dicta foras eliminet" (there will be no one who will blab what is said among faithful friends—*Epist.* 1.5).[40] Jonson owes to Horace not only this emphasis on *libertas* but also the peculiarly fictive quality of the invitation. Gordon Williams, discussing a poem in which Horace invites Maecenas to supper (*Odes* 3.8), argues that the poem is not "occasional" at all. It is not an invitation to an actual supper but rather "a dramatic evocation of an occasion imagined as now taking place."[41] The immediacy of the Horatian "hic dies" argues not for the reality of the occasion but its imaginary, fictive character. This same blend of immediacy and imagination marks Jonson's poem, which begins and ends with the word "tonight."

Martial's invitational poems also stand as a model for Jonson's epistle. It has long been recognized that many details of the London supper are taken from three of Martial's epigrams (5.78, 10.48, 11.52), but it is important to notice just how Jonson adapts his classical sources.[42] In the first of these epigrams, Martial admits the poverty of his larder but promises freedom from literary readings and pedantic critical debate. The second epigram emphasizes the freedom and security, trust and discretion, that will mark the feast. In both poems, *libertas* depends on the tact, discretion, and integrity of the host. What Martial offers, far more than wine, even more than freedom, is himself. His epigrams do more than describe a feast; they dramatize and define the poet. The double action of description and self-dramatization that Jonson was to find so important is especially pronounced in the third of these epigrams (11.52), the text Jonson used most extensively. Jonson follows the outline of Martial's menu, with its promise of fat birds from poultry yard and marsh. Martial admits, as Jonson will, that the array of delicacies may be more wishful ploy than promise: "Mentiar, ut venias" (I will lie so that you will come). For Martial and for Jonson, the menu is a fiction, a wish, a fantasy; what is true in each case is the poet's eagerness to win his guest's approval.

Although Jonson could find in Martial a model for his own pattern of poetic action, their poems differ significantly in tone, concept of occasion, and purpose. Whenever Martial declares that there will be no poetry readings at any party he gives or attends, his tone borders on arrogant contempt for any work others might read. Jonson, promising not to recite his own verses but to have his man read Tacitus instead, displays an uncharacteristic reticence. Pastry, he jokes, is more enticing than his "paper," which would be better used to line a pie tin than to contain his lines of verse. More important, however, are the different attitudes these poets have toward the nature of the occasion.[43] Martial values the created play-world as a temporary refuge from the public world. His idea of *libertas*, therefore, is defined negatively: nothing his guest says will be spread abroad. The supper has a deeper significance and a more important purpose for Ben Jonson. He wants to describe an occasion and a way of life that epitomize the Humanist ideal of community. His idea of *libertas* refers not only to private pleasure and secure refuge from the world but also to the true basis for participating in the world. In this poem, and throughout Jonson's work, "liberty" designates freedom and liberality: free thought and action for oneself but also for others.[44] Its opposite is the "license" that Jonson often associates with the fear of commitment that he is quick to condemn in his satiric epigrams.

Jonson may have found the ideals of Horace more congenial than those of Martial, but it is evident from Jonson's text that his version of Horace was mediated by Erasmus. For Erasmus, as for Jonson, Horace was the classical paradigm of friend, poet, and moral spokesman for society. Jonson echoes the substance of Martial's feast and the tone of Horatian invitation, but he also alludes both to the substance and to the tone of Erasmus. The tone of the poem, now serious, now playful, enacts the *libertas* emblemized by the Humanist feast. True to the spirit of Erasmian colloquy, Jonson's overstatements are playful, his serious themes understated. If he errs, it is in eagerness and generosity.

The *libertas* dramatized in Jonson's poem derives most directly from the festive colloquies of Erasmus. Originally written as Latin primers, the colloquies developed into major illustrations of Humanist ideas. These works became extremely popular; Ben Jonson owned a copy of the 1527 Paris edition, only one of the many editions available during the Renaissance.[45] Several of the colloquies describe dinner parties: *The Godly Feast* (*Convivum religiosum*, 1524), *The Fabulous Feast* (*Convivium fabulosum*, 1524), *A Feast of Many Courses* (1527), *The Sober Feast* (1529), and *The Profane Feast* (*Convivium profanum*, 1518, 1522). Of special importance is Erasmus's final colloquy, *The Epicurean* (*Epicurus*, 1533), which was not included in the edition Jonson is known to have owned, but which was published in an enlarged edition of the colloquies during Erasmus's lifetime.

It has not been noticed, so far as I am aware, that Jonson alludes to several of these colloquies in his poem of invitation, summing up in one poem what Erasmus explores on separate occasions. The pattern of these allusions suggests that Jonson is defining both the supper and friendship in Erasmian terms. A major issue in the colloquies is the proper way to reconcile virtue and pleasure, which Erasmus depicts as a struggle between the Stoic and Epicurean ethical systems.[46] "On Inviting a Friend to Supper" shares the Erasmian preference for a Christian version of the Epicurean scheme, a morality of indulgence. Virtue, that highest of pleasures, does not exclude such other joys as good food, good wine, and good talk. To the contrary, it is what makes them "good."[47]

Augustinus, a central figure in *The Profane Feast*, insists on his right to have it both ways: "I praise Zeno," he declares, "but I live like Epicurus."[48] Augustinus is no hypocrite but rather a man who can distinguish between Epicurean indulgence and license. He advocates pleasure that can be reconciled to Stoic moderation, though not to Stoic indifference. Erasmus's last colloquy, *The Epicurean*, sets forth a dialogue between the Stoic Spudaeus (whose name means "sober") and the Epicurean Hedonius ("hedonist"). Hedonius carries the day, arguing that godly Christians are the true Epicureans, that pleasure is the natural and proper response to virtue, indeed that only virtue can give true pleasure.

An earlier colloquy defending Christian Epicureanism, *The Godly Feast,* provided Jonson with several details and much of the tone of his poem. Eusebius, the host of the Erasmian supper, invites his friends to share a modest meal of eggs and lettuce, followed by "a small but excellent shoulder of mutton, a capon, and four partridges. Only the partridges were bought at market; my little estate here supplies the rest" (p. 62). Jonson promises a similar menu but gives more prominence to the market. As a typical city dweller, he depends entirely on the foodstalls of London: "a coney / Is not to be despaired of, for our money," fowl are scarce but the (sales) clerks are optimistic. Eusebius, like Jonson, does not denigrate the importance of good food in large measure but shifts the emphasis to food for thought: "You shall hear, if you don't object, a short passage from Sacred Scripture, but in such fashion that this won't interfere with your eating eggs and lettuce if you like" (p. 56). Jonson is equally deferential in offering similar entertainment: "a piece of Virgil, Tacitus, / Livy, or . . . some better book"—perhaps a reference to the Bible (20–23). More important than the similarity of details in the Erasmian colloquy and Jonson's poem is the similarity of atmosphere and ideals. Eusebius promises his guests a party that will offer just the right blend of indulgence and moderation, not only in diet but also in free conversation: "And truly enjoyable conversations are those which are always pleasant to have held or heard and always delightful to recall, not those which soon cause one to be ashamed and conscience-stricken" (p. 56).

Martial and Horace emphasize escape from importunate clients, spies, and gossips, Erasmus the virtuous pleasures of guest and host. Martial and Horace promise discretion; Erasmus is more concerned with the moral tone and substance of the conversation. Martial promises an evening free from unlooked-for consequences; Erasmus (for Eusebius is his surrogate) cares more for a proper consequence, the edification of his guests. Both the classical poet and the Christian Humanist set forth the ideal of *libertas,* but Martial's vision seems more limited, certainly more secular.

The distinctively Christian character of Erasmian *libertas* becomes clear in the last segment of the colloquy. Eusebius and his guests discuss a famous Biblical text, "No man can serve two masters." It has been the purpose of the entire dialogue to discern how the proper choice of master can enable a person to know virtue and pleasure, to have the best of both worlds. The godly feast symbolizes the godly life, in which the soul enjoys the presence of Christ, the most worthy of all guests. The symbolic function of the feast is made explicit when Eusebius explains why the feast includes a discussion of Biblical texts: "That he may please to come, and we make ourselves the reader for so great a guest" (p. 56).

Although Jonson's poem mutes the Christian typology that marks Erasmus's *Godly Feast,* there remain indirect suggestions of that conceptual framework. In addition to the possible reference to a Scriptual reading after dinner, the poem opens with lines that, in their blend of deference and enthusiasm, echo the centurion's invitation to Christ: "Lord, I am not worthy that you should enter under my roof" (Luke 7:6–7), a passage used to introduce the Communion service. Later in the poem, celebrating Canary wine, Jonson exuberantly declares that it would have given eternal life to Horace and Anacreon. Any other drink is only "Luther's beer" (34), a cheap substitute. A common Elizabethan saying, "Beer and heresy came hopping into England the same year," linked German beer to Luther's denial of transubstantiation.[49] Even the exclusion of traitors like Poley and Parrot (36) may remind us that Judas was present at the original Communion Supper. Jonson's dinner party is not a Mass, the "grave sir" is not Christ, and Canary wine is not Christ's blood. Nor does Jonson satirize the Communion Supper. He offers his guest a gracious compliment by playfully alluding to a far greater feast than he can offer. Indulging the Renaissance penchant for analogy and emblem, Jonson deftly suggests a larger importance for his feast without lapsing into pretentiousness, blasphemy, or folly.

Jonson's extravagant claims for the properties of "a pure cup of rich Canary wine" (29) owe more to *The Profane Feast* of Erasmus than to Christian liturgy. This festive colloquy begins with a discussion of Stoic and Epicurean ethics, describes the menu, discusses poet's devotion to wine, comments on men's preferences in food, and concludes with remarks on rhetoric and an example of rhetorical copiousness. The two men in the colloquy offer interesting parallels to the portraits of host and guest in Jonson's poem. Christianus, the host in the Erasmian colloquy, has been described as almost too convivial, with too ready a wit, and his guest, Augustinus, has been accounted a moderate, sober, but unpedantic classicist.[50] Both Jonson and Christianus try to win the favor of a grave guest. Jonson makes extravagant promises but admits he may be forced to settle for a modest menu. Christianus, on the other hand, promises "a Platonic dinner at which there'll be plenty of learned stories but little food," but then provides a lavish spread. He has therefore satisfied all the tastes of Augustinus, who declares himself both Stoic and Epicurean. Both Jonson and Christianus, however, provide the excellent wine that Christianus declares essential to poets: "Drinking wine rids our minds of cares and anxieties and induces a certain cheerfulness. . . . Wine both arouses invention and ministers to eloquence, two things very suitable to a poet" (pp. 596–97). A conversation may disappoint; not so a cup of "rich Canary wine":

> Digestive cheese and fruit there sure will be;
> But that which most doth take my muse and me
> Is a pure cup of rich Canary wine,

> Which is the Mermaid's now, but shall be mine;
> Of which had Horace or Anacreon tasted,
>   Their lives, as do their lines, till now had lasted.
>
> (27–32)

Wine can nourish and inspire the ethical Horace and the erotic Anacreon, the Stoic and the Epicurean. Indeed, both poets had sung its praises. As a poet, Jonson transforms Erasmian generality to personal statement: Canary wine "doth take my muse and me," and this poem is the eloquent invention that can result just from its promise.

"On Inviting a Friend to Supper" also owes some of its specific details to yet another Erasmian colloquy, *The Poets' Feast*. There Erasmus describes a meal featuring a hen still capable of producing eggs—a profligate choice of entree. As one guest remarks, "She didn't deserve a death sentence" (p. 169). Jonson seeks for his table just such a "short-legg'd hen . . . full of eggs" (11–12). Erasmus also promises that after supper a boy will read from classical literature, or the guests will provide puzzling texts for analysis, and all will speak their minds amidst their meat. Justifying this dialogue to his detractors, Erasmus would later declare, "I know what sort of feast scholars should have: frugal, but gay and mirthful; seasoned with learned stories; without quarrels, bickering, or slander" (p. 630).

By alluding to these three disparate colloquies, Jonson brings together in his poem three different models of feast and of self-definition. He promises a dinner equally satisfying to the Christian, the scholar, and the poet, to the Stoic and the Epicurean. This blend of ideas kept separate in the colloquies of Erasmus signals Jonson's ability to assimilate the work of Erasmus and form out of it a work entirely his own. This kind of imitation is itself a feast, and Jonson describes it so in his *Discoveries*. The poet, he writes, imitates "Not, as a Creature, that swallowes, what it takes in, crude, raw, or indigested; but, that feedes with an Appetite, and hath a Stomacke to concoct, divide, and turne all into nourishment" (2472–75).

This poem defines a set of values to be shared, and a value of sharing, through a dramatic process of promise and qualification, one good enabling another.[51] The test of its morality lies not entirely in the isolated, protected world of the dinner party, but in the ability of that world and its values to prevail over the harsh reality outside. The friendship and trust celebrated in this poem are even rarer than delicacies in the food stalls of Fleet Lane. The crude woman who represents the crude way of the world had the last word in "A Celebration of Charis," but this poem banishes all those who would violate the morality and freedom of friendship's charmed circle:

> And we will have no Poley or Parrot by;
> Nor shall our cups make any guilty men,

But at our parting we will be as when
We innocently met. No simple word
That shall be uttered at our mirthful board
Shall make us sad next morning, or affright
The liberty that we'll enjoy tonight.

(36–42)

Poley and Parrot, the only contemporaries Jonson names in this poem, were probably the spies who informed on Jonson while he was imprisoned for his part in writing *Eastward Ho!*[52] These men intruded on whatever liberty the poet could maintain in jail, and by naming them Jonson makes very specific one kind of liberty he values and the kind of betrayal he despised. His dramatization of freedom in this poem gains intensity and point from his allusion to a time when he was not free, when he was vulnerable to those spies he derides in another epigram as "base stuff" who "Stink, and are thrown away" (*Ep.* 59). However, these men are not mentioned last. They do not pose the greatest threat to *libertas,* any more than prison is the true antithesis to freedom. The worse threat comes from within: to degrade oneself or to betray one's friend, to violate "fair acceptance."

The security of mutual trust and generous acceptance enables the poet's vision to survive the pressures of the outside world—the economic, social, and political versions of actuality alluded to in the poem. If the dinner is to be "Something . . . of esteem," a reality equal to the other "things" of the world, then the poet's fantasy must take them into account. It is noteworthy in this regard that the works read after supper are interpretations of Roman history from the beginnings to the Empire: Virgil, Tacitus, Livy. These three writers offer a range of attitudes toward the world, but they have in common an emphasis on ethics and morality. Virgil envisions his ethical ideal of Rome in the sixth book of the *Aeneid.* Tacitus and Livy occupied opposite ends of the spectrum of Humanist historiography. Livy, after Virgil the most widely read of Roman historians, was admired for his magnamity, his tact, and his emphasis on Roman morality. Tacitus, renowned for his terse epigrammatic style, was the most psychological of the three; he combined a certain disillusionment and cynicism with firmly held moral principles and resentment of tyranny. Jonson's choice of these three historical writers would be especially appropriate if Jonson wrote this poem to a friend who was a Humanist hisorian: perhaps Sir Henry Savile, who translated Tacitus; or William Camden, the foremost antiquarian in England; or John Selden, an authority on legal and linguistic history and a noted antiquarian. If the "better book" does refer to the Bible, Jonson appropriately includes the book of sacred history that provided Humanists with a measure and a context for all secular history.

These literary references may also play an indirect role in relating Jonson's fictive occasion to the political world he inhabited. He values the literature that can interpret and judge that world and incorporates it into the sheltered play-world of the supper party and the poem. One withdraws from the world, or so the Humanists argue, not only to escape but also to gain the strength to reenter it. Jonson's references to the Roman historians are not arbitrary: these were the writers favored by the scholarly and political coterie of the Essex-Sidney circle, which Jonson sought to enter in the 1590s. Their interest in interpretations of the Roman past masked their own analysis of the English present.[53] Members of the Essex circle were at risk for their opposition to Elizabethan policy; they relied on friendship and intellectual indirection to maintain their own safety. Jonson's poem reflects his sympathy with this coterie, not only by his indirect references to Humanist authorities but by his direct endorsement of Humanist ideals.

Jonson grounds his poem in three Humanist ideals that make its endorsement of serious play possible: *humanitas, simplicitas,* and *libertas.* Each ideal is dramatically represented in narrow and then in comprehensive terms. The poet enacts *humanitas,* or cultural study, by promising that the entertainment will include a discussion of literature and the Bible. In larger terms, the supper occasions *humanitas* by occasioning moral excellence in host and guest. *Simplicitas* can be construed narrowly as a reference to plain food, the absence of a richly laid table and a lavish estate, and the poet's dependence on shopkeepers. As a Humanist ideal, however, *simplicitas* implies allegiance to essential truth, and gives a deeper meaning to the "simple word" (39) to be spoken at Jonson's table. *Libertas,* in its strictest sense, is demonstrated in the host's promise that his guests will "sup free, but moderately," But again, a larger concept informs the poem, a style of life signified by a meal in which men can speak without constraint or fear, sharing a belief in virtue as the highest form of pleasure. *Libertas* is made the explicit ideal of the poem in the final line. "The liberty that we'll enjoy tonight" (42) sums up the shared freedom of this occasion and the Humanist vision it embodies.

Two later poems echo the vision fully realized in this poem. One is a far lesser poem, summarizing what makes a pleasant life:

> A quiet mind; free powers; and body sound;
> A wise simplicity; friends alike-stated;
> Thy table without art, and easy rated;
> Thy night not drunken, but from cares laid waste.
>
> (*Und.* 90, 6–9)

The other is Jonson's majestic ode commemorating the Cary-Morison friendship. Jonson describes that friendship in terms of a feast like the one he promises in "Inviting a Friend to Supper":

> No pleasures vain did chime,
> Of rhymes, or riots, at your feasts,

Orgies of drink, or feigned protests:
But simple love of greatness, and of good;
That knits brave minds and manners, more than blood.
                                                    (*Und.* 70, 102–6)

Whether praising the friendship of other men or creating an image of his own, Jonson recognizes the Aristotelian distinction between friendships of utility and casual pleasure, which cannot endure, and those founded on virtue, which will.[54] In all three of these poems, Jonson dramatizes the act of judgment and selection that is prologue to true friendship. "On Inviting a Friend to Supper" stands out because it includes such a wide range of tone, balancing negative and positive, promise and qualification, and puts into just proportion all the feelings that can be indulged in the privileged world of friendship.

The poems that follow "On Inviting a Friend to Supper" in Jonson's *Epigrammes* praise other men and women who would lend grace and dignity to such a feast: the Earl of Pembroke, Lady Mary Wroth, the Countess of Montgomery, Sir Edward Herbert, Sir Henry Nevil, Clement Edmondes, Sir William Jephson, Sir Ralph Shelton, Benjamin Rudyerd, Sir William Uvedale and his wife, Lord Aubigny, William Roe, Alphonso Ferrabosco, and Josiah Sylvester. Many are members of Pembroke's circle; others are scholars or colleagues of Ben Jonson. The satiric epigrams attack men who would defile the feast, who would not recognize its value or the ethical ideal it embodies. Captain Hungry barters juicy slander for meat; Gut indulges heedless gluttony; Mime imposes his raucous antics on other guests (*Ep.* 107, 118, 129). The Town's Honest Man "Talks loud and bawdy," gives himself over to "the anarchy of drink" and "watches / Whose name's unwelcome to the present ear, / And him it lays on; if he be not there." Instead of enjoying a "simple word" around the "mirthful board," he claims the center of attention and "in the fit / Of miming, gets the opinion of a wit" (*Ep.* 115). *Humanitas, libertas, simplicitas*—the qualities essential to friendship—the knaves ignore, even in the narrowest sense of civil behavior. They prefer license to liberty, bawdy to courtesy, affectation to sincerity.

If "On Inviting a Friend to Supper" can be itself considered a feast, and the poet a host, then the final guest at Jonson's feast is the reader, who accepts the invitation and enjoys the feast by reading the poem. The first reader, the "grave sir," may have been a particular friend, perhaps Sir Henry Savile, John Selden, William Camden, or the Earl of Pembroke. But by publishing the poem, Jonson invites every reader to imagine and enjoy his feast. The reader completes Jonson's description of the supper, and of ethical friendship, by granting it "fair acceptance." Jonas Barish, discussing the relationship between feasting and judgment in Jonson's plays, argues that poetic justice in the great comedies "fosters our festive responses as well as our judicial approval; it enables us to relish the follies of the fools and the peculations of the knaves without making us feel that we are endorsing the inadmissible."[55] In this poem, Jonson evokes in his readers a festive response that leads to judicious approval. Pleasure and virtue are not only reconciled but shown to be inseparable. We can appreciate an opportunity to "speak our minds, admidst our meat" (23) with a poet who can subordinate his verse to pastry: "if aught appear which I not know of, / That will the pastry, not my paper, show of" (25–26). The joke that poet and reader share, of course, is the understanding that no pastry can appear apart from the paper of this poem. Similarly, despite the fiction of this poem that poetry serves its occasion, all occasions also serve the poetry they evoke. Poem and occasion "equally desire" the company of one another. Friendship and feasting signify Jonson's commitment to Erasmian values, and ultimately to his own poetry as well. The poem, as an act of feast and friendship, offers the reader a direct experience of the community Jonson advocates. He uses the occasion of our reading to secure our "fair acceptance" of his festive language. In his Humanist poetry he offers us a poetics of grace and pleasure, freedom and esteem.

3

"Times and Occasions": History as Subject and Context of Poetry

> There is a greater Reverence had of things remote, or
> strange to us, then of much better, if they bee nearer, and
> fall under our sense. Men, and almost all sort of creatures,
> have their reputation by distance.
>
> (*Dis.* 1489–92)

The double actions of description and self-dramatization that constitute a Jonsonian poem occur in the context of a larger doubling: the poem as act that mimetically presents historical reality and as act that participates in that reality. As occasional poetry, Jonsonian texts stand at the boundary of the two worlds we customarily designate as "art" and "history." His poems are occasioned by history: circumstance is their *raison d'être*. Not only fact, however, but a particular understanding of fact—an idea of history—governs Jonson's treatment of occasion and his concept of his own role as poet. The dialectic of art and history in his poetry permits us to enlarge our definition of Jonsonian poetry beyond its internal dynamic and its affirmation of the Humanist program of language and interpretation. His poetry can be placed in the context of the interpretive model that it exemplifies and endorses, as well as in the context of circumstances that are the object of interpretation. Jonson adapted to his study of the present the methods and values developed by historians for their inquiry into the past.

A new historical method of inquiry can be detected almost everywhere in late Elizabethan and Jacobean writing: in the correspondence and diaries of Cecil, in the new histories of Savile and Ralegh, in the poems of Jonson. It is a method of indirection, working through to probable causes and probable judgments, through amplification and elimination of possibilities. The Tudor historians, as F. J. Levy points out, weigh negative and positive alternatives

before venturing an interpretation of events; these historians abjure speculation on the hidden or secret causes of events, but exhaustively probe various
explanations of every historical act.[1] Ben Jonson is notorious for beginning
his complimentary poems with several lines that detail what he chooses not
to write. No psychological explanation for that mode of epideictic art
suffices; too many of his contemporaries in different disciplines act the same
way. The explanation for his choice of this particular rhetorical strategy lies
rather in the new empiricism that underlies the revolution in discourse that
occurred during the late Renaissance.

Jonson and the new historians share a belief in history as drama not only
because they subscribe to the Humanist "exemplar" theory of history, but
also because they endorse the new empiricist theory of history as the
personal discovery and enactment of universal truths through the slow,
complex process of investigating particulars.[2] Only personal action connects
the "light of truth" to the "life of memory."[3] Literature, whether fictive or
factual, at once reflects and constitutes culture.[4] Jonson's poetic voice, like
that of a historian, is embedded in the culture that is embedded in the work.

The terms of this claim are familiar to students of cultural anthropology.
The argument, stated most clearly by Clifford Geertz in the fourteenth
chapter of *The Interpretation of Cultures,* holds that ideas important in a
culture are developed and sustained only in social speech and behavior.[5]
Jonson, as a "participant observer," adopts the techniques of "thick description" to map the values of Jacobean society. What he sees and what he does—
his decisions to address specific categories of people in specific ways, his
attitudes toward name, appearance, speech, place, his creation of a distinctive "voice" in poetry—enable us to apprehend his culture more surely
than any sweeping narrative would allow. Jonson writes the world that he
lives: his experience of its rituals, its signal events, its most honored members, its stereotypes, even its jokes. His poems document the fictions of
power and friendship (the figure of a relationship that can dispense with
power) that are discovered, imposed on, created by, the poet. The dramatic
character of Jonson's social poetry derives not only from the playwright's
predisposition toward the theatrical, and not even from the action of theatrical self-fashioning and world-fashioning that dominates Renaissance
culture, but also from the inevitably dramatic and active relationship, which
we half-perceive and half-create, between circumstance and its art, fact and
idea, world and self.

Because Jonson writes in the urgency and richness of specific circumstance, the explication of his poetry often requires the retrieval of information: who was Clement Edmondes, or Sir Henry Savile, or "Elizabeth, L.
H."? what kind of book was Camden's *Britannia,* or Ralegh's *History of the
World?* A historical reading of Jonson's poetry requires both information
about the specific occasion of a text and attention to the theoretical puzzling

over facts that marks Tudor-Stuart historiography. Ben Jonson's struggle to write a poetry adequate to his own age should be considered in the context of the attempts being made by men important to him—Camden, Selden, Savile—to shape a new way of writing history, both in substance and in style. They paid new attention to artifacts and material circumstance, to texts and records, to context as well as event. These antiquarians, no mere collectors, replaced the historiography of narrative chronicle with interpretation. They weighed the causes and meanings of events, seeking in specific detail the bases for understanding the past and its continuity with their own present.

As scholars, they sought a warrant for their work in the classical tradition, which they regarded not as a monolithic set of values but as a record of political struggles like their own. Because they read widely in the literature of Rome, they understood its variety and could select those writers whose situation mirrored their own. The historians' perception of what was new about their work can be located in the new pattern of classical allusions in their texts: references to Tacitus, Sallust, and Caesar replace allusions to Livy. Livy's history emphasized chronicle and event, Tacitus's and Sallust's the possibility of multiple interpretation. In substance, Tacitus and Sallust wrote of empire but shared the moral values of republicans; in style, they were inclined toward maxim, epigrammatic brevity, and dramatic characterization. These Roman historians wrought a revolution in historical method and rhetorical discourse; their Renaissance translators sought and won a similar radical change.

The making of a new history was not a neutral act; many of the radical historians were associated with the Essex circle. F. J. Levy summarizes the importance of Tacitus, in particular, as a political touchstone: "When Essex became ascendant, so did the Taciteans. The earl himself encouraged politic history—there is some evidence that he wrote the preface to Savile's translation of Tacitus—and his followers, Francis Bacon, Sir Henry Savile, John Hayward, and Henry Cuffe, all wrote in the same genre. Cuffe went further, urged Essex forward, and was executed with his master; Savile and Hayward were both imprisoned. Tacitus had become practical politics, and the historians had left their posts as observers and had stepped into the arena. The danger was such that when, later, Isaac Dorislaus, the first history lecturer on Fulke Greville's foundation at Cambridge, began by analyzing Tacitus, the king sent word 'to prohibit the history-reader to read.' "[6]

The overt idealism of Jonson and his contemporaries combines with their covert pragmatism. A rhetoric of indirection at once protects the writer and encourages the reader to emulate what is being described, to bring memory to life. Such a rhetoric might be transparently topical: Queen Elizabeth knew the pertinence of Shakespeare's *Richard II*, James I the danger of analyzing Tacitus. Jonson's poetry is indirect both in the personal realm, as in his epitaph on "Elizabeth, L. H." and in the political sphere, as in his compliments to the historians whose work had such contemporary force. The simultaneity of idealism and pragmatism, of eliminating whatever strategies of action would be untactful, inadequate, or inappropriate, and of choosing instead a mode of praise at once practical and ethical, marks the personal action of poet, subject, and reader.

Ben Jonson wrought in poetry a change in method and language comparable to the change in historiography achieved by the scholars he admired. Like them, he valued interpretation over chronicle. Like them, he sought a style of moral maxim and epigrammatic brevity. Like them, he found a warrant for his work in the classical tradition. As he writes to his "Mere English Censurer," "To thee my way in epigrams seems new, / When both it is the old way and the true" (*Ep.* 18). Again and again Jonson adopts an epigrammatic, rigorously selective language precisely analogous to the Tacitean style or code for "history" advocated by the English historians he valued.

His idea of history, like his poetry, is dramatic. Like Sir Francis Bacon, another adherent of the Tacitean style, Jonson remains an advocate of the Humanist "exemplar" theory of history.[7] People, not abstract forces or ideas, generate events. Moral maxims mean little apart from the complexity and flux of the human community. What matters to Jonson is the ability of individual people to exemplify by enactment the truth of moral ideas. He addresses particular people, either real people he knew or exaggerated types of those he could expect to meet in his daily life. His preface to *Epigrammes* compares his book to a "theatre," and gives his readers the multiple roles of characters, actors, and audience.[8] His cast of characters can be compared to the *dramatis personae* of a Renaissance history play, in which the public figures of the main plot coexist with the fictive clowns and knaves of the subplot. As a playwright, Jonson may have found the historians of the Sidney circle especially congenial because they replaced the old narrative style of the chronicles with the new mode of dramatic episode. His own poetry enacts a dramatic idea of history.

In order to demonstrate the importance of circumstance and occasion in Jonson's work, I have chosen for discussion texts that both require information and that specifically address the problematic relationship of art and history. In a group of poems to Robert Cecil and in "To My Muse," Jonson ponders the role of art and its contingency. His poems to historians and scholars—John Selden, Sir Henry Savile, Clement Edmondes—find their method of history an analogue to his method of art. His clearest formulation of a view of history can be found in the poem commenting on the frontispiece to Ralegh's *History of the World*. Jonson himself seems to have undertaken the writing of history at least once; he would later claim to have written the draft of the section on the Punic Wars for Ralegh's book (*Conv.*

Dr. 200–201). The relationship between poetry and history becomes a central issue in Jonson's own commemorative epigrams to the living and the dead. He affirms the adequacy of poetry to even the most complex situation in the tactful simplicity of his deliberately enigmatic "Epitaph on Elizabeth, L. H."

Throughout this chapter, I use "occasion," "circumstance," and "history" interchangeably to designate the context of fact that precedes a Jonsonian text. This usage may seem to conflate two different ideas of history: the immediate experience that elicits a specific poem and the general arena of circumstance in which the poet lives and writes. Such a conflation is justified because that larger arena impinges on the poet only as specific event or person. It is only in the particular that we can apprehend our world; that is, our history is our experience. Jonson implicitly argues from this assumption in all his poetry.

I

What strikes any reader of Jonson's poetry is the unshakeable self-confidence he displays. Forthright and plainspoken, sincere, sure of his own integrity, he declares himself "no child, no fool" (*Ep.* 65). He bases his autonomy on his moral integrity, professing himself "in love / With every virtue . . . at feud / With sin and vice" (*For.* 13). Yet something in the very nature of occasional poetry renders those statements suspect. Is not the Humanist act of praise to some extent a complicity in the social puffery he abhors? Does not Jonson's occasional angry outburst—the protest "To My Muse" (*Ep.* 65), the odes to himself—spring from the awareness that as author he can claim no authority except that authorized by his noble patrons? Or does Jonson shape his own authority so as to authorize his patrons' sense of themselves? How much, in other words, does the world shape the poet, and how much does he give it form and substance?

The language Jonson must use in claiming authority provides a starting point for a discussion of these questions. For example, he must establish for himself a moral stature at least proportional to the social rank of his noble readers before he can seek the delicate balance of deference and rectitude that can gain him a hearing. At the same time, he must identify himself with the best in them before he can urge them to enact that best. And all the while, he must distinguish his praise from "sordid" flattery (*Und.* 70), which is but a "false light" (*Und.* 52) and "common poets' shame" (*Ep.* 43). He must distance himself from poetasters who "lose the forms and dignities of men / To flatter my good lord" (*Und.* 15). Once the poet has lost his own dignity, he cannot authorize anyone else's worth. "An Epistle to a Friend to Persuade Him to the Wars" (*Und.* 15) bitterly condemns not only the corrupt world

but also the flattery it engenders and rewards. "Bought flatteries" haunt the pur-
chaser and become his "curse," inevitably reducing the world, poetry, and
the poet himself to "nothing." To counter that "nothing," to replace the
debased language of the depraved world, Jonson offers the "one" of integrity: "Be always one" (186).

The ideal of the one true self, gathered, centered, marks not only Jonson's
praise of other people but also his vision of himself.[9] Only his insistence on
his integrity enables him to avoid the extremes of flattery and malice.
Although Jonson shares the Humanist creed that the poet has a necessary
and powerful place in society, as a poet-commoner he knows himself doubly
an outsider. The temptation to bitter disillusionment comes not only from
the world's corruption but also from its indifference. The virtue he celebrates
does not require his celebration; vice prefers cut-rate art or none at all. The
first kind of indifference can be turned to advantage: if virtue does not
require the poet's praise, the poet requires virtue as the proper subject of his
art.

Jonson defines that relationship between virtue and art in his first epigram
to Robert Cecil, the powerful Earl of Salisbury (*Ep.* 45). Two other epigrams
praise Cecil's judgment, his disregard of flattery, and his well-rewarded
"worth" (*Ep.* 63, 64). Bitterness interrupts this comfortable affirmation as
Jonson is forced to confront the diminished role of art in a world that assigns
an economic value to every action, and to confront his own complicity in
that world. Enraged at being betrayed into a betrayal of his art, Jonson
berates his muse:

> Away, and leave me, thou thing most abhorred,
>   That hast betrayed me to a worthless lord,
> Made me commit most fierce idolatry
>   To a great image through thy luxury.
>
> (*Ep.* 65, 1–4)

He resolves to forgo poetry for hire and to embrace Poverty, a new muse
who will free him "to write / Things manly, and not smelling parasite" (13–
14). In the last lines of the poem, Jonson reconciles the religious and
economic idioms that had clashed in the opening lines:

> But I repent me: stay. Whoe'er is raised
> For worth he has not, he is taxed, not praised.
>
> (15–16)

His initial rage against the sin of betraying his art is replaced by repentance
for the further sin of blaming his art. He reclaims his muse, turning the
language of economics to an attack on the lord who buys the poet's praise.
At the same time, Jonson's pun on the word "tax" distances his art from the

language of economics. The economic meaning is linked to the lord, the moral evaluation (tax as criticism or burden) to the poet's authority. The economic and religious idioms that were intertwined in the opening lines seem to merge in the pun, but in dramatic terms remain quite separate, or at least serve to separate lord from poet. The point of the last couplet is to dramatize the contradictory situation of the lord, which is presented through the rhetoric of self-canceling paradox, and at the same time the ethical clarity of the poet, which is presented as his recovery of calm ironic humor. The dramatic progress of the poet from outrage to calm affirms not only his own authority but also, through his reliance on a rhetoric of moral commonplace, his authorization by a community of readers. The double negation of the last line enables Jonson to distinguish his art from its subject, thereby making the value of a poem less contingent on his subject's worth.[10]

Because this epigram follows two complimentary poems to Cecil, it has been argued that Jonson intended this poem as an attack on Cecil.[11] However, there is no compelling reason to conclude that the "worthless lord" of *Epigram* 65 must be Cecil. There is no doubt Jonson would later speak bitterly of him. The *Conversations with Drummond* record Jonson's opinion that "Salisbury never cared for any man longer nor he could make use of him," and also the poet's self-satisfied reminiscence of remonstrating with Salisbury at dinner: "You promised me I should dine with you," Jonson had said, "but I do not" (*Conv. Dr.* 317–21).[12] Cecil, however, had not secured Jonson "the court's ill-will," whether that phrase alludes to lawcourt or king, but rather had helped secure Jonson's release from prison during the *Eastward Ho!* affair.[13] Any attempt to read this poem as unequivocal evidence about Jonson's attitude toward Cecil seems doomed to fail.

More important, such an attempt disregards the primary action of the poem and its placement in *Epigrammes*. Even if "To My Muse" does not attack Cecil, Jonson's decision to place this poem among complimentary epigrams invites the reader to consider the worth of all the people he praises. They may be (or may later become) undeserving of the praise he lavishes on them, in which case their failure converts his praise to an ironic "tax." It could be argued that the poem renders the preceding poems independent of Cecil's worth. A poem, that is, may be good even if its subject is not. Certainly Jonson takes care throughout *Epigrammes* to demonstrate his own authority and judgment, to shape a poetry for a world that seemed, if not oblivious or hostile, all too eager to shape art to its own ends. "To My Muse" resolves this question only by way of rhetorical witticism. The contingency of his occasional poetry remains an issue throughout his book. His purpose, moreover, may not be to solve the problem of the relationship between history and poetry, but to make his collection livelier and more challenging for the reader, who is more detached than either poet or subject and who is free to use the connections between a specific poem and its context to develop a general understanding of the connections between poetry and history.

Jonson's belief that history is both true and dramatic may seem inconsistent to a modern reader accustomed to doubt both the stability of fact and the adequacy of interpretation. Jonson, however, wanted to bring together both "the language and the truth," arguing that a true, objective history can be described only by a historian of special subjective power. His poems to historians dramatize and describe the union of self and world he admired in their work and sought to achieve in his own.

Each of his poems to historians is occasioned by the publication of a book: the English translation of Camden's *Britannia*, Selden's *Titles of Honour,* Savile's translation of Tacitus, Edmondes's *Caesar's Commentaries Observed and Translated.* Together these poems reflect Jonson's understanding of what the job of historian requires: respect of the past as an integral world in itself; an independent spirit and intellectual courage; a blend of empathy and a capacity for disinterested judgment; and a sense that style is a cognitive skill. The historian must know not only texts and information but also the task of presentation, "the several graces / of history, and how to apt their places" (*Ep.* 95).

The qualities of the ideal historian are essential ingredients of Jonsonian *imitatio* as well. Imitation of the sort that is Jonson's major contribution to English literature requires a sense of the distance and integrity of the historical source. The classics must be appreciated for what they are in themselves, admitting their difficulty and remoteness, before they can be revived and assimilated to and for the present, vernacular moment. Jonson's allusions to classical texts in his poems for historians illustrate the simultaneous deference and appropriation that mark his imitative method. The poem to his old teacher, William Camden, echoes two of Pliny's letters praising effective teachers.[14] It is not enough, I think, to point out Jonson's appropriation of classical texts written for analogous occasions. He honors the classical model to which the contemporary occasion aspires and by which it must be judged. In order to retain its value as a measure of present art and occasion, the classical text must to some degree resist appropriation, remaining outside the bounds of Jonson's poem. If allusions (and poetic imitation in general) reflect his desire for identity through identification, he can achieve his own identity only when he can differentiate identity and identification. Jonson's self-confident presence can be achieved only in a system of reciprocity between his authority and the authority of the texts he cites. Each authority both enables and resists the other.

The epigram to Sir Henry Savile (*Ep.* 95) both describes and dramatizes what Jonson understood as the relationship between historian and poet. Savile had translated the first four books of Tacitus and added an original section, "The End of Nero and Beginning of Galba." In the first twelve lines of the epigram, Jonson playfully speculates that the soul of Tacitus is reincarnate in Savile, proved not only by the translation but even more by the writing original to Savile. In the second section (13–24), Jonson does more than praise Savile's "antiquity of voice." The poet urges Savile to write his own history of England: both skill and moral stature qualify him to undertake such "Newness of sense." Skilled in judgment, free from ambition and factional loyalty, untainted by any hint of corruption, Savile could be not only a Tacitus but a Sallust. Jonson concludes his poem with a definition of the ideal historian:

> We need a man that knows the several graces
>   Of history, and how to apt their places:
> Where brevity, where splendour, and where height,
>   Where sweetness is required, and where weight;
> We need a man can speak of the intents,
>   The counsels, actions, orders and events
> Of state, and censure them; we need his pen
>   Can write the things, the causes, and the men.
> But most we need his faith (and all have you)
>   That dares nor write things false, nor hide things true.
>
>   (25–36)

This ringing conclusion adds to the ideals outlined to Selden a concern with cause and intention, with a judgment that can perceive the hidden truth as well as the accurate disposition of facts and events. In moving from a praise of Savile's works to a praise of Savile's character, from classical predecessors to contemporary promise, Jonson dramatizes his own effort to do the "things" he describes and celebrates in Savile. What Savile can achieve as historian, Jonson will try to emulate in the discrete moment of occasional art.

An allusion to Sallust links the double actions of description and self-dramatization in this poem. Jonson compares Savile to Sallust in an effort to describe Savile's detached probity. The allusion pays special tribute to Savile: in *Discoveries* Jonson had singled out Livy as the historian for beginners, Sallust for the more advanced reader (1796–98). Here Jonson appropriates lines from Sallust in order to dramatize his own response to Savile. In this act of allusion and imitation, Jonson enacts the style he has urged on Savile in the second section of the epigram. If the historian offers a model to the poet, so also the poet can offer a model of imitation to the historian.

Jonson's "Epistle to Master John Selden" brings together the poet and the historian as true interpreters. "I know to whom I write," Jonson declares, and, having learned by trial and error, "I turn a sharper eye / Upon myself. . . . So that my reader is assured I now / Mean what I speak" (*Und.* 14.1, 23–28). As Jonson chooses which books to review and how, according to the norms of his own judgment, so Selden can be praised for constant judgment:

> What fables have you vexed, what truth redeemed,
> Antiquities searched, opinions disesteemed,
> Impostures branded, and authorities urged!
> What blots and errors have you watched and purged
> Records and authors of!
>
> (39–43)

Selden maintains a consistent style as well, "not one while / With horror rough, then rioting with wit" (56–57). He not only ferrets out the truth but shapes a style adequate to it:

> to the subject still the colours fit
> In sharpness of all search, wisdom of choice,
> Newness of sense, antiquity of voice!
>
> (58–60)

"Newness of Sense, antiquity of voice" sums up not only Jonson's praise of Selden but also the poet's own ideal of the relationships between his occasional art and literary tradition. His poetic voice, made strong by its informed echo of classical art, makes antiquity new—shaped by his own accent, applied to his own occasions.

Because Selden serves as a model for the kind of authority Jonson himself sought, it would not have been surprising if Jonson had chosen to make that connection the climax of his poem. Instead, he defers to a third person, Edward Hayward, the close friend to whom Selden dedicates *Titles of Honour* (the book Jonson here praises). If Selden is a model for the poet, Hayward embodies the ideal reader:

> He thou hast given it to,
> Thy learned chamber-fellow, knows to do
> It true respects. He will not only love,
> Embrace, and cherish, but he can approve
> And estimate thy pains, as having wrought
> In the same mines of knowledge, and thence brought
> Humanity enough to be a friend,
> And strength to be a champion and defend
> Thy gift 'gainst envy.
>
> (71–79)

Hayward and Selden: "two names that so much understand!" (82). The tribute to Hayward echoes Jonson's first epigram, his own wish for a reader who will "understand" his book. Early in the poem, Jonson described the difficulty he faced when he had to judge harshly the work of a friend. The temptation to go easy is hard to resist: "it doth or may / Chance that the friend's affection proves allay / Unto the censure" (9–11). By introducing another friend of Selden at the end of the poem, Jonson distances himself dramatically from the occasion and theme of the poem. He had begun this epistle, as he begins so many of his complimentary poems, with a set of negatives: a description of false judgments and false, because compromised, friendships. Instead of setting himself up as the example of the true judge and the true friend, he praises Selden as a model of judgment and Hayward as a model of friendship. They represent those qualities he would indeed want most for himself; at least he has their friendship. The last line of the poem indicates at once the separation and the union of these two men and the poet: "You both are modest: so am I. Farewell" (86). It is one thing to praise someone else's modesty, another to claim your own. Jonson's playful self-mockery indicates both intimacy and distance. Selden and Hayward provide models for the judgment and the friendship he finds at the base of all true interpretation.

Clement Edmondes, like Sir Henry Savile, is praised as a translator and commentator. In two poems prefaced to Edmondes's *Caesar*, Jonson explores different approaches to the relationship between past and present. Historians have two modes of procedure: they can study the past and its texts in order to understand the present, like Edmondes and Savile, or, like Selden and Camden, they can search deeply into the past in order to understand the past itself. They can work from the assumption that the past is wholly Other, or from the opposite assumption that past and present are continuous. Jonson's first epigram for Edmondes's book argues from the first assumption, the second epigram from the second. The second assumption rests on the successful overcoming of the first. Because Edmondes can make "Caesar speak," Jonson can argue for Caesar's contemporaneity.

Jonson's two epigrams to Clement Edmondes do not place the poet on center stage but juxtapose Edmondes and Caesar in order to explore commonplace paradoxes about the relationship between history and the present. The first poem, like so many of Jonson's complimentary epigrams, begins with a series of negatives, each paying a tribute to Caesar: "Not Caesar's deeds . . . In these west parts . . . [Nor] Rome and her liberty / All yielding to his fortune . . . [nor] To have engraved these acts with his own style . . . Nor that his work lived in the hands of foes . . . Not all these, Edmondes, or what else put to, / Can so speak Caesar as thy labours do" (*Ep.* 110, 1–12). Deeds yield to words in Jonson's praise, the language of Caesar and his contemporaries overmatched by Edmondes's English. The map of praise begins in Roman Britain and reaches to Rome itself, only to find its present place and present moment in Jacobean Britain.

If Caesar's deeds warrant immortality, Edmondes confers it in his book, not only recording but creating them for present and future understanding:

> They learned hand and true Promethean art
>   (As by a new creation) part by part,
> In every counsel, stratagem, design,
>   Action or engine worth a note of thine,
> To all future time not only doth restore
>   His life, but makes that he can die no more.
>
> (17–22)

The historian mediates between past and future, shaping a new and immortal hero from the ashes of the past. The Promethean historian who restores the truth of old time paradoxically conquers all time, giving new human life to the dust of the past.

The second epigram to Edmondes (*Ep.* 111) replaces the common conflict between mutability and eternizing art with the equally commonplace idea that nothing ever really changes. When Edmondes accurately describes Caesar's martial strategies, he describes modern warfare as well: "in action there is nothing new / More than to vary what our elders knew" (4–5). When Jonson makes this specific comparison between Roman and Jacobean military methods, he echoes Edmondes's own *Observations*. The shift in the epigram occurs when Jonson turns to the other famous event of Caesar's life—his assassination. Jonson compares Edmondes to Caesar, suggesting that Edmondes may also attract resentment and rage, that he may be betrayed by the judgment of those who feel his work has betrayed them:

>   To those
> Caesar stands up, as from his urn late rose,
> By thy great help, and doth proclaim by me,
>   They murder him again that envy thee.
>
> (11–14)

In this last modification of the analogy, Jonson finally enters the poem himself. Caesar as the murdered hero may be analogous to Edmondes, but as the speaking voice brought to new life by Edmondes, Caesar is also analogous to the poet. If modern soldiers repeat the martial actions of Caesar, modern critics repeat the unjust envy of Caesar's murderers. What happens in the brazen world of action is not opposed to what can happen in the supposedly golden world of written language. The events of history can be repeated in the experience of the historian. Jonson's compliment, a blend of praise and warning, mutes the difference not only between past and present, but also between history and art.

Edmondes, an Oxford graduate, had been associated with Sir Francis Vere in the Netherlands campaign.[15] The first edition of the *Observations* (1600) is dedicated to Vere, whose brother Horace Jonson would praise in *Ep.* 91 for his "Humanity and piety, which are / As noble in great chiefs as they are rare" (15–16). Edmondes, a pragmatist in politics as well as in military strategy, dedicated the second edition of his *Observations* (1610) to Prince Henry, doubtless mindful of the royal heir's militant Protestant ambitions. Edmondes seems to have been one of those who saw in the militant young man not only a patron of scholarship but, more important, a spiritual heir of Sidney, and a new hope for Protestant Europe. Edmondes's work may have been one component in a Protestant strategy to ennoble the political present by linking it to a martial past.

At the time Jonson composed these epigrams, he had himself converted back to Protestantism. Although a cluster of epigrams—to Sir Horace Vere, to Sir John Radcliffe (who also served in the Netherlands), to Sir Henry Nevil (imprisoned for his role in the Essex rebellion), to "True Soldiers," to Clement Edmondes—document Jonson's relationship with Protestant activists, the poet himself seems to have remained a moderate, closer in spirit to the centrist royal court that seemed to many English Protestants so suspect, so tainted with Catholic sympathies. Even his works for Prince Henry—the *Barriers* (1609) and *Oberon* (1611)—seem designed to counter the militancy of the Protestant advisors distrusted by James.[16] However, Jonson probably succeeded to some degree in maintaining good working relationship with both the Court and the household of Prince Henry. Jonson carefully balances poems to Catholics (e.g., Aubigny and Shelton) and Protestants in his collection of epigrams. He owed much to people on both sides and indeed had been a member of both sides himself. As he would later remark to Drummond, Jonson was "for any religion as being versed in both" (*Conv. Dr.* 690).

His decision to convert to Catholicism and then back to Protestantism, each at precisely the "wrong" political moment, indicates that integrity, not expediency, motivated him on both occasions. I think it proper to argue that the presence of poems to Catholics and Protestants in *Epigrammes* is not a matter of mere chronology or disinterested aesthetic judgment, or even a calculated attempt to appeal to both sides, but rather a clear sign of Jonson's idea of history. Individual people, not abstract beliefs or conflicts, compel his attention and his loyalty.

In 1616, however, his primary allegiance was to England and to Protestantism. "After he was reconciled with the Church [of England] and left of to be a recusant," Drummond writes, "at his first communion in token of true Reconciliation, he drank out all the full cup of wyne" (*Conv. Dr.* 314–16). That allegiance influenced his literary style as well as his religious practice. The methods he admired in the Protestant historians he emulated in his own poetry. It was Sir Walter Ralegh who brought that historical rhetoric to its highest point in his *History of the World*.[17] Ralegh wrote the book while he was imprisoned in the Tower, and he fervently hoped that his work would secure him the favor of Prince Henry. Jonson, who was on the Continent with Ralegh's son when Prince Henry died in 1613, was one of the few English poets who did not compose a eulogy for the royal heir. Jonson's prefatory poem for Ralegh's *History of the World* (1614) seems to have served that function. The poem, less about Ralegh than about the writing of history, sums up the ideals Jonson shared with the Taciteans. He presents it as a gloss on the frontispiece of Ralegh's book, an engraving that depicts History holding up the world, watched over by the all-seeing eye of Providence, flanked by figures that represent Experience and Truth, and surmounting skeletal figures labeled Death and Oblivion.[18] Jonson's poem gives special emphasis to the light of truth and to the reliability of experience, "whose straight wand / Doth mete, whose lines doth sound the depth of things" (*Und.* 24.11–12).

Jonson's final definition of history, however, can be traced not to the Taciteans but to Cicero, whose periodic style they and the poet had emphatically rejected: "Time's witness, herald of antiquity, / The light of truth, and life of memory" (17–18). This definition, taken from Cicero's *De Oratore*, fits Jonson's occasional poetry as well. The revolution in historical and poetic discourse from the elaborate periodicity of the Ciceronians to the plain style of the Taciteans nonetheless maintained a Ciceronian concept of history as "The light of truth, and life of memory." The particular way of addressing history changed, but not the value attributed to history.

II

As a Humanist poet, Jonson places his poems squarely in the actual world. The fictive men and women he satirizes, however caricatured the portrayal, were at least types of the people he could expect to encounter in the world. The men and women he praises, however idealized by his verse, were his actual patrons, colleagues, and friends. Because of his commitment to a poetry of interpretation, his response to a particular occasion may seem incomplete. Truth to the occasion of a poem may require tact and discretion rather than lavish praise, and may even require a certain muting of the occasion. Such is the case with one of his most famous and puzzling poems, "An Epitaph on Elizabeth, L. H." Critics unable to identify the lady have concluded that her identity is unimportant to the poetic and moral artistry of the poem. The epitaph is said to move beyond occasion, to deny the importance of ephemeral earthly life.[19] Yet throughout *Epigrammes* Jonson emphasizes the identity of the people he praises. David Wykes aptly terms the collection "a book of names," and describes the poems as variations on the theme of naming.[20] The epitaph is one of those variations. Jonson sets up a riddle; its solution depends on the reader's knowledge of the lady's identity. He thereby affirms the power of historical occasion and circumstance to test and complement the moral truth of his art.

From the title to the closing lines, the poem insists on the importance of the lady's half-revealed, half-concealed name:

Epitaph on Elizabeth, L. H.

Wouldst thou hear what man can say
   In a little? Reader, stay.
Underneath this stone doth lie
   As much beauty as could die;
Which in life did harbour give
   To more virtue than doth live.
If at all she had a fault,
   Leave it buried in this vault.
One name was Elizabeth,
   The other let it sleep with death:
Fitter where it died to tell,
   Than that it lived at all. Farewell.

(Ep. 124)

Read thematically, without regard for its historicity, the epitaph seems to be only a set of commonplaces: virtue (interior beauty) and physical beauty are congruent; a poet can compass a life and confer immortality, determining what endures and what fades; a poet should judge generously—*De mortuis nihil nisi bonum.*[21] However, forging these ideas into a powerful poetic statement is only part of the poet's action. Only if the lady's identity is known can a reader judge her beauty, her virtue, and "If at all she had a fault." Beauty, virtue, and fault are inseparable from the drama of specific circumstance, time, place—and name. The occasional origin and historical particularities of the poem give substance to its conventional rhetoric and moral commonplaces. No mere conventional exercise on the death of a nameless lady, Jonson's poem offers a complex response to a complex historical occasion.

John Major has suggested that any proposed identification of "Elizabeth, L. H." should satisfy three conditions. To be an appropriate subject of this epitaph, a woman would have died before 1616 (preferably before 1612, when *Epigrammes* was entered in the Stationers' Register), would have had some association with Ben Jonson, and would have the title "Lady H———."[22] However, Jonson's riddling treatment of that title requires that the third stipulation be modified. If "L. H." refers in a direct and unambiguous way to a Lady H——— whose name has merely slipped out of memory, then Jonson's elaborate enigma would have no point. It is more probable that "Lady H———" is not a straightforward formal title, but a name associated with the lady in some other way. In the closing lines of the poem, Jonson associates the lady and the name with the place "where it [the name] died," even hinting that the name is "Fitter" to designate that place than to identify the lady. As a means of identification, "H———" may not be entirely appropriate to the lady. Such a speculation argues for a fourth condition, perhaps the most important, that any hypothesis about "Elizabeth, L. H." should meet. It should enhance our understanding of the text—its obscure lines, its shifting tone, its blend of specific allusion and generalized praise.

There have been several attempts to identify "Elizabeth, L. H.": Cecilia Bulstrode, the Countess of Bedford, Lady Hatton, Lady Hunsdon, even Queen Elizabeth have all been proposed as Jonson's subject. Yet all proposals have foundered, in part because a specific lady's initials or date of death rule her out, but most of all because nothing known about the lady helps untangle the meaning of the poem.[23] There is one woman whose name can solve the riddle of Jonson's epitaph: Elizabeth Talbot, Countess of Shrewsbury, commonly known as Bess of Hardwick.[24] She died in 1608, four years before *Epigrammes* was registered. Her family and associates were among Jonson's most important patrons: *Epigrammes* is dedicated to Pembroke, who was married to her granddaughter, and more than half the complimentary poems are addressed to members of her circle. She ranked second only to Queen Elizabeth among the powerful and wealthy women of the 1590s and was unique in her rise from untitled poverty to high rank and immense wealth. She was famous for the great houses she built, especially Hardwick Hall, the most egregiously personal of all Elizabethan prodigy houses. If "L. H." does refer to "Lady Hardwick," then the last four lines of the poem can be explicated as a gloss on the Hardwick name and the circumstances of the lady's death. Other enigmatic lines in the poem can be understood as allusions to her complicated, often troubled relationship with her family. The epitaph recognizes and is rooted in her history.[25]

Given Jonson's familiarity with many people who knew Bess and had very disparate opinions of her, it is probable that he knew the turmoil that marked her life. His riddling wit and his counsel, "If at all she had a fault, / Leave it buried in this vault," convey one meaning to the cognoscenti and another to the general reader, thereby establishing Jonson as a poet at once knowledgeable and discreet, master of any occasion. He says just enough. It is this kind of mastery that secured Jonson the respect of the small group of aristocrats who supported English poets. Lord Falkland later remarks in *Jonsonus Virbius*, "How the *wise* too, did with mere *wits* agree, / As *Pembroke*, *Portland*, and grave *Aubigny*." These were men who knew Bess well—two of them her heirs, Aubigny her enemy—and who "daily flockt" to Jonson and gave him "reverence."[26]

At first glance, Bess does not seem to have the proper initials. Of all her titles, the one that would not have been sanctioned by correct usage was "Lady Hardwick." However, Jonson may have coined the name "Elizabeth, L. H." as an illicit formalization of her common nickname, "Bess of Hardwick." In an early epigram, he claims such poetic license: "May none whose scattered names honour my book / For strict degrees of rank or title look; / 'Tis 'gainst the manners of an epigram; / And I a poet here, no herald am" (*Ep.* 9).[27] "Bess of Hardwick," the only one of her several names that could not properly be prefaced "Lady," was the only one that endured in common use.[28]

Identifying "Elizabeth, L. H." as Bess of Hardwick enables a modern reader to understand what is "wrong" with the lady's name without resorting to lurid suggestions that are not congruent with the poet's confident, magisterial tone. The name "Hardwick" solves the riddle of the last lines, which solemnly declare that the name should sleep with death, as fitter to tell "where it died . . . / Than that it lived at all." The Hardwick name is fit to tell "where it died" because Bess died at Hardwick Hall and there were no men to carry on the family name. Hardwick, moreover, is the place she emphatically identified with herself. It designates not only where she died, but everything about her: wealth, power, strength, beauty, and the ambition for self-commemoration and aggrandizement that had finally alienated her from her large family. She founded a dynasty that spread and endured; she saw her children wealthy and titled; yet she died alone. The last lines may pay Bess a special tribute on her own terms, praising Hardwick Hall as the emblem of the Hardwick name. On the other hand, those readers who despised Bess may well have taken the last lines of the poem as a criticism of her. Jonson contrives an enigmatic mode of poetry that can acknowledge the lady's importance without offending his own patrons in either camp.

Only historical information can clarify the last lines of the poem. Without such clarification, the poem remains at once platitudinous and pointlessly enigmatic, subject to inappropriate hypotheses. A more difficult problem remains: to specify how the poem as a whole is enriched and altered by the hypothesis that Bess of Hardwick is its subject. When this question is raised, the epitaph becomes a kind of test case for the importance of occasion in Jonson's poetry. In this poem, he addresses the occasion in an unusual way. He does not seek to transcend it, as Donne would, but neither does he bluntly encompass Bess in his poem: there is no list of her attributes, no trumpeting of her name. Moving from formulaic praise to an admonition that her name "sleep with death," the poem becomes at once more insistently specific and more hushed in its allusion to its half-concealed occasion. Jonson wants his readers to bring their own knowledge of the occasion to the poem, wants them to solve the riddle of the lady's name. Occasion and lady remain outside the poem, transcending it, conferring meaning on the poet's art. His plain style does not presume to overgo its subject, but rather seeks to impress the reader with the lady's ineluctable actuality. The occasion must be recognized as more than a gloss on the closing lines of a conventional epitaph. The occasion provides its origin, the test of its success, and its primary subject.

Epitaph is by convention an inscription on a tomb that bids the passerby stay to hear a name or brief summation of a life. The *multum in parvo* topos (the idea that art can say "much in little") follows naturally enough (though not inevitably), as in Jonson's "Epitaph on Cecilia Bulstrode" (*U. V.* 9): "Stay, view this stone; and if thou beest not such, / Read here a little, that thou mayst know much." The epitaph for Cecilia Bulstrode is "little" only in length; it magnifies its subject as a paragon who might have become a fourth Grace, "Taught Pallas language, Cynthia modesty," and even "increased the harmony / Of spheres." In the "Epitaph on Elizabeth, L. H.," Jonson makes *multum in parvo* a stylistic norm. He gives the poem its distinctive intensity by simultaneously evoking and restraining both conventionally extravagant elegiac sentiments and the massive historical presence of Bess of Hardwick. He renders the conventional opening in a way that calls attention to this accomplishment: the poem will demonstrate "what man can say / In a little." The lines that follow emphasize not the conventional topics of praise and consolation, but the delicate task of saying just enough to respond adequately to the occasion.

The demonstration of his virtuosity begins with the conventional association of beauty and virtue. The grave contains "as much beauty as could die." This line leads a reader to expect some affirmation of the beauty that could not die, the spiritual beauty of the lady's virtue. But this expectation is not fulfilled.[29] Instead, it is canceled by another, potentially more extravagant compliment: when she died, the poet declares, most of the world's virtue died with her. This conceit, so hyperbolic in Donne's *First Anniversary,* here has the effect of understatement because of the way it turns the expected affirmation of immortality into another acknowledgement of death. The grave receives both her beauty and her virtue—as, later in the poem, it is to receive her fault and name. The effect of restraint is furthered by the use of the comparative mode where one might expect the superlative, and by a parallelism that judiciously balances her qualities. These two stylistic features of the poem combine to suggest a precise ratio for measuring the lady's excellence against the totality of Beauty and Virtue:

> Underneath this stone doth lie
> As much beauty as could die;
> Which in life did harbour give
> To more virtue than doth live.

The effect of this ratio is to emphasize how much has been lost. The word "harbour" is unusual in this context. It is tempting to speculate that Jonson, who by his own admission was recusant when this poem was written, may be referring obliquely to Bess's difficult years as guardian of the Scottish Queen.[30] Mary is identified with Virtue; a piece of needlework, sent to Norfolk by Mary, features her motto, *Virescit Vulnere Virtus* (Virtue flourishes by wounding).[31] The allusion to Mary, if there is one, is not the main point of the lines but a reverberation of historical circumstance that might have suggested to readers how deftly Jonson could say much "In a little."

The poem's central couplet, "If at all she had a fault, / Leave it buried in this vault," denies a ratio of loss and enduring presence, introduces a new qualification of praise, and signals a movement from carefully restrained elegiac commonplaces to the particular circumstances of the lady's life and death. The couplet makes the conventional plea for generosity toward the dead, but phrases it as a warning not to speak ill of her, not to unearth her fault. This warning evokes the origins of epitaph in ritual admonitions not to disturb the remains of the dead.[32]

The admonition grows stronger in the final lines of the poem as Jonson's allusions to her life become more precise. The parallelism of the lines connects her fault to her name (both are to be buried) and also to the place where beauty, virtue, fault, and name all died. As Jonson becomes more specific, he becomes more discreet as well. In the first poem of *Epigrammes*, he warns his audience to "take care, that tak'st my book in hand, / To read it well: that is, to understand." The epitaph demands a special understanding of proper judgment, as well as demanding the historical knowledge that makes understanding possible.

Jonson has commemorated a lady; he has also judged language. The name as all-powerful word, in some ways analogous to the poem itself, has governed the meaning of the poem and exemplified Jonson's affirmation of language. This epitaph presents a powerful display of the plain style that Wesley Trimpi has shown typifies so many Jonsonian poems: the chaste, subdued, confident choice of precisely the one word appropriate to the poet's subject.[33] To demonstrate the adequacy of language is to defend poetry against the charge that it is trivial, merely a leisure pastime. Geoffrey Hartman has suggested that this epitaph recognizes the limitation or "littleness" of art and affirms it: "The recurrent and operative topos of 'much-in-little' constitutes a poetics as well as a theme; it is a defense of poetry's *ignobile otium*, the trivial yet mystical or contemplative nature of art."[34] Hartman assumes that the lady of this poem cannot be known, and that the epitaph is a meditation on the "littleness" of identity, knowledge, and art. If she can be known, then the emphasis shifts to the "much" of "much-in-little" and locates it in the richness of history and action rather than in detached poetic contemplation. This epitaph celebrates the ability of understated language to suggest the richness of history. By implying that Elizabeth has done much and that her name thereby signifies much "In a little," Jonson makes her name analogous not only to the poem but also to language. The lady's name may govern the meaning of the poem; history governs the meaning of the name.

When this poem is read only as a series of conventional motifs, it is judged only as an act of disengaged language, its only context literary tradition. As an occasional poem, however, its language must be described as a response to a particular person, a particular moment in history. This poem explores the possible relationships between its occasion and the resources of language. Given Bess of Hardwick's forceful character and given an audience of her family and associates, Jonson ran as great a risk of saying too much as he did of saying too little. Relying entirely on literary convention, he would have said too little; alluding to specific details of her life, he might have said too much. In riddle, he found the solution to the problem of just how much to say "In a little."

Hugh Maclean, discussing the principles that underlie Jonson's complimentary poetry, cites Jonson's definition of poetic *Discretio:* "Respect to discerne, what fits your selfe; him to whom you write; and that which you handle, which is a quality fit to conclude the rest, because it does include all."[35] In this riddling epitaph, Jonson serves himself, his audience, and his subject. Scrupulously faithful to the occasional origin and requirements of the poem, and therefore equivocal in his judgment of Bess, Jonson achieves through deliberate, restrained, confident language the aesthetic distance that O. B. Hardison finds typical of successful epitaph.[36]

The hypothesis that "Elizabeth, L. H." is Bess of Hardwick places Jonson's poem in a historical context without which the full measure of its art goes untaken. It can, of course, be argued that a poetic idea or problem can serve as the enabling occasion of a poem and that no historical extrinsic occasion is required. However, even in the poetic context of this poem, Jonson's volume of epigrams, a historical referent of the epitaph is appropriate if not required. *Epigrammes* is more than a book of names; it is also a book of occasions. These occasions are more than the common run of circumstance; they present the poet with moments when he must consider how to know and judge another person. In this epitaph, the riddle of the lady's name becomes part of a larger riddle introduced in the opening lines: how much poet or reader can know of another person, and how much of that knowledge can be said "In a little." Even as Jonson shows that language can say much, he affirms that more remains unsaid. There are limits to what can be known, but Jonson suggests that there are also limits to how much of what is known should be said: "Leave it buried in this vault," "Let it sleep with death," "Farewell." In this poem, silence is as deliberate an act as speech. The poet's reticence directs the reader beyond his text to his subject, beyond the riddle of a lady's name to the riddle of the lady herself.

The dialectic of history and poetry is never meant to be resolved, but reciprocity rather than opposition is finally the appropriate word to define their relationship. History occasions and enables poetry; poetry probes, preserves, defines history. If history is "The mistress of man's life" (*Und.* 24), poetry can "honor, serve, and love" (*Ep.* 76) those it finds worthy. Unlike Sidney, whose *Apology for Poetry* sets the golden world of poetry against the brazen world of fact, Jonson tries to bring both worlds together to show their "true relation." A Jonsonian poem marks out the boundaries of its golden world, in part to determine its power to act upon the world of circumstance. History in turn acts upon the poem, evoking poetic action and rendering it significant. History shapes the poem; the poem shapes what will endure of that history.

When the "Epitaph on Elizabeth, L. H." is read as the last of the epitaphs scattered through *Epigrammes*, it can be seen as the last step in a developing idea of the role of poet and the power of his art. The first epitaphs, on his children, assert the personal force of poetry, but Jonson's feelings as father constantly threaten to overwhelm his poetic design. In the "Epitaph on Elizabeth, L. H.," Jonson addresses an occasion that evokes his feelings about poetry rather than about the lady. This poem bears witness to his faith in the public, impersonal force of art. The epitaph offers no clue to his feelings about the lady, but confines itself to an affirmation of art as speech and discreet silence. We may regard this willingness to submit himself to the otherness of the lady as a tribute to her,[37] or (as I have suggested) as a gesture toward his understanding of her complex circumstances and the attitudes of his audience. The poet's reticence certifies his knowledge of the lady and the occasion. His assertions claim his authority as poet and the larger authority of art to address history. As the last and least personal of the epitaphs in *Epigrammes*, this poem is designed to bear witness that art can reverence as well as redress the inevitable distance of circumstance.

"The Whole Piece": Epigram and *Epigrammes*

Then as all actions of mankind
  Are but a labyrinth, or maze:
So let your dances be entwin'd,
  Yet not perplex men unto gaze
But measur'd, and so numerous too,
  As men may read each act you do.
                    (Pleasure Reconciled to Virtue)

Jonson gathered 133 of his "ripest . . . studies," composed in different moods for different occasions, into a book which at first glance may appear no more than a maze of texts, a sketchbook of Jacobean moments. Some poems are narrative, others descriptive. Some dramatize dialogue, others explicate a pun. There are epitaphs, epistles, even a scatological mock-epic. *Epigrammes* includes poems of praise and blame, compliment and condemnation, formality and intimacy. Jonson portrays most of the commonwealth: lord, lady, servant, gambler, Puritan preacher, braggart coward, politicians, alchemists, bawds, hustlers, userers, plagiarists, poetasters, scholar, actor, musician, and poet. He himself plays many roles, speaking as professional poet and man of letters, loyal subject, sincere admirer, caustic satirist, bereaved father, loyal friend. Although he usually writes iambic pentameter couplets, *Epigrammes* includes other poetic forms as well: iambic tetrameter, trochaic couplets, mixed meter, and quatrains. The variety of his book is hardly surprising, since "epigram" was traditionally an umbrella term sheltering many kinds of poems. An epigram could be long or short, satiric or complimentary, sober or playful, and could be adapted to any major literary genre. The accepted forms of epigram included epitaph, epicede, monody, threnody, eulogy, elegy, and palinode; and epigrams could be constructed to accord with the principles of judicial, deliberative, or epideictic rhetoric. One modern critic surveying these Renaissance ideas of epigram concludes that "Its very value rested in an adaptability that defied classification, its usefulness on all occasions for all purposes"; another defines epigram as "a technique rather than a form, subject matter, or attitude."[1]

Jonson's readers would not have expected more from *Epigrammes* than a book of discrete texts, a haphazard miscellany. John Weever, another Jacobean epigrammatist, defends his own book as a deliberate hodge-podge:

> If you looke for some reasons because I keepe no order in the placing of my Epistles and Epigrams, let this suffize, I write Epigrams, and there is an old saying:
>
> > Non locus hominem, sed homo locum, &c:
> > —The placing gives no grace
> > Unto the man, but the man unto the place.[2]

It is enough for Weever that his poems display his wit, and he regards his book as no more than a showcase for each poem.

Jonson undertook no less than a renovation of epigram when he gathered his poems into a meticulously crafted book. He begins by admonishing his reader to study *Epigrammes* as a unified work:

> Pray thee take care, that tak'st my book in hand,
> To read it well; that is, to understand.
>
> (*Ep.* 1)

To a certain extent, the poems of *Epigrammes* are unified by the repetition of moral themes and the recurrent action of pointed wit. When the collection is considered as a coherent "book," its variety of form, incident, and tone are seen in their proper setting, a framework of consistent values and techniques. Most readings of *Epigrammes* have centered on the nature and development of Jonson's moral and social themes.[3] The themes that bind together these separate poems gain their force from the subtle and varied techniques for achieving point that diversify Jonson's work in epigram. As event, each poem records an instance of the poet's speech which his audience is invited to "hear" (*Ep.* 27). The pointedness of epigrammatic closure sets each utterance apart from the rest of the book and confers on each poem a coherence and completeness of its own. As part of the larger text that is the book, however, each epigram contributes to the development of the reader's judgment, which is demanded in the first epigram and tested in the mock-epic that ends the volume. One way to identify the simultaneous double actions that unify *Epigrammes* is to consider the poems as moments of speaking to the world and writing to the reader.

Whatever the length or tone or mode of an epigram, its distinguishing mark is the technique of pointed wit. Jonson abstracts from the rich circumstance and possibility of an occasion its single point. He also abstracts from his own possible responses to an occasion the one crucial component. The point of epigram marks the intersection of the occasion and the poet's response. *Epigrammes* is an intensive investigation of a single poetic form, whatever its capaciousness, and is even more focused because it imitates the work of a single poet, Martial, who was the first to perfect the art of pointed wit.[4]

Yet neither the reiteration of moral themes nor the recurrent technique of pointed wit can entirely account for the unity that allows Jonson to call *Epigrammes* a "book." The very idea of a book of epigrams seems paradoxical: this is a genre for the discrete moment, the detached aphorism, the achievement of "point." The effect of epigram is to dislodge and disperse moral themes, to locate their enactment in separate, fleeting moments. Jonson apprehends the importance of moral norms and themes only in specific moments: "This morning, timely rapt with holy fire" (*Ep.* 76); "Idiot, last night I prayed thee but forbear / To read my verses; now I must to hear" (*Ep.* 58). Epigram plays point against line, word against sentence, part against whole. The pleasure of such an exercise of mind, suggests Geoffrey Hartman, lies in what can only be a "provisional act of mastery."[5] The poet who can gather together these actions into a cohesive book can claim an even greater mastery.[6]

It is tempting to locate the coherence of *Epigrammes* in the figure of the poet. Ben Jonson plays many roles in his book, and given his massive presence in his poetry, it is not surprising to find many critics turning to psychological description. Yet Jonson never presents his experience for its own sake, and he has little interest in probing his own psyche. He becomes instead a normative character, his voice the signature that, in Harman's phrase, "saturates the text."[7] Such normative self-presentation buttresses Jonson's contempt for the ragtag plagiarisms of Poet-Ape: "Fool, as if half eyes will not know a fleece / From locks of wool, or shreds from the whole piece" (*Ep.* 56).

His voice, not his psychology, orders the book, as it disciplines his encounter with history and shapes the moment into poetry. Tradition and circumstance, theme and image, culture and self, brought together into a book of spoken, written occasions, gathered in clusters, in strands, in complementary or clashing pairs, voice Jonson's metamorphosis of history into art, of man into poet. He writes so that "Truth might spend all her voice, Fame all her art" (*Ep.* 106). He seeks a "public voice" adequate to "private fact" (*Ep.* 63) and declares its necessity: "Cursed be his muse that could lie dumb or hid / To so true worth" (*Ep.* 63). He endorses the promotion of the Earl of Suffolk (perhaps to Lord Treasurer in 1614, more probably to Lord Chamberlain in 1603), echoing the King's, and God's, and

the people's "voice" (*Ep.* 67). He satirizes other voices: the pompous whispers of young statesmen, the formulaic phrase of Lieutenant Shift, the easy
self-justifying tones of Don Surly, Sir Voluptuous Beast, Lady Would-Be.
He describes his own work as the voice of truth, fame, aftertimes, and
affection. As he writes to Sir Henry Goodyere, praising his scholarship and
friendship, "Now I must give thy life and deed the voice / Attending such a
study, such a choice" (*Ep.* 86).

An argument for the unity of *Epigrammes* must not only acknowledge but
insist upon the tension located at the interstices of each poem and the book as
a whole. One must attend to the voice of the poet and also to the silent action
of the poet-editor who sets these poems in place. Although Jonson intends
his book to be more than a miscellany, the source of its simultaneous unity
and variety is the individual poem. The pointed ending of epigram insists on
closure, each text autonomous in its wit and vigor, yet surrounding poems
adumbrate the meaning of each poem, and each poem in turn contributes to
the intricate web of relationship and cross-reference, analogy and echo,
repetition and contradiction, that constitutes the book. The significant warp
and woof of this book are history—the occasions of these poems—and the
book itself.

Although each poem originates in what Sidney terms the "brazen world"
or "bare was" of historical circumstance, the created context of the book
enables Jonson to suggest that occasional art need not be entirely contingent
on its origin. It is a sign of his success that critics have not found it necessary
to seek out historical information about the people he addresses. It has not
seemed important to consider *Epigrammes,* for example, as a testimony to
Jonson's relationships with the Pembroke circle (although more than half the
complimentary poems are addressed to them) or to evaluate Jonson's inclusion of poems to Protestants and Catholics as an act that positions him as a
member of both groups or, on the other hand, that enables him to escape any
position at all. By placing his poems in a book of epigrams, Jonson emphasizes their relation to poetry rather than to their originating occasion.
Whatever the vagaries of history, in the new context of the book each poem
can endure. Its meaning for future readers will depend more on its placement
in the book than on its relation to a specific occasion.[8] More is at stake here
than a claim that art conquers time. "Occasion" refers not only to the
originating circumstance or event of a poem but to the reason for poetry. The
relationships between history and poetry are replicated, or given mimetic
representation, in the double action of each epigram as a discrete text and as a
component of a book. Just as history (in all its tellings) confers meaning on
the events that constitute it, so these poems are at once autonomous and
contingent on their place in Jonson's book and on those who read it.

Jonson's organization of his book consistently attends to this double
action of the poetry. To heighten the effect of each poem and of the collection

as a whole, Jonson organizes his book in several different ways. First, he adopts the usual polarity of epigram, including poems of praise and blame. He also juxtaposes poems that contrast with or intensify each other; many of the most vivid moments in *Epigrammes* result from the pairing of poems. Third, Jonson groups several poems that explicate a single theme or situation.[9] Finally, woven through *Epigrammes* are recurrent types of poems: satiric attacks on those who are controlled by their own desires, compromising their human dignity; loving epitaphs for children and revered friends; and ethical poems, both satiric and complimentary, that dramatize and define the act of reading.

Repetition is not merely a trait of this book but its central, complex action. The original Latin meaning of the word, "to ask again," suggests the dynamic, incomplete probing of circumstance and poetic form enacted in *Epigrammes*. Jonson gathers together in one intensive collection his studies in one poetic form, however elastic, studies necessarily limited in type. He writes only a few types of satiric epigram: abrupt couplets, intensely focussed descriptions, concise narratives. His complimentary poems depend on a few formulaic devices: the significance of a person's name, the superfluity of Jonson's praise, the importance of the person as social exemplar. As poet, Jonson values the intensive investigation of a single form and a few poetic ideas. Here, by way of illustration, is his account of poetic practice:

> Repeat often, what wee have formerly written; which beside, that it helpes the consequence, and makes the juncture better, it quickens the heate of imagination, that often cools in the time of setting downe, and gives it new strength, as if it grew lustier, by the going back. (*Dis.* 1709–14)

Juncture and consequence: these form the structural basis of Jonson's book. Some connections reinforce or develop a single situation: Jonson writes three poems to Salisbury, three to Sir Benjamin Rudyerd, two to Alphonso Ferrabosco. Some junctures intensify a contrast. "English Monsieur" (*Ep.* 88) wears his identity in his clothing; costume becomes a metaphor for the fame Jonson urges Edward Alleyn to accept: "Others speak, but only thou dost act. / Wear this renown" (*Ep.* 89). Surly's whore "in her new silks" and the Countess of Bedford's generous grant to Jonson frame the poet's sardonic retort to a would-be bowdlerizer whose squeamishness at reading the word "whore" has little to do with genuine regard for women. Rebuking his oversensitive "Friend," Jonson declares his regard for the integrity of words. Complimenting the Countess of Bedford, he demonstrates his regard for women (*Ep.* 82–84).

Jonson's decision to address a relatively small number of kinds of occasions, to repeat key phrases and rhetorical techniques, and to affirm only a few moral ideas is a deliberate poetic strategy, not what Freud would call a "compulsion to repeat." Lester Beaurline finds the same strategy prominent in Jonson's masques and plays.[10] *Epigrammes*, even more than they, can be described as a "compact series," a set of possibilities developed within a carefully defined framework. The poet creates an "illusion of completeness" by intensively exploring one situation, attitude, or form in all its variety.

I

When Jonson organized his epigrams into a book, he shifted the locus of poetic meaning to the poet's act in its particular character as poetry. The newly created context of the book preserves the ethical significance of the occasion in the new aesthetic context of the printed book. Each text, more-over, contributes to the general dialectic of history and poetry worked out in his book. Jonson's attempt to explore that dialectic sets him apart from other English epigrammatists, who were content to consider their work ephemeral. To quote John Weever again:

> Epigramms are much like vnto Almanacks serving especially for the yeare for the which they are made . . . being for one yeare pend, and in another printed: are past date before they come from the presse.[11]

Jonson, unlike Weever, shared the classical view that epigram, a form derived from inscriptions on tombs, should pay lasting tribute to its subject. As he writes to his "Mere English Censurer,"

> To thee my way in epigrams seems new,
>> When both it is the old way and the true.
> Thou say'st that cannot be: for thou hast seen
>> Davies and Weever, and the best have been,
> And mine come nothing like. I hope so.
>
> (*Ep.* 18, 1–5)

This exchange exemplifies a typical technique of dialogue in Jonsonian epigram. What is most characteristic is the turn of language in Jonson's cryptic comment, "I hope so." By seeming to agree with his critic, he maintains and clarifies the difference between them. His acerbic comment removes epigram from its place in the ephemeral world of circumstance and novelty, and claims for such poetry a place in the timeless world of literary tradition.

This claim invites a further consideration of the importance of Martial as a source of Jonson's idea and practice of epigram. For Jonson, a return to "the old way and the true" meant imitating Roman epigrams, and the design of *Epigrammes* documents his claim to be England's Martial.[12] The prefatory letter to Pembroke and the first four poems in the book (to reader, book, bookseller, and king) replicate the opening of Martial's first book of epi-grams. Martial insists that no self-respecting reader will take offense at his playful, if frank, poems; moralists like Cato should either avoid his theatre or enter and join into its spirit. Disavowing any ambition to be thought clever, finding his own warrant for epigram in his Greek predecessors, Martial consigns his name and his book to his reader's judgment (1.1), advertises his book and his bookseller (1.2), and, in a wry address to his book, mocks the presumption that it (he) could possibly command the attention of the sneering, supercilious Roman audience. Jonson also wel-comes Cato to the theatre of his book, appeals to the same kind of audience, refuses to play the role of mountebank, seeks a warrant for his work in the tradition of epigram, and mocks his own hope for attention.

Although Jonson apprenticed himself to Martial, he did not hesitate to distinguish himself from his classical predecessor. He follows the advice he gives to a young writer:

> I know Nothing can conduce more to letters, then to examine the writings of the Ancients, and not to rest in their sole Authority, or take all upon trust from them. . . . For to all the observations of the Ancients, wee have our owne experience: which, if wee will use, and apply, wee have better meanes to pronounce. It is true they open'd the gates, and made the way, that went before us; but as Guides, not Commanders. (*Dis.* 129–39)

In the epigram "To My Book," for example, Jonson acknowledges the importance of his own authorship and offers a personal apologia that super-sedes its model, Martial's preface to his first book of epigrams, and owes little to Martial's poem to his book (1.3). Jonson ruefully admits that most readers will take up *Epigrammes* only because the reputation of both genre and author lead them to expect what they will not find: malice, wormwood, and gall. Yet he admits that readers are right to equate the author and his book. Jonson's address to his book is in fact a personal defense: "By thy wiser temper let men know / Thou art not covetous of least self-fame / Made from the hazard of another's shame" (*Ep.* 2).

He follows Martial in seeming in jumble together poems radically dif-ferent in tone and occasion, but rather disingenuously contrasts himself to Martial by labeling *Epigrammes* "my chaste book." Martial more often mocks the embarrassments of human sexuality and desire with brutal images of bestiality, disease, appetite, and perversion; he includes seven such to every one in Jonson's book. Jonson draws more often on Martial's satire of pla-giarists, poetasters, and readers of little or no taste. Although both writers scatter self-reflexive poems through their books, keeping before the audience the claim of epigram as art, they foreground poems of human intimacy, whether depicting the intimate supper as an image of ideal community and

friendship or mourning children in tender epitaphs. These poems of friendship and family establish the ideals that demand and support the satire of
greed, exploitation, and the violation of human love.

Jonson owes less to the plot or pattern of Martial's book than to the
brevity and pungent language perfected there. The distinguishing mark of
epigram is its pointed ending, the surprising conclusion so neat as to seem
inevitable. The effect is usually achieved by syntax. A damning balance of
terms or the alteration of one word in a phrase will do: "Cum tua non edas,
carpis mea carmina, Laeli. / carpere vel noli nostra vel ede tua" [Although
you don't publish your own, you carp at my poems, Laelius. Either do not
carp at mine, or publish yours] (1.91). Sometimes the point is hammered
home by blunt repetition, as in this epigram, so often translated into English: "Non amo te, Sabidi, nec possum dicere quare: / hoc tantum possum
dicere, non amo te" [I do not love you, Sabidius, nor can I say why. I can
only say this much: I do not love you] (1.32).

Although he explicitly honors Martial's work as "far nobler" than his own
(*Ep.* 36), Jonson characteristically creates poetry that is much more dramatic.
Martial describes or declares a judgment; he does not enact the process of
encounter and response. His epigram *is* point; Jonsonian epigram *achieves*
point by unfolding and then reducing a complex drama to its final significance. A brief comparison of two epigrams satirizing lawyers can illustrate
the difference. Martial mocks Aelius: "Quod clamas semper, quod agentibus
obstrepis, Aeli, / non facis hoc gratis; accipis, ut taceas" [That you always
shout, that you disrupt the pleaders, Aelius, you do not do for nothing: you
take pay to keep silent] (*Ep.* 1.95). Jonson's dramatic version of this poem
unfolds the act and consequence that Martial had condensed into a quick
succession of verbs:

> No cause nor client fat will Cheverel leese,
> But as they come, on both sides he takes fees,
> And pleaseth both: for while he melts his grease
> For this, that wins, for whom he hold his peace.
>
> (*Ep.* 37)

Jonson shows us both parties to a lawsuit, the lawyer in the middle.
Cheverel sweats and his client's fat purse melts away: Jonson has added to
Martial's idea a proverbial image ("He has a conscience like a cheverel's
skin") to make the bond of exchange physically vivid.[13] Jonson's metaphor
of "grease" equates the client's money and the lawyer's language. Against the
false, melting languages of money and argument Jonson sets his own lean
muscular language of poetry. By using a single metaphor and virtually a
single rhyme for all four lines of his epigram, Jonson packs the dramatic
process of perception and explanation into what finally seems a single

statement, distilled and complete. He then can turn away, can hold his own peace.

Jonson imitates the form and often the tone of Martial's epigrams, but his poetic concerns owe more to the Erasmian Humanists of the Renaissance. Jonson studies "humanity," he declares in his prefatory letter to Pembroke. The term signifies culture, not simply the topical events of Jacobean London.[14] His book is a theatre, a commonwealth, a portrait of his world as it was and as he would have had it be. Jonson is observer, explorer, judge. He presents his encounters not to investigate his own response for its own sake, as Montaigne might have done, but to depict his culture and to instruct his readers in judgment and in public action.

II

Because Jonson approaches the tasks of praise and blame very differently, this set of oppositions can be used to demonstrate some of the ways he achieves "point" in epigram. Name, narrative, dialogue, and catalogue are four of his characteristic techniques. All four are prominent in his satiric verse but occur in quite different forms when the poem is complimentary.

So many of Jonson's epigrams constitute acts of naming that the collection has been called a "book of names."[15] Jonson's complimentary poems celebrate real, named contemporaries. His descriptions of aristocrats, however, are rarely precise or concrete. Instead, he allegorizes these real people through allusions to mythical divinities, classical virtues, or historical heroes. Lady Mary Wroth is "nature's index" (*Ep.* 105), William Roe a "good Aeneas" (*Ep.* 127). Horace Vere and Lady Susan Montgomery attain iconic stature because their names ally them to Roman or Biblical greatness. When a name does not provide an analogue, Jonson converts it to a metaphor: "If men get name for some one virtue, then / What man art thou, that art so many men, / All-virtuous Herbert!" (*Ep.* 106). Or again: "I do but name thee, Pembroke, and I find / It is an epigram on all mankind" (*Ep.* 102). Fact overgoes fantasy and myth, real name displacing conventional metaphors. When Jonson imagines the ideal woman, he finds her in real life: "My Muse bad, *Bedford* write, and that was she" (*Ep.* 76).

One of Jonson's most appealing poems in this view is his graceful compliment to Mistress Cary, later married to Sir William Uvedale:

> Retired, with purpose your fair worth to praise,
>   'Mongst Hampton shades and Phoebus' grove of bays,
> I plucked a branch: the jealous god did frown,
>   And bade me lay the usurped laurel down;
> Said I wronged him, and, which was more, his love.

I answered, Daphne now no pain can prove.
Phoebus replied, Bold head, it is not she:
Cary my love is, Daphne but my tree.

(Ep. 126)

The world of myth and fact are reversed in this deft compliment. In the grove of Phoebus, the real lady has displaced the fictive Daphne. The name "Cary" has been confirmed in mythic status. Daphne, in turn, is relegated to the world of fact and dismissed as a mere tree. The poet, too, is driven back into the world of fact, and is left alone holding a broken branch.

In satiric epigrams, Jonson often invents a name and unfolds its allegorical meaning, or he justifies his refusal to grant his subject the privilege of any name at all. Allegorical names identify a physical feature (Gut, Groin, Cod, Cob, Lippe), personal trait (Don Surly, Lieutenant Shift, Captain Hungry, Lady Would-Be), behavior (Sir Luckless Woo-all, Annual Tilter, Prowl Plagiary, Old-End Gatherer, Mime), or damning analogy (Sir Voluptuous Beast, Court-Worm, Hornet, Colt). To name is to judge, as Jonson reminds "My Lord Ignorant": "Thou call'st me poet, as a term of shame; / But I have my revenge made in thy name" (*Ep.* 10). When he refuses to assign someone a name, he pronounces the harshest judgment of all:

You wonder who this is, and why I name
    Him not aloud that boasts so good a fame,
Naming so many, too! But, this is one,
    Suffers no name, but a description:
Being no vicious person, but the vice
    About the town; and known too, at that price.

(Ep. 115)

"It" is further labeled "A subtle thing," its behavior a catalogue of items culled from earlier satiric epigrams. As the description proceeds, mocking the mime who "acts old Iniquity," the false friend who "is its own fame's architect," and the "engineer in slander," Jonson makes it obvious that his target is Inigo Jones. Yet the poem ends with an act of definition that avoids the name: "Described, it's thus; defined would you it have? / Then the town's honest man's her arrant'st knave."

Jonson had a pragmatic motive for refusing to satirize anyone by name: satire was outlawed. However, he turned this rude necessity to his satiric advantage. By refusing to name "Something that Walks Somewhere" or "The Town's Honest Man," he heaps insult on insult, denying them their very existence. The poet makes them "real" by describing in detail their appearance, behavior, speech, and beliefs, but turns against them their own constricting self-interest: English Monsieur cares only for clothes, Don Surly for greatness, Lady Would-Be for sport. The poet takes such people on their own terms, and never extends their importance by comparing them to figures of myth or history.

By honoring the names of those he praises and assigning derogatory names or denying names to those he condemns, Jonson intends to forward the moral education of his readers. If poetry is to have a significant effect on society, the forces of vice must be shown in their full strength, not linked to any single person but evident again and again in recognizable, "typical" instances, and the ideals the poet advocates must be attainable, shown to exist—however rarely—in the actual world. The satiric epigrams end in confirmed isolation; the complimentary poems celebrate community and growth. Praising Pembroke as "an epigram on all mankind" (*Ep.* 102) or lady Mary Wroth as "nature's index" (*Ep.* 105), Jonson seems to refine their actuality into iconicity.[16] What creates the "realism" of such poems is the specific drama of the poet's response. He feels compelled to write: "[Who] can to these be silent?" (*Ep.* 63). His purpose, he declares in the prefatory letter to Pembroke, is to lead forth "many good and great names . . . to their rembrance with posterity." He never presumes to create a name for the men and women he praises but prides himself on explicating their actual names.

Jonson's epigram to the Countess of Bedford illustrates the dramatic relationship between actual life and the poet's impulse to idealize it:

> This morning, timely rapt with holy fire,
>   I thought to form unto my zealous muse
> What kind of creature I could most desire
>   To honour, serve and love, as poets use.
> I meant to make her fair, and free, and wise,
>   Of greatest blood, and yet more good than great;
> I meant the day-star should not brighter rise,
>   Nor lend like influence from his lucent seat.
> I meant she should be courteous, facile, sweet,
>   Hating that solemn vice of greatness, pride;
> I meant each softest virtue there should meet,
>   Fit in that softer bosom to reside.
> Only a learned and a manly soul
>   I purposed her, that should, with even powers,
> The rock, the spindle and the shears control
>   Of destiny, and spin her own free hours.
> Such when I meant to feign and wished to see,
>   My muse bade, *Bedford* write, and that was she.
>
> (*Ep.* 76)

A variation on the Pygmalion theme, the poet's fantasy of the ideal woman finally pales next to the real woman he addresses. Throughout the poem, he emphasizes his own shaping imagination: "I meant . . . I meant . . . I meant" enumerate every quality of the lady. He insists on the power of imagination to body forth an ideal; there is nothing vague or unformed in his account. He concludes his wishful creation by naming a real woman: what he wished for in imagination he finds outside its sphere. Her name satisfies his wish to "see" as well as "feign" her. All his mythmaking is fulfilled and excelled by her fact. His fantasy has wished her free: "I meant to make her fair, and free, and wise," he writes, able to "spin her own free hours." The one innovation in his inventory of feminine beauty, "Only a learned and a manly soul / I purposed her," permits his fantasy of a conventional passive object of love sonnets to yield to the fact of an active woman who could control her own destiny. In consequence, what has been a poem of creation becomes one of response. The poet, not the lady, has been transformed.

This form of compliment combines hyperbole and understatement, giving the impression of tasteful restraint, deference, and economy. The poet forgoes monotonous catalogues of virtuous deeds, yet the act of naming transforms his general statements into personal and specific praise. Jonson uses this technique to set up a correspondence between a person's internal, unarticulated idea of self and the poet's articulation of the world's idea of that person at his or her best. Jonson recognizes the simultaneous hyperbole and restraint of his method, as his epigram to Lady Mary Wroth confirms:

> How well, fair crown of your fair sex, might he,
>   That but the twilight of your sprite did see,
> And noted for what flesh such souls were framed,
>   Know you to be a Sidney, though unnamed?
> And, being named, how little doth that name
>   Need any muse's praise to give it fame?
> Which is itself the imprese of the great,
>   And glory of them all, but to repeat!
> Forgive me, then, if mine but say you are
>   A Sidney; but in that extend as far
> As loudest praisers, who perhaps would find
>   For every part a character assigned.
> My praise is plain, and wheresoe'er professed
>   Becomes none more than you, who need it least.
>
> (*Ep.* 103)

This Petrarchan sonnet features none of the intricate self-definition and detailed catalogue of the lady's "every part" common to that mode of compliment. Aside from the pun on "twilight" to suggest the double spirit of the lady, her own and her noble father's, the poet seems not to strain to produce the poem. His ease emphasizes his sincerity and highlights her nobility of station and the merit of her heritage. She does not need or demand his art. He presents it to her as his "spontaneous" response to her excellence. Because the poem is neither demanded nor required, its praise is plain and free.

Like the complimentary poems, which often turn on a reinterpretation of their subject, Jonson's satiric narratives generally end with the poet's interpretation or re-description of the story he has told. "On Mill. My Lady's Woman" (*Ep.* 90) traces the long affair of Mill and her lady's page, ending in their marriage when he has "Blown up" and "got the steward's chair." In the last couplet Jonson compares Mill to Milo, using a classical paradigm of physical strength to describe her sexual endurance. Lieutenant Shift avoids paying his debts by repeating his "charm," "God pays." Jonson describes this rake's progress in detail, until the motto shifts: "But see! the old bawd hath served him in his trim, / Lent him a pocky whore. She hath paid him" (*Ep.* 12). Some satiric narratives end with this kind of address to the reader, others with a rebuke to the person who has been described. Don Surly's ambition to be "great" becomes an ironic refrain counterpointed to his every inglorious act: he violates all bonds of courtesy, hospitality, and fidelity. After itemizing Surly's abusive, pompous efforts to seem great—forgetting men's names, eating alone, disliking Jonson's epigrams (the worst crime of all), the poet turns on him in disgust: "Surly, use other arts; these only can / Style thee a most great fool, but no great man" (*Ep.* 28).

Jonson's portrait of Don Surly is one of several satiric epigrams that counterpoint description and evaluation, giving the impression of encounter and dialogue. The satirist often begins by seeming naive, but his judgments grow increasingly severe as he completes his portrait of an English Monsieur, Sir Annual Tilter, or Lady Would-Be. Each of these poems presents mocking questions that culminate in a damning answer or a definition. English Monsieur proves neither statue—"it doth move, / And stoop, and cringe"—nor man, but mannequin: "The new French tailor's motion, monthly made, / Daily to turn in Paul's, and help the trade" (*Ep.*88).

The three conventional voices of satire Maynard Mack has labeled the *naif,* the *vir bonus,* and the hero.[17] In Jonson's satiric epigrams, irony mediates between the *vir bonus* and the *naif;* Jonson usually speaks his blunt conclusion as a satirist-hero, the idealistic man fully cognizant of vice. Many satiric epigrams are constructed as dialogues, in which the poet interrogates someone in increasingly brutal language. The process of the inquiry occasions the poet's development from naif to blunt-spoken hero. Such satiric epigrams include "To Sir Voluptuous Beast" (*Ep.* 25), "To Person Guilty" (*Ep.* 38), and "To a Weak Gamester in Poetry" (*Ep.* 112). The most effective is "To Fine Lady Would-Be," whose name seems at first no more than a sign of her ambitions, but finally comes to stand for her devaluation of life itself:

> Fine Madam Would-Be, wherefore should you fear,
> That love to make so well, a child to bear?
> The world reputes you barren; but I know
> Your 'pothecary, and his drug says no.
> Is it the pain affrights? that's soon forgot.
> Or your complexion's loss? You have a pot

That can restore that. Will it hurt your feature?
To make amends, you're thought a wholesome creature.
What should the cause be? Oh, you live at court:
And there's both loss of time and loss of sport
In a great belly. Write, then on thy womb:
Of the not born, yet buried, here's the tomb.

(Ep. 62)

The rhythm of these questions ironically suggests familiar nursery rhymes; harsh irony mediates between his plainness and his naive rhythm. From mocking questions to final blunt prescription, the satirist takes both roles in the dialogue. In the octave of this truncated sonnet, the poet's compliments sardonically refute the lady's reasons for wanting to avoid motherhood. In the last four lines, the poet repeats the lady's imputed language—"Oh, you live at court"—and draws away from her by redefining the sense of "live." Lady Would-Be presumably intends this as no more than a casual statement of her residence, or, to go one step further, her pleasure ("sport"). The poet forces on her the fact of life itself, which her would-be child has lost.

Jonson explains his motive for writing satire in his epigram "To Captain Hungry": "I oft look on false coin to know't from true: / Not that I love it more than I will you" (*Ep.* 107). A desire for knowledge and mastery, not pleasure, compels him to confront what he condemns. When Jonson truly loves the people he praises, he does not presume to speak for them. Instead, his poetry follows the intricate rhythms of his own intimate speech—elliptical and recursive, blending assertion and qualification, hyperbole and reticence. One example is the epigram to Francis Beaumont:

How I do love thee, Beaumont, and thy muse,
　　That unto me dost such religion use!
How I do fear myself, that am not worth
　　The least indulgent thought thy pen drops forth!
At once thou mak'st me happy, and unmak'st;
　　And giving largely to me, more thou tak'st.
What fate is mine that so itself bereaves?
　　What art is thine that so thy friend deceives?
When even there where most thou praisest me
　　For writing better, I must envy thee.

(Ep. 55)

In an epistle to Jonson, Beaumont had abjured any claim to have the kind of learning he found evident in *Volpone* and *Catiline:* "I would let slippe / (If I had any in mee) schollershippe, / And from all Learninge keepe these lines as [cl]eere / as Shakespeares best are. . . ."[18] Beaumont sent two manuscript copies of unfinished comedies along with a letter that accompanied this poem, and Jonson probably composed his poem in reply. Beaumont fears that his artless lines may prove tedious to the learned Jonson, but excuses himself in the name of friendship: "But I know I write not these lines to the end / to please Ben: Johnson but to please my frend."[19] In Jonson's reply, the friend in him can admit the embarrassment and the envy of the writer in him. The embarrassment Jonson details in his poem results less from real discomfort than from courtesy and literary tact. He arranges the poem as a set of antitheses: "How I do love thee, Beaumont" and "How I do fear myself." He is made happy and unhappy, seeing Beaumont's gift as "giving largely" yet taking even more. Jonson tries to resolve his antithetical feelings by distancing them from him, externalizing his fate as "itself," yet his question, "What fate is mine, that so itself bereaves," forms part of a new antithesis: "What art is thine, that so thy friend deceives?" He resolves the conflict not by appealing to general principle but by admitting his own disparate feelings. The poet in him seems to triumph over the friend: "Even there, where most thou praysest me / For writing better, I must envy thee" (*Ep.* 55). Yet in a single phrase, "For writing better," both poets meet: syntactically, the phrase designates at once Beaumont's compliment to Jonson and Jonson's assessment of Beaumont.

Whether writing to Beaumont or Donne, Lady Wroth or the Countess of Bedford, Thomas Roe or Alphonso Ferrabosco, Jonson adopts the rhythms of personal speech to pay his friends the compliment of intimate disclosure. Many of Jonson's poems to friends, especially to learned men like William Camden, John Selden, and Sir Henry Savile, establish a kind of dialogue between Jonson's own speech and the speech of classical poets on similar occasions. Jonson's "Mere English" readers are likely to miss an important dimension of these epigrams if they "let slippe" their scholarship, for "antiquity of voice" is especially important to his "Newness of sense." Jonson's praise of Camden alludes to Pliny the Younger's praise of learned men, including his own teacher. The compliment to Sir Henry Savile, a historian and translator of Tacitus, echoes Pliny's praise of Pompeius Saturninus, a Roman historian. Such allusions have a double effect: they pay the reader the compliment of assuming the allusion will be recognized, and they occasion a new step in the poet's development of a strong voice.

Name, narrative, dialogue, and familiar address are usually constructed in a spare, linear progression of thought, but expansive catalogue can also be found in Jonsonian epigrams, both satiric and complimentary. Itemizing the goddesses superseded by Lady Mary Wroth (*Ep.* 105) or the pretentious follies of Don Surly (*Ep.* 28), detailing the follies of young politicos in "The New Cry" *(Ep. 92)*, or planning the evening's festivities in "On Inviting a Friend to Supper" (*Ep.* 101), Jonson embeds his acts of satire and compliment, his affirmation of moral norms, in the thick description of his world. What Jonas Barish argued in his study of Jonson's comic prose holds for the poetry of catalogue as well: the poet delights in the texture of language for its own sake as well as for its role in the full portrayal of his world. Language is feast as well as judgment.[20]

The poetic actions of naming, narrative, dialogue, familiar address, and catalogue share a common ending, the achievement or revelation of epigrammatic point. Each epigram comes to rest on one word or phrase, one act of mind and language that at once synthesizes and differentiates the languages and events of the poem. Through these various types of epigram, Jonson interrogates the possibilities of his world and his poetic voice. One set of possibilities affirms variety and the uniqueness of every utterance, another the unity Jonson sought both in art and in human community. Through the interplay of point and richly varied circumstance, Jonson enacts both components of possibility for his poetry.

III

Opposed to both the rich life of the world and the aesthetic wit of epigrammatic point is the single fact of death. Because epitaphs were traditionally regarded as the original of epigram, one might expect a book of epigrams to include a selection of epitaphs. Jonson scatters through his collection epitaphs for friends, for a child actor in his company, for "Elizabeth, L. H.," and for his own children. Two of these poems, those for "Elizabeth, L. H." and Lady Margaret Radcliffe, seem more an exercise in riddle and anagram than poems of deep personal feeling. But in the context of *Epigrammes* as a whole, the epitaphs of loving grief for his friends and children gain a special force. The expression of grief is somehow made possible because of his mastery of the epigrammatic form in all its various capabilities. Moreover, because the epigrams of praise and blame address and judge life, they highlight those moments when the poet mourns a life that might have been.

To mourn his daughter, Jonson echoes in more personal terms two of Martial's epigrams. Martial describes the grief of Faenius, whose daughter Antulla lies in a grove consecrated to her memory: "Ad Stygias aequum fuerat pater isset ut umbras: / quod quia non licuit, vivat, ut ossa colat" [It should have been the father who passed to the shades of Styx: but since that could not be, let him live to honor her bones] (1.114). He speaks of the fertile acres untilled for her and of the grief-stricken parents who will join her one day (1.116). Martial describes the grief of someone else, Jonson his own. Martial, moreover, is telling a third person (Faustinus) of the death, while Jonson speaks directly to the reader.

The poet makes his only gesture of reticence when he shifts from the immediacy of the title, "On My First Daughter," to the impersonal third person of the *Hic iacet* formula:

> Here lies to each her parents' ruth,
> Mary, the daughter of their youth;
> Yet, all heaven's gifts being heaven's due,
> It makes the father less to rue.
> At six months' end she parted hence
> With safety of her innocence;
> Whose soul heaven's Queen (whose name she bears),
> In comfort of her mother's tears,
> Hath placed her virgin train;
> Where, while that severed doth remain,
> This grave partakes the fleshly birth;
> Which cover lightly, gentle earth.
>
> (*Ep.* 22)

"Severed": parent from child, husband and wife from their own youth, heaven from earth, soul from body. This overwhelming fact of separation, summed in a word, Jonson finds in his own life, not in classical poetry.[21] His belief that life is a thing but lent and his relief in her secure innocence comfort him only a little. In the original text of *Epigrammes*, "less" is set off from the rest of line 4 by commas—the two pauses declare the difficulty of that comfort. Even that solace seems denied the mother. To quiet her tears, Jonson appeals to the love of his daughter's other mothers, Heaven's Queen and the gentle earth. The formal process of the poem bespeaks the painful process of mourning: after three awkward couplets, rudely yoked together, three lines for the child's soul and three for her body, the central couplet (9–10) splits like the soul and body of the infant girl. Remain, partakes, cover: these words are set against the parting of parents from child, of her soul from her body. Her body, at least, remains on earth with them, and the horror the father confronts in the penultimate line—"This grave partakes the fleshly birth"—he can accept only by appealing to the loving mercy of earth. His last line echoes another epitaph of Martial, written for the young slave girl Erotion (5.34,9–10), but combines its appeal to earth with a final recognition that we can know only earth, gentle or no.[22]

The placement of this tender epitaph, framed by a satiric attack on "Reformed Gamester" and a compliment to John Donne, enhances the effect of all three poems. Gamester, a born-again Puritan, has suddenly converted after being cudgeled by men who want their winnings: "The body's stripes, I see, the soul may save" (*Ep.* 21). The contrast between false and true salvation, between Gamester's hypocrisy and the infant's innocence, is so extreme that the poems seem hardly related at all. This kind of pairing, like the juxtaposition of Jonson's epitaph for his son with a satiric vilification of the way Chuff disinherits his children (*Ep.* 43–44), illustrates the radical separations, even the failure of coherence that Jonson sees in his world.[23]

The juxtaposition of the epitaph for his daughter and the compliment to John Donne achieves quite a different effect. Jonson pays tribute to Donne's youthful achievement: "Every work of thy most early wit / Came forth example, and remains so yet" (*Ep.* 23). Donne's name will last longer "than most wits do live," and even Jonson's "affection" cannot praise him "enough." Jonson can do little but mourn the loss of his daughter as the lost promise of her youth and that of her parents. By contrast, there is almost too much to say of a gifted poet. His "language, letters, arts, best life" all merit praise. To read these poems next to each other is to be torn in two directions, forced to know what we cannot, but must, say.

Nowhere are style and poetic convention put to the service of deep feeling more than in Jonson's epitaphs for his children. In the poem for his daughter, Jonson had severed even the first-person reference of the title from the third-person language of *Hic iacet*. In the intensely personal, even self-absorbed epitaph for his son, the poet merges himself with his son in a poignant wish to deny the permanence of his loss:

> Farewell, thou child of my right hand, and joy;
>   My sin was too much hope of thee, loved boy.
> Seven years thou wert lent to me, and I thee pay,
>   Exacted by thy fate, on the just day.
> O, could I lose all father now! For why
>   Will man lament the state he should envy?
> To have so soon 'scaped world's and flesh's rage,
>   And, if no other misery, yet age?
> Rest in soft peace, and, asked, say here doth lie
>   Ben Jonson his best piece of poetry;
> For whose sake, henceforth, all his vows be such,
>   As what he loves may never like too much.
>
> (*Ep.* 45)

The poem is constructed around a series of puns: on the name of the boy (Benjamin: "son of my right hand"), on the contrast between a contractual bond between God and man and the familial bond between father and child, and on the implicit analogy of father and poet as makers. The poem can barely contain his feelings: he blames himself for the boy's death ("My sin was too much hope of thee"); he wishes he could somehow free himself of grief: "O, could I lose all father now." But neither the line nor the grief can end. The consolations that he could bring to bear on his grief for his daughter here seem harshly thrown up against his wish to deny and escape the feelings that overwhelm him. He presents the conventional themes of consolation not as statements but as questions: "For why / Will man lament the stage he should envy? / To have so soon 'scaped world's and flesh's rage,

/ And, if no other misery, yet age?" The questions go unanswered, as he finally moves beyond protest to a hollow recognition of his loss.[24]

His tender variation on *"Requiescat,"* "Rest in soft peace," resembles the plea to "gentle earth" in the epitaph for his daughter. In both poems, the simple adjectives alter the classical formula to evoke some sense of the child's innocence and the parent's love. But Jonson does not conclude his epitaph for his son on this note. The inscription that ends the poem both rebukes and embraces the act of language, as the poet forces language to bring his son to life to voice the father's grief. These lines embody a clash of personal feeling and convention, the interplay of public formula ("Here lies") and the intensely private "Ben Jonson." The name designates both the little boy and the poet, shifting from nominative to genitive: their identities blur. Jonson's grief strains the limits of his poetry. Only as poet can he express the grief he feels as father, yet he seems unable to speak in his own voice. Imputed speech, so common a vehicle for satire in *Epigrammes,* here enables the poet to express *as his son's words* feelings that might otherwise exceed the power of his own making. Jonson reverts to the third person he had used to designate himself in the title of the epitaph, forcing an illusory disengagement no more effective than that suggested by the equally forced antithesis of "loves" and "like." The poet stands alone, but he is not disengaged.

The other epitaphs in *Epigrammes* move further and further away from the drama of grief and hard-won restraint enacted in the epitaphs for his children. Moral generalizations dominate the epitaphs for Sir John Roe, aesthetic pattern the epitaph on Margaret Radcliffe, fictive "story" the epitaph for Salomon Pavy (*Ep.* 27, 33, 40, 120). The "Epitaph on Elizabeth, L. H." (*Ep.* 124) uses riddle to conceal whatever the poet may have felt in favor of a demonstration of his poetic authority. These poems thereby achieve what O. B. Hardison, Jr., describes as a consoling aesthetic distance: "The reader's attention is subtly shifted from life to literature—from the pain of personal loss to the impersonal world of art."[25] Although the epitaphs remind the reader of the classical origin of epigram as tomb inscription and demonstrate Jonson's skill in writing this traditional type of epigram, they do more than document the power of impersonal art. Because the epitaphs place Jonson's portraits of living men and women in the context of life and death, time and eternity, they give added point to his two general poems about mortality, "Of Death" (*Ep.* 34) and "Of Life and Death" (*Ep.* 80). Both reiterate the value of life, especially in the face of death and judgment. Unlike classical poets who advocate ethical action for its own sake, Jonson grounds his judgments and exhortations in hope for a life to come. That hope frees him to indulge an aesthetic impulse toward wit and form, and at the same time serves as a counterweight to any overvaluing of the poetic act. The poet can commemorate; he cannot revive the dead. The fact of death, at once certain and unknowable, cannot be compassed in epigram.

IV

The unity of form and value in *Epigrammes* can be discovered only through the process of reading closely the individual poems and investigating their specific place in Jonson's book. At first glance, the book presents an epideictic spectrum of blame and praise. Satiric poems dominate the first half of the book, complimentary poems the second. However, there is no clear linear progression from blame to praise. Any argument to the contrary crashes on the rock of "The Famous Voyage," the scatological "progress piece" that ends the book. Alternation, rather than progression, best describes the procedure of Jonson's epideictic collection. The alternation ensures that readers will recognize his capacity to respond appropriately to different occasions, his consistent response to similar occasions, and his intolerance of any easy, secure fiction of progress. As he remarks in *Discoveries*, "I know not truly which is worse; hee that malignes all, or that praises all. There is as great a vice in praising, and as frequent, as in detracting" (1632–35). If one were to seek a linear progression in *Epigrammes*, it would be discernible as an increased quality, complexity, or clarity of judgment in both satiric and complimentary poems, rather than an escape from either kind.

"My Lord Ignorant" (*Ep.* 10) is only the first of many portraits of readers who do not "take care . . . to understand" Jonson's book (*Ep.* 1).[26] Mere English Censurer (*Ep.* 18), Playwright (*Ep.* 49), Censorious Courtling (*Ep.* 52), Groom Idiot (*Ep.* 58), Fine Grand (*Ep.* 73), Weak Gamester in Poetry (*Ep.* 112), even Don Surly (*Ep.* 28), either misread or misappropriate Jonson's work. Some, like Gamester and Playwright, Old-End Gatherer (*Ep.* 53) and Prowl the Plagiary (*Ep.* 81), are not only thieves but tasteless as well: they cannot distinguish true art from false, and assume the same of their audience. Critics like Mere English Censurer and Courtling apply false criteria to Jonson's poetry: they look for themselves in every line, undervaluing Jonson's poetic achievement. Other readers—King James, Sir Henry Goodyere, the Countess of Bedford, "Learned Critic"—perceive the truth of Jonson's book. Jonson relies on the act of reading to test its worth and to reenact the experiences it records. Poetry is occasioned by history but itself occasions reading.

Jonson's epigrammatic couplets bring together poet and world in a coupling and an uncoupling, at a point just at the edge of disjunction. Then he turns the act of naming, both judgment and feasting, to the reader. The clusters and contrasts, reinforcements and oppositions everywhere in *Epigrammes* mirror the reader's attempt to make sense of the world. In reading the most idyllic long poem in the book, "On Inviting a Friend to Supper" (*Ep.* 101), I suggested that all the subsequent epigrams describe people who would or would not deserve an invitation. "On the Famous Voyage" (*Ep.*

133), the even longer mock-epic that ends the book, offers the acid test to such a claim. It could be argued that the poem is "complimentary," but its celebration of two drunks who row up Fleet Ditch to visit a brothel hardly seems congruent with the sober praise of virtue and achievement in the complimentary poems that precede it. Although most critics have dismissed the poem as "hideous and unsavoury burlesque," it has been suggested that the mock-epic is a kind of palinode, a deliberate contrast to everything that has gone before: the other side of Jonson's poetic coin, a realism to counter an idealism perhaps too facile.[27] I want to propose that "On the Famous Voyage" has a more complex relationship to *Epigrammes*. The poem gains special meaning from its placement at the end of the book. Jonson requires from readers a firm understanding of the other poems and the book as a whole. He burlesques classical poetry, his own work, and the aesthetic ideal of literature itself.

"On the Famous Voyage" should first be appreciated, if that is the word, as a typical Renaissance parody. Writers of the English Renaissance and their audience delighted in translation and parody, in reverence and mockery of the same texts. It should not surprise us to find these attitudes side by side, for reverence requires attention to its limits. Jonas Barish gives as an example the parodic puppet show in Jonson's *Bartholomew Fair*, but "On the Famous Voyage" can be cited to the same effect.[28] Both reduce the major themes of Renaissance literature to raucous bawdry: friendship and love in the puppet show, heroism in the "Famous Voyage." Moreover, both parody specific texts: the puppet show offers a Bankside "Hero and Leander," the poem a rude approximation of Joshua Sylvester's "The Furies," a translation of one section of du Bartas's *La Seconde Semaine ou Enfance du Monde*. Jonson's epigram commending that translation (a commendation he retracted in conversation with Drummond) immediately precedes "On the Famous Voyage" (*Ep.* 132).[29]

A parody can be understood only when it is set against the text it mocks; the very word "parody" derives from the Greek word for juxtaposition. As a literary parody, "On the Famous Voyage" clearly assumes the reader's familiarity with Virgil's *Aeneid*. Jonson models his narrative on Aeneas's journey to the underworld (Book 6). Shelton and Heyden, the noble voyagers, row up Fleet Ditch past a throng of damned souls and fantastic monsters whose Virgilian ancestry is explicitly remarked. Jonson's poem destroys the decorous congruence of poetry and history established in serious literature, whether the *Aeneid* or *Epigrammes*. He does not just misapply lofty language to a vulgar or trivial subject but overwhelms literary language. Horrendous encounters with mundane facts that dwarf Virgilian fiction follow thick and fast in Jonson's narrative. Jonson does nothing to compromise its mock-epic humor. He does not parody the most memorable episodes of Book 6—the hero's meetings with Palinurus, with Dido, with Anchises, with the boy Marcellus. Book 6 ends with a prophetic vision of Rome as an ideal and idealized society, but Jonson's parody remains firmly rooted in London's urban underworld.

Jonson's decision not to parody important episodes in Book 6 implies that his poem might depend on a relationship to a text other than the *Aeneid*. When "On the Famous Voyage" is read in light of the Jonsonian poems that precede it, it seems clear that his mock-epic mocks his own book. Jonson parodies the major action of the epigrams, the evaluation of a person's life and character. The satiric condemnation and didactic praise that alternate throughout the rest of *Epigrammes* are brought together in the unlikely form of mock-epic celebration. Their "transmigration" into a jest is rather like the metempsychosis of Banks and his horse into the sewer-diving cat that occasions the vilest pun of the poem (155–84). This burlesque lifts to mock-epic heights a single obscene pun as the "occasion"—the origin and the reason—for poetry. Just so had many epigrams pivoted on a single name or word. The act of naming, the moral imagery, all the carefully articulated techniques of praise and censure are displayed in a new, entirely inappropriate context, disengaged from their customary didactic function. Such parody lifts the heavy mantle of moral judgment from the poet's shoulders. At the same time, he uses inversion, contrast, and exaggeration to clarify the means of judgment he has developed elsewhere in his book.

Transforming earnest into game throws into high relief the techniques of his serious poetry. In his satiric epigrams, he had used images of "stench, diseases, and old filth" (70) to condemn moral depravity. Sir Cod's foul breath, Gut's lechery, Playwright's gluttony, and the Courtier's "flesh and blood" emblemize their folly and vice (*Ep.* 19–20, 100, 118, 11). No one is treated so abruptly or so emblematically in the mock-epic. Images of "stench, diseases, and old filth" are not employed as vehicles of moral judgment but signify only gross physical reality and are exploited for their coarse comic value. Shelton and Heyden are fellows with the poet rather than the object of his abuse, and Jonson's characteristic moral fervor—only hinted at in passing references to "women, and men / Laden with plague-sores and their sins" (16–17) and to "famine, wants, and sorrows" (71)—is overwhelmed by the impulse to tell a merry tale.

If Jonson fails to make the equation of physical decay and moral turpitude that has been customary in his satiric epigrams, he insists on the equation of past and present excellence prominent in his complimentary poems. Edward Alleyn, Sir Henry Savile, the Countess of Montgomery, Lady Mary Wroth, and Benjamin Rudyerd (*Ep.* 79, 95, 104, 105, 122) are only a few of the exemplary people praised for surpassing the virtue and "pure gold" of their real or mythical forebears. Jonson praises Shelton and Heyden for the same achievement, comparing them to their epic precedessors. Although the parody is grounded in a contrast between the voyagers and the epic heroes they are said to excel, the explicit comparison between them rests on the poet's serious moral principles: the dependence of the present on past exemplars, the precedence of merit over title ("Pity 'tis I cannot call 'em knights"), the need for endurance and nobility in the face of vulgarity, and the primacy of life over the art that judges it. Shelton and Heyden, after "ploughing the main" like Castor and Pollux, deserve apotheosis. Jonson hopes to emulate in art their achievement in life, to equal for their sakes the epic greatness of Homer, or at least of Sir John Harrington:[30]

> I could wish for their eternized sakes,
> My muse had ploughed with his, that sung A-jax.
>
> (195–96)

The counterpoint of classical idealism and scatology, of celebration and degradation, sustained throughout the poem, is resolved in that final pun.

Moral heroism has been the major theme of *Epigrammes*, and Jonson's poems trace his quest for examples of great virtue. Each poem marks a step on his journey, as he praises those who achieve heroic stature and condemns those who fail. The moral significance of such poetry demands the scope of epic, and the epic dimension of the book is suggested by its frequent images of quest. "Of Life and Death" (*Ep. 80*) depicts life as a perilous voyage through "death's region." Elsewhere Jonson compares William Roe to Aeneas, and puns on "travail" to suggest the relationship between an epic voyage and a life's work (*Ep.* 128). Sir Ralph Shelton (who is probably not the Shelton of the "Famous Voyage") is valued for maintaining his integrity in a corrupt world. Shelton is one of the few who

> Dar'st breathe in any air, and with safe skill,
>   Till thou canst find the best, choose the least ill;
> That to the vulgar canst thyself apply.
>   Treading a better path, not contrary;
> And in their error's maze thine own way know:
>   Which is to live to conscience, not to show.
>
> (*Ep.* 119, 9–14)

In the epigram to Shelton the imagery of heroic quest is so strictly subordinated to its rhetorical function and moral significance that it scarcely calls attention to itself as imagery. We are, as Jonson intends, more consciously impressed with his subject than with the poetry which describes it.

In the "Famous Voyage" the figurative journey becomes literal. The voyagers indeed apply themselves "to the vulgar," seek a path through their "maze," and dare "breathe in any air." Literalizing the quest metaphor emphasizes the substance from which Jonson has abstracted his moral language. He thereby quickens our awareness of that language and of the

imaginative energy which in preceding poems was subdued by the requirements of the plain style. The unbridled extravagance of the parody helps us
value, in retrospect, restraint and decorum as another kind of poetic energy,
one which seeks its fulfillment in moral realities and which lives "to conscience, not to show."

At the same time, however, Jonson disengages himself from restraint and
decorum. He seems to throw his carefully nurtured techniques of judgment
into Fleet Ditch along with the grease, garbage, and melted pewter that clog
its stream. His egregious admiration of the voyagers allies him to them, so
that the mock-epic mocks his own poetic authority. Jonathan Culler argues
that any parody places in tension two authorial perspectives, "the order of
the original and the point of view which undermines it."[31] "On the Famous
Voyage" sets Ben Jonson's festive voice against the voice of judgment he had
so carefully established in the rest of *Epigrammes*. The issue then becomes
not what he does, but why he does it. Parody, because it inverts accepted
literary standards, serves by its very nature to liberate poets from their own
dogmas. That is not to say Jonson uses parody to reject the value of classical
texts or of his own book. Poets best parody what they best know and most
value. Parody enacts freedom, not nihilism. Parody may free a poet from a
private demon, exorcising a fear of authority,[32] but such an interpretation
would be difficult to formulate for this poem. Virgil and other Roman poets
did not obstruct Jonson's work but enabled him to claim his own authority.
Moreover, a psychological explanation grounded in some idea of the self of
the poet cannot, finally, be validated.

If, instead of locating the object of parody in the poet, we posit the poet's
voice in *Epigrammes* as the object of parody, then we can begin to understand the poem not just as the misapplication of his epideictic techniques and
values but as the last, necessary test of their effectiveness. Parody implicitly
depends not only on other texts but on the reader's knowledge of what is
being parodied. Jonson has carefully nurtured the reader's moral understanding by dramatizing his own responses to specific occasions and by
creating instructive vignettes of fit and unfit readers. Now, through this
parody, he disengages himself from the role of judge and transfers the
burden of judgment to the understanding reader of his book. Such a reader
can go forth to build a proper "pyramid" that will commemorate men more
noble and feats more worthy than the voyagers and their "liquid deed" (193).
Such a reader also knows when to laugh and how. That laughter will depend
less on a recognition of specific topical references or literary allusions than
on a solid awareness of moral norms and their proper use. The mock-epic
tests the capacity of "lordings" to "listen well" (28), just as *Epigrammes*
challenges its audience "To read it well: that is, to understand" (*Ep.* 1). By
transferring authority to the reader, Jonson breaks what could have been a
confining intensity, a hermetically sealed glass sphere in which atoms of wit

endlessly bounce off one another. "On the Famous Voyage" provides Jonson not only a means of poetic closure but escape as well, or at least an opening out into a larger landscape, a longer narrative, a suggestion of extensive range rather than concentrated point.

The closure provided by parody is indirect: the disparity of subject and style within the poem can be understood as analogous to the disparity between the poem and the rest of the book. Yet this very obliqueness is formally useful in concluding a large, apparently formless collection of epigrams. The sequence of poems has not followed a clear narrative or thematic progression toward a natural or inevitable conclusion. The impulse toward an integrative conclusion is always strong, but in this kind of book can be satisfied only through indirection. For example, Jonson might have chosen a religious poem that looked beyond his book, setting it in the context of eternity. He adopts just such a strategy in *The Forrest,* concluding with a meditation on Heaven rather than a descent into the urban hell of Fleet Ditch. The effect will be another kind of disengagement, a sense of borders transcended by the poet and imposed on the reader. He could have summed up *Epigrammes* in general terms, placing "Of Life and Death" or some such epigram in the final position. Or he might have chosen a direct comment on his self-presentation in the book. Herrick ends *Hesperides* with a personal evaluation: "To his Book's end this last line he'd have plac't, / Jocond his Muse was; but his Life was chast."[33] Parody provides closure of a different kind. Its disparity of subject and style is more than a reflection on the poetry and the poet. It requires that we make that reflection while sharing the poet's capacity for disengagement.

To make such an argument in the teeth of grinning parody is to risk seeming moralistic, sentimental, or foolish. However, "On the Famous Voyage" can be read with other poems about the disengagement of the artist that are clustered near the end of *Epigrammes.* The "Epitaph for Elizabeth, L. H." (*Ep.* 126) is the last and least personal of the epitaphs in the book. The poems to Alphonso Ferrabosco (*Ep.* 130–31) urge independence (even as the poet admits a degree of dependency). In an amusing epigram to Joshua Sylvester, the translator of Du Bartas (*Ep.* 132), Jonson even disengages himself from the act of praise: since he does not know French he cannot judge Sylvester's translation, but he calls up the ghost of Du Bartas to do the job. Epitaph, commendation, and mock-epic, in their radically different voices, at once affirm and qualify not only the authoritative voice of epi-grammatic poet but the illusion of poetry itself. That is, they test the aesthetic idealism and the privileging of art that otherwise dominate *Epigrammes.* Without such a test, the real power of art to press against the limits of history goes unregarded.

"Authors of the Feast": Horace, the Sidneys, and the Poet of Jonson's *Forrest*

> These things agree, and hang together, not as they were
> done; but as seeming to be done; which made the Action
> whole, intire, and absolute.
>
> (*Dis.* 2802–4)

English poets conventionally gathered their short poems into two kinds of books: collections of works in a single genre (sonnets, epigrams) and miscellanies, "works of divers nature, and matter congested."[1] Jonson himself applied this latter phrase to *The Forrest*. Although his comment and the title place it firmly in the tradition of *silvae*, or poetic miscellanies,[2] *The Forrest* stands out among such books because Jonson rigorously edited it to demonstrate his poetic virtuosity and to establish a new paradigm of order and coherence. The few critics who have argued that *The Forrest* should be discussed as a unified whole base their claim on major themes that unify the book: the ideal society, the ideal self, and the ideal love that informs self-respect, desire, community, and art.[3] In addition to the thematic links among poems different in genre and tone, a complex of related actions unifies *The Forrest*. These actions mediate the generic diversity and thematic repetition in the book and account for the placement of particular poems as well as for the dramatic coherence Jonson achieves here. He invents in *The Forrest* the kind of coherence that readers have since come to expect from a carefully wrought collection of poems.[4]

Three actions unify *The Forrest*. First, Jonson documents his extensive imitation of Horatian poetry; second, he celebrates his long association with the Sidney family; and third, he outlines his ideal of a poetic voice. To a Humanist like Jonson, these actions are closely related. He imitates Horace, for example, in order to serve the Sidneys as Horace served Maecenas. The classical tradition of Horatian poetry and the contemporary patronage of the Sidneys shape the idea of himself that Jonson enacts in this book, as man (lover, houseguest, counselor, satirist, idealist, struggling Christian) and as poet, at once dependent and free, capable of imagining himself an Orpheus: "For I shall move stocks, stones no less than he" (*For.* 12). Common to all these actions, as we shall see, is Jonson's inquiry into the power of language. Competing codes of discourse clash within a poem, modes of voice shift from text to text. Jonson explores the double action of poetry as speech and writing. He finds in poetic occasions different uses for metaphor as a rhetorical trope or a mode of poetic intellective action. Separately and together, the poems in Jonson's *Forrest* define actions constitutive of his poetic theory and practice.

Each of the fifteen poems in *The Forrest* contributes to the three main actions of the book, and each gains new meaning from its placement there. The acts of imitation, address, and self-definition develop recursively in Jonson's book, each now augmenting, now resolving, issues raised by the others. Moreover, because these poems retain a double character as autonomous texts and as components of a poetic book, the action of the book itself remains indirect, worked out by readers as they interpret the possible reasons that underlie the order of the poems, the juxtaposition of similar texts, the repetition of situations and words in apparently dissimilar poems. Just as *The Forrest* both fulfills and transforms the idea of the poetic miscellany, so Jonson's rhetorical acts of imitating Horace, addressing the Sidneys, and defining his own poetic voice are both fulfilled and transformed as this book proceeds.

The development of these actions proceeds, paradoxically, even as Jonson seems to turn away from them, even as he includes poems that are not apparently Horatian, that do not address the Sidneys, or that are not written in his own personal voice. These seeming discontinuities in the main rhetorical actions of *The Forrest* remain of central importance to any argument about the unity of Jonson's book and crucial to our understanding of the actions themselves. An argument that *The Forrest* presents a record of Horatian imitation, for example, must confront the non-Horatian songs to Celia. An argument claiming that *The Forrest* records Jonson's involvement with the Sidneys must consider his epistle to Lady Katherine Aubigny (*For.* 13), who was not a member of their circle. Jonson's inclusion of a poem spoken by a "gentlewoman" (*For.* 4) and two of Volpone's songs to Celia (*For.* 5–6) challenge any easy hypothesis that *The Forrest* traces the poet's ideal development of his own poetic voice. "To Heaven," the meditative lyric that ends the book, at first glance refutes the importance of all three actions I find central to *The Forrest.* Jonson seems to abandon Horatian imitation and to turn away from the Sidneys even more decisively than he had by addressing Lady Katherine Aubigny. He also seems to abandon his definition of himself as a poet who addresses and judges society. Yet a careful reading of Jonson's book can show how these three patterns of action, woven together throughout *The Forrest*, find their appropriate summation and reconciliation in Jonson's final poem. What is true of "To Heaven" can be argued in the case of the other poems as well. Jonson does not in fact swerve from his major concerns, nor does he defer the central meanings of his text. These apparent discontinuities clarify and differentiate, rather than detract from, the three central actions of his book. To make this claim is not to justify critical cleverness or intricate argument, but to give the poet credit for a clear and deep understanding of the actions he has undertaken in his book. In every case, I shall argue, Jonson probes the relationship between fact and symbol as the grounds of poetic meaning.

I

The first three poems in *The Forrest* establish the three actions that will be central to the book, and provide initial examples of how these actions will be variously developed. These three poems illustrate different aspects of Jonson's Horatian imitation: the first distills a much longer Horatian epistle, the second emulates Horatian poetry without alluding to a specific text, and the third transforms a satiric Horatian monologue into a straightforward complimentary epistle, converting the "trick ending" of Horace's second epode into serious moral counsel. "Why I Write not of Love" (*For.* 1) rejects the poetry of private desire and prepares us for the moral celebration of the Sidneys in the two epistles that follow. Jonson forgoes personal action in the epistle to Wroth, using a Horatian text as his model for a celebration of Wroth's moral choice "To do thy country service, thy self right." Only in "To Penshurst" does Jonson imitate Horatian poetry, address the Sidney way of life, and consider his own role as poet.

Jonson's theory of poetic imitation, clearly set forth in *Discoveries*, underlies his imitative practice in these three poems and throughout *The Forrest*. For Jonson, *imitatio* consists of two related activities. First, it signifies the essential action of poetry in response to the world outside poetry, "expressing the life of man in fit measure, numbers, and harmony," presenting in a feigned image "things like the Truth" (*Dis.* 2349–54). *Imitatio* also designates a relationship between texts: poets imitate other poets, assimilating other texts into their own work. The process of poetic imitation begins in the apprehension of affinity with another poet, leads to immersion in that person's work, and ends in a renewed, revised, comprehended affinity. For Jonson, this process is not a psychological struggle grounded in anxiety about self or art, but proceeds from an initial integrity and serves an aesthetic community.[5] As he writes in *Discoveries*, citing Scaliger and Seneca, "To judge of Poets, is only the facultie of Poets; and not of all Poets, but the best" (2578–79).

As his own exemplar of poetry Jonson chose Horace. Jonson describes Horace as "an Author of much Civilitie, and (if any one among the heathen can be) the best master, both of vertue, and wisdome; an excellent, and true judge upon cause, and reason; not because he thought so; but because he knew so, out of use and experience" (*Dis.* 2590–95). Jonson's assessment, coupled with his poetic imitations of Horace, suggests that admiration, not Oedipal competition, provides the appropriate analogue for his relationship to other poets.[6] Just as the identification of poetic influence does not explain the origin of a poetic text, so also poetic self-fashioning cannot be traced solely or necessarily to an origin in intertextuality. Jonson's poetry is not metapoetic; he does not take his medium as his subject. Jonson admired Horace not only becuase he wrote both poetry and poetic theory but also because he affirmed the importance of experience. "Experience," although it can obviously include the poetry he encounters and the response that other people have to his work, remains for Jonson a realm outside poetry which the poet addresses in his art.

Although the Renaissance practice of imitation would seem to permit any writer to imitate any predecessor, Horace presents special difficulties. Unlike Ovid and Virgil, for example, Horace creates a compelling personal presence in his work. It is not just that he fills his poetry with details of his life, his tastes, his physical traits. His voice captures the twists and turns of thought and speech, now formal, now intimate, ranging in tone from slang to elegance, yet always recognizable as uniquely his own. He does not take himself as his subject for his own sake—that is, he does not write private lyric—but shows himself engaged with his world: inviting a friend to supper, mourning a child, mocking fools or knaves.

To imitate Horace is at once a literary and a moral project, not merely an exercise in literary craftsmanship but an encounter of personalities and a commitment to a moral stance. Jonson writes about the same sort of events that engaged Horace and develops a Horatian tone to shape his own experience. The often unruly Jonson might have admitted with his critics that he was not by nature Horatian (Marston's Captain Tucca, in *Satiromastix*, declares to the Jonson-surrogate that "Thou hast no part of *Horace* in thee"), but in Horace Jonson saw the "civilitie" he most admired. By imitating Horace, Jonson honors the precept that Horace advocated and exemplified: "To make choise of one excellent man above the rest, and so to follow him, till he grow very Hee: or, so like him, as the Copie may be mistaken for the Principall. No, as a Creature, that swallowes, what it takes in, crude, raw, or undigested; but, that feedes with an Appetite, and hath a Stomacke to concoct, divide, and turne all into nourishment. Not, to imitate servilely, as

Horace saith, and catch at vices, for vertue: but, to draw forth out of the best, and choisest flowers, with the Bee, and turne all into Honey" (*Dis.* 2466–82).[7]

It has long been a commonplace that Jonson modeled his ideal poetic self on Horace, but critics have not recognized that Jonson conceived *The Forrest* as an extensive imitation of the forms and temper of Horatian poetry. The book includes examples of the most important Horatian genres: ode, epode, satire, and epistle. Some, like the ode and epode, Jonson introduced into English poetry, and he was the first English poet to master the Horatian verse epistle. In *The Forrest* he documents his success in this form by juxtaposing two poems written ten years apart for similar occasions: the epistle to the Countess of Rutland and the epistle to Lady Katherine Aubigny. His borrowing from Horace ranges from close imitation of specific Horatian texts ("To Sir Robert Wroth," "Epistle to Elizabeth Countess of Rutland") to general emulation ("To Penshurst," "Epistle to Katherine, Lady Aubigny") to limited allusion ("To the World," "Come My Celia").

At least as important as form and phrase is the distinctive Horatian tone that Jonson chose to imitate. Horace begins his first book of epistles by announcing he will no longer accept commissions to write love poetry. He finds it tiresome to keep writing the same old songs, and he is old as well: "Non eadem est aetas, non mens" (My years, my mind, are not the same). What he will not do, he perhaps should not: "Est mihi purgatam crebro qui personet aurem; / 'solve senescentem mature sanus equum, ne / peccet ad extremum ridendus et ilia ducat' " (Someone there is who is always dinning in my well-rinsed ear: "Be wise in time. Turn loose the ageing horse, lest at the last he stumble amid jeers and burst his wind"). Morality offers poets a refuge; moral, therefore, Horace intends to be: "Quid verum atque decent curo et nogo et omnis in hoc sum" (What is right and seemly is my study and pursuit, and to that am I wholly given). Both self-mocking and determined, serious and comic, Horace invents a 'concerned friend' to whom he can defer but in such a way that the reader will mock the friend, mock love, even mock morality, but sigh sympathetically with the poet.

It has not, so far as I know, been recognized that Jonson opens *The Forrest* with his own condensed version of Horace's first epistle.[8] Like Horace, Jonson explains "Why I Write not of Love." No longer can he pursue Cupid convincingly or enthusiastically: "Then wonder not, that since, my numbers are so cold / When Love is fled, and I grow old" (11–12). Unlike Horace, Jonson leaves his new agenda for poetry unspoken. He centers instead on the moment of decision and his nostalgic memory of his one success in love poetry. However, this anacreontic narrative clears a path to a new poetry and a new subject matter, both Horatian. As Horace writes in his second epode (I quote Jonson's translation in *Underwood*):

Who, amongst these delights, would not forget
Love's cares so evil, and so great?

(*Und.* 85, 37–38)

The delights Horace affirms in his first epistle are moral, and Jonson's imitation of that text invites his readers to expect in *The Forrest* the intimate but chaste tone common to that poetic form. Yet Jonson was hardly "old" when he wrote the poems of *The Forrest;* most were composed years before the 1616 *Folio.* Many of them, moreover, do concern love, either human or divine. By opening *The Forrest* with a distillation of Horace's first epistle that includes the Horatian lament but not the explicit agenda for moral poetry, Jonson adopts a poetic stance that will permit him in subsequent poems to formulate an idea of moral community which can contain, if not contradict, the pleasures of erotic love lamented in this poem and celebrated in the songs to Celia.

Jonson's apprenticeship to Horatian poetry coincided with his close association with the Sidney circle. Although the Sidney family and the Sidney estate figure prominently in *The Forrest,* the connection between the family and the book has never been fully explored.[9] Drummond's conversations with Jonson (1619) provide circumstantial evidence linking the poems of *The Forrest* to the Sidneys. Clustered together in one section of the *Conversations* are references to the Sidneys, to Essex, and to several poems in *The Forrest.*[10] Stronger evidence, though still circumstantial, for a connection between *The Forrest* and the Sidney circle can be found in the contents of a Bodleian commonplace book, Rawlinson MS 31, a collection of poems by members of the Sidney circle. This manuscript also includes five poems from *The Forrest* in texts that are especially significant. The epistle to Wroth is juxtaposed to its main source, Jonson's translation of Horace's second epode. The epistle to the Countess of Rutland is present in its entirety; this manuscript contains the only extant text of Jonson's original ending. The songs to Celia are the extended versions which were printed in *The Forrest,* not the abbreviated texts in *Volpone.*[11]

The Forrest itself provides the strongest evidence that Jonson intended his book as a tribute to Sir Philip Sidney, to his family, and to Sidney's poetic ideals. Several of the poems address members of the family: the Countess of Rutland, Sir Robert Sidney, Sir Robert Wroth, Sir William Sidney. The Countess of Rutland was Sir Philip Sidney's daughter; Sir Robert Sidney was his brother, lord of Penshurst and father-in-law of Sir Robert Wroth. Sir William Sidney, son of Sir Robert Sidney, was one of the children whose upbringing Jonson praises in "To Penshurst."

The pressures of loss and mortality heighten the force of these idealizing poems. By the time Jonson published these poems in *The Forrest,* several of the people he addresses were dead: Sir Robert Wroth died in 1614, the

Countess of Rutland and Sir William Sidney in 1612. Elizabeth and Essex (the Phoenix and the Turtle of the epode) and Sir Philip Sidney himself, whose "god-like" (*For.* 12) presence looms so large in this collection, had died years before. Although Jonson composed these poems while his subjects were alive, his published book has something of the commemorative spirit of *Il Cortegiano*, which unfolds under the shadow of Castiglione's declaration that the ideal courtier lived, but lives no more: "And, as the savor of Duke Guido's virtues was fresh in my mind, and the delight that in those years I had felt in the loving company of such excellent persons as then frequented the Court of Urbino, I was moved by the memory thereof to write these books of the Courtier."[12] Jonson sets his book of the courtier at Penshurst. He describes those who live and visit there, suggests the ambience of wit and play that marks life in its sheltered community, and even claims a place there as its poet.

Although actual events seem to have occasioned several of the poems, the symbolic importance of the Sidneys counterbalances historical fact. Jonson not only describes the reality of Penshurst but transforms the estate into a symbol of the Sidney way of life. This collection of poems, like the Sidney family, finds its ideal figure in Sir Philip Sidney, "where all the Muses met" (14), its ideal place the Sidney estate. The analogues between the account of Penshurst and the varied tones and actions of Jonson's book suggest that the book, too, has a capacity to symbolize the Sidney excellence. Life at Penshurst, like the poetry of *The Forrest*, includes wit, song, judgment, and concord; a day at Penshurst ends, like Jonson's book, in prayer.

Jonson's various poetic responses to the Sidneys are congruent with their historical reality and their symbolic importance. His association with them meant more to him than financial patronage and prestige. Their patronage elevated him to the privileged realm of those who, like him, cherished the classical tradition of poetry and morality and valued the making of literature as more than a professional career.[13] In some ways, Jonson out-Sidneys the Sidneys, and we can learn much about his sense of himself as a poet by removing him from the crowd of London hopefuls and regarding him instead as someone who also functioned as a member of the Sidney circle. Jonson frequently expressed admiration for Sidney's poetry, and even compares himself to Sidney in this poem from *Underwood:*

> Hath our great Sidney Stella set,
> Where never star shone brighter yet;
>
> . . . .
> And shall not I my Celia bring
> Where men may see whom I do sing?
>
> (*Und.* 27, 25–32)

Jonson, however, rarely writes in Sidney's style, and owes more to his intellectual patronage than to his poetry. In *An Apologie for Poetry*, Sidney had urged the attainment of an excellent English verse as a patriotic ideal, arguing in expressly Horatian terms:

> they that delight in Poesie it selfe should seeke to knowe what they doe, and how they doe; and, especially, looke themselues in an vnflattering Glasse of reason, if they bee inclinable vnto it. For Poesie must not be drawne by the eares; it must bee gently led, or rather it must leade. Which was partly the cause that made the auncient-learned affirme it was a diuine gift, and no humaine skill . . . *Orator fit, Poeta nascitur.* Yet confesse I always that as the firtilest ground must bee manured, so must the highest flying wit with haue a *Dedalus* to guide him. That Dedalus, they say, both in this and in other, hath three winges to beare it selfe vp into the ayre of due commendation: that is, Arte, Imitation, and Exercise.[14]

Most poets of the Sidney circle responded to this challenge by attempting to recreate classical literature in English: Daniel's Senecan tragedies, Lady Elizabeth Falkland's *Miriam Queen of Jewry*, and Spenser's and Sidney's experiments in quantitative verse are but a few familiar examples. But of all the classically minded writers in the Sidney circle, Jonson had the greatest success in guiding English verse through imitation of Latin: *The Forrest* comes closer than any other work to the kind of achievement Sidney advocated. Jonson's book is at once Horatian and quintessentially English.

This dual achievement is nowhere more evident than in "To Penshurst" (*For.* 2), a monument to English life and Horatian art. Jonson does not allude to any Horatian text, yet this poem is rightly celebrated as the first truly successful English epistle in the descriptive, discursive mode of Horace. Behind Jonson's poem stand the many Horatian invitations to enjoy country life, poems that range freely and associatively from factual descriptions of Horace's Sabine farm to anecdotes, allusions, metaphors, and memories.[15] Jonson writes as though he had accepted such an invitation to Penshurst, and he presents himself as a grateful guest.[16]

As a place, Penshurst makes possible, indeed invites, poetry that blends description and myth, fact and fancy, incident and principle. The conventional languages of pastoral and satire and the allusive narrative of anecdote each contribute to a particular phase of the poem, but no one of them entirely defines it; together, however, they afford Jonson an indirect way to work out his response to the reality he addresses. This indirection, in turn, permits and even requires his return to the language of direct statement. Jonson learns from Horace how to write poetry that seems discursive, ordered by association and experience rather than logic or principle, subordinating his associative imagination to the "reality" of his subject. Penshurst elicits from Jonson many different modes of imaginative response, but "To

Penshurst" remains a poem more about an estate than about imagination. The poet finds satisfaction not in discovering the power of his imagination to create a fictive golden world, but in responding to one that truly exists. By returning again and again to a "flat" mode of description, Jonson enhances the portrait of Penshurst's reality being created in the poem. He also keeps before his readers a stable sense that the estate is his true subject. Its reality as fact serves as the strong foundation of its capacity for symbolic meaning.

Although Jonson is not the subject of this poem, he uses the fiction of his own experience at Penshurst to organize the different idioms of the poem into coherent narrative. As a visitor just down from London, he is easily diverted from the realism "of soil, of air, / Of wood, of water" (7–8) to the idealizing conventions of pastoral, the city-dweller's language for the country. He dots the landscape with Pan and Bacchus, fauns and satyrs, dryads and sylvans. Because Penshurst pours forth its abundance to him, he pulls back from that language of conventional imaginary landscape and finds a truer poetic language in listing its resources and naming its family landmarks: deer and conies, "purpled pheasant" and "painted partridge," cattle feeding in the meadow "that to the river bends," the oak commemorating Sir Philip Sidney's birth, the Gamage, Ashour, and Sidney copses (19–29).

Still an outsider, still an observer, Jonson stands at the boundary between country and urban life. His awareness of the disparity between these two appears as he shifts from the indulgent language of pastoral to the judgmental language of satiric allegory. He begins his account of fishing with what seems a simple, direct statement—"Thou hast thy ponds that pay thee tribute fish" (32)—but in that word "tribute" introduces the political idiom of power and competition. Court and city, still foremost in his mind, provide the context in which he experiences life at Penshurst. He is surprised, for example, that the fish here forgo their predatory, competitive ways: pikes weary of eating lesser fry, "Bright eels" emulate their elders. Jonson speaks of the court using exactly this image in *Discoveries:* "The great theeves of a State are lightly the officers of the Crowne; they hang the lesse still; play the Pikes in the Pond: eate whom they list" (1306–8). Prepared to find in nature an analogue to the rapacious human world of London and the Court, he finds instead game and fish so "willing to be killed" (30) that they seem to him to "leap on land / Before the fisher, or into his hand" (33–38). The object of his satire remains the urban world, with at least a mocking glance at the homocentric enthusiasm of his own imagination. But he restrains his imagination and reverts to simple, direct description: "Then hath thy orchard fruit, thy garden flowers." He lists them: cherry, plum, fig, grape, quince, apricot, and peach. It is enough to list them. When image does creep into his description, it does so merely as realistic vignette: a child plucks a "woolly peach" (39–44).

The abundance of the estate lures Jonson to participate in its life. Treated like a king, he acts like one. He imagines legendary dalliances in the oak grove, casts an appreciative glance at the village maidens, and enjoys everything from the lavish supper to the fragrant candles that light him to a bed of fresh-laid linen. But his pleasure in the estate belies a ruder reality: the maidens have come to seek husbands, the long-suffering servant who seems so generous "knows below he shall find plenty of meat" (70). More is at work here than fancy, and Jonson's verse comprehends the rich network of motives and satisfactions that marks life for everyone at Penshurst.[17]

At the moment when he most participates in the life of the estate, Jonson most participates in literary tradition as well. Allusions to classical literature, particularly to Martial's invitational poems, inform Jonson's account of supper at Penshurst. The allusions here seem inextricable from fact: Jonson presents as his own experience anecdotes from Martial's poetry.[18] If Penshurst at first served the imagination, by the end of the poem Jonson has found a way to make his literary imagination, and literary language, serve the estate.

It would not be useful to describe this poem as a series of rejected, inadequate langauges.[19] Penshurst offers itself in abundance, and Jonson returns to it every poetic gift he can muster. If he mocks his initial enthusiasm, he nonetheless indulges it and is indulged; his first response to Penshurst is, after all, legitimate praise. By expressing each phase of response, and allowing each its value, Jonson describes the estate in its own dimensions like itself and participates in it not "as if" he ruled there but as a guest who has come to know, if only for a while, what it means to "dwell" there. Penshurst as a place for poetry enables him to fashion his own ideal poetic voice. As the village maidens bring to Penshurst gifts of plum and pear, "An emblem of themselves" (56), so Jonson brings this poem, an emblem of his desire, his knowledge, and his authority to speak the value of the place.

The poem participates in each of the three actions that dominate *The Forrest,* and the particular relationships among these actions in this text establish a model for their relationships in the rest of Jonson's book. Don E. Wayne and Stanley Fish have recently argued that Jonson's classicism provides him a measure of independence from the patronage he sought and required.[20] On the other hand, by imitating Martial and Horace, who themselves write poetry for patrons, Jonson seems to embrace a poetry of dependency. In addition, it is his classicism that gives him access to the Sidneys. Perhaps the key to this double-edged art is Jonson's decision to couple arts of description and self-dramatization in his poetry. In dramatizing his own poetic choices and his own experience of the Sidney estate, as well as itemizing its topography, its "country stone" and its "liberal board," he both resists being an outsider and retains the otherness his integrity requires. By imitating Horace, Jonson honors the poetic values of his patrons and his own as well. The relationship between the Horatian and

Sidneyan actions of the poem can also be approached from the opposite perspective. That is, Jonson gives life to what would otherwise be no more than a literary imitation by submitting his Horatian art to English reality. What can be concluded, at least provisionally, is that Jonson establishes Horatian poetry and Sidneyan community as the two contexts in which he will form his idea of a poetic self.

That idea of self, even at this stage of *The Forrest*, should be distinguished from autobiography or personal desire. What is being defined is an ideal of poetic voice, not a model life to be achieved in the world of circumstance or literary history. The poems that follow "To Penshurst"—the epistle to Sir Robert Wroth, the dramatic monologue of a "gentlewoman," and Volpone's songs to Celia—do not concern the poet's own experience at all. If, however, these poems as a group refute any claim that every poem in *The Forrest* constitutes an episode in the poet's self-dramatization, that seems to be the only thing that they have in common. Faced with Horatian epistle, Christian complaint, and Catullan love song, a reader cannot but declare that *The Forrest* is a miscellany after all. So it is, but by turning to other connections between these poems and the rest of *The Forrest* I hope to demonstrate that these poems do contribute, if only by indirection, to all the actions that unify the book, the definition of poetic voice as well as Horatian imitation and Sidneyan compliment.

The first step in making this argument is to explore the relationship between "To Penshurst" and the epistle to Sir Robert Wroth. Both poems are Horatian in form and tone, but the epistle to Wroth imitates a specific Horatian text, the second epode, which Jonson had already translated (*Und.* 85). Jonson does not merely "English" this familiar Horatian text but transforms its enigmatic narrative into a consistent moral argument by converting Horatian fact to an idiom of Christian metaphor. This transformation is based in Jonson's decision to abandon the Horatian fiction of dramatic monologue in favor of direct address and argument.

The difference between the indirect mode of "To Penshurst" and the direct address to Wroth may reflect the different circumstances of Sidney and Wroth. Although Jonson describes Penshurst as a dear perpetual place for the Sidney family, they had acquired it only a few generations before and its resources were sorely taxed by Sir Robert Sidney's frequent absence and heavy financial obligations at court. As J. C. A. Rathmell has noticed, the pressures of quotidian reality—debt, professional disappointment, family disagreements—threatened the life Jonson portrays in the poem.[21] His apostrophe to Penshurst is more than a generalized celebration of its beauty; he implicitly counsels Sir Robert Sidney to turn away from the court and to "dwell" at home. Rathmell's survey of the Sidney correspondence reveals that Jonson's general statements in the poem often veil astute comments on particular conditions facing the Sidney family. The idealized portrait of the

estate disguises counsel as description. Quite different circumstances occasion Jonson's epistle to Wroth, a young man who had less ambition than his
father-in-law and who had only recently inherited his father's rich estates. In
addition, the political climate had changed. King James expressly and repeatedly ordered members of his court to take up residence in the country, and
this epistle could even be read as a document of Jacobean domestic policy.[22]
Wroth, a dedicated sportsman with no particular interest in the arts or court
affairs, would have had little trouble following the dictates of that policy. We
know from surviving correspondence, moreover, that King James and Prince
Henry were fond of visiting Wroth for hunting expeditions, and in 1605
James would appoint Wroth a "forester," whose duty was to scout for
hunting parties in the royal forest at Essex.[23] Just as significant, Jonson was
on more intimate terms with the young Wroths than with the older Sidneys.
Lady Wroth danced in several Jonsonian masques, and she is the only
woman to whom he dedicated a play—*The Alchemist*. He admired both the
lady and her poetry and addressed two epigrams to her. Unlike her mother,
Lady Barbara Sidney, who is so prominent in "To Penshurst," Lady Mary
Wroth is mentioned only once in the epistle to Wroth, as his "noblest
spouse." The reason may be that the Wroth marriage was already founder-
ing; Jonson himself would confide to Drummond that "my lady Wroth is
unworthily maried on a Jealous husband."[24]

Whatever the difference of occasion and circumstance, both poems are
Horatian in idea and tone. Jonson praises Wroth for taking the counsel that
underlies his tribute to Penshurst, choosing a life justly and generously
proportioned:

> Thy peace is made; and when man's state is well,
> 'Tis better if he there can dwell.
>
> (93–94)

Dwell. For Jonson this word summed the values of life at Penshurst: "Thy
lord dwells" (102). Here he uses the word to designate not only life at a
country estate but also a state of mind. Durrants, the country estate Wroth
chose as his chief residence, mirrors his moral values. It becomes, in Jonson's
poem, a metaphor for the ideal interior state of its lord. This shift to
metaphor distinguishes Jonson's text from its Horatian predecessor.

Horace and Jonson confront the same problem: how to balance satire and
idealism in portraying the contrast of city and country life. On the one hand,
it is crucial to avoid mere idealization of country life. On the other hand,
satiric denunciation of the rest of the world must not be allowed to take over
the poem. The two poets solve this problem in different ways. Horace found
his solution in an apparent change of speaker. For most of the poem, he
seems to speak in his own voice. However, in the famous "trick ending" of

the epode he reveals that Alfius the moneylender has been the person singing the praises of country life. His dream indulged and his debts collected, Alfius returns to business as usual. The nostalgic longing for rural simplicity and abundance is entirely free from satire or qualification until the ending throws a shadow over the preceding text. The sudden infusion of satire invites several interpretations. We may admit the claims of "reality": other appetites and desires outweigh what seems, finally, an escapist fantasy of a cynical or harried businessman. At the same time, the ideal can be reaffirmed precisely because an Alfius requires it—even, or especially, if only in imagination. Finally, the reader can redeem the celebration of country life by disengaging it from the speaker. The speaker, that is, not the idea, becomes the object of satire: Alfius is too corrupted by worldly greed to recognize his true good. Whatever interpretation(s) we choose, drama, not metaphor, remains the core of the Horatian poem.

As argument rather than narrative, Jonson's poem contrasts different forms of gratification. He brings the competing values of urban and rural life explicitly before the reader (and Wroth), juxtaposing satire and idealism throughout the epistle. The poem is written in four parts: an attack on court and city life; a celebration of life at Wroth's country estate; satiric portraits of men who define success only as glory, power, competition, and wealth; and a final homiletic admonition. Satire dominates the first and third sections, praise the second and fourth. No dramatic revelation compels us to revise our reading of Jonson's poem, and no sudden shift in narrative stance undermines our appreciation of Durrants or Wroth. The epistle to Wroth celebrates country life and mocks court and city life, including the entertainments Jonson himself helped create: "the jewels, stuffs, and pains, the wit / There wasted, some not paid for yet!" (11–12). But aside from the personal overtones of these satiric comments on masquing, this poem does not dramatize Jonson's experience. This poem is not self-referential: Jonson does not trace his own interior progress, as he had in "To Penshurst." Wroth, not Jonson, is the person whose choices are described and endorsed. Moreover, those choices have already been "made" (1).

All four sections of this poem operate the same way to transform Horatian narrative into metaphor. Jonson does this first in a satiric catalogue of urban vices, castigating city feasts and court masques, militarists, lawyers, misers, and court sycophants. This inventory, which has no counterpart in Horace's second epode, does more than illustrate the disdain of urban life so characteristic of Horatian epodes. Jonson defines the value of country life by contrasting it to the perverse alchemy of greed that reduces urban life to an aggregation of commodities. There is no value but price, no goal but exchange:

> Let this man sweat and wrangle at the bar
> For every price in every jar,

And change possessions oftener with his breath
    Than either money, war, or death . . .
Let that go heap a mass of wretched wealth
    Purchased by rapine. . . .

                                                                    (73–82)

There is a striking difference between these lines and Jonson's close translation of Horace's second epode. In the translation, Jonson anticipates the
satiric point of the Horatian text by opening Alfius's reverie with a specific
allusion to usury: "Happy is he, that . . . is not in the usurer's bands" (*Und.*
85.1–4). The epistle to Wroth does not require this kind of narrative prolepsis
but argues vigorously its own idea of virtue as the discipline of true hap-
piness. Jonson uses direct satire to invest his Horatian poetry with moral
urgency. By transforming fact to symbol, Jonson makes metaphor enact
what it describes: the mind's liberation from the oppressive materiality—
"the mass of wretched wealth"—heaped up in his satiric catalogue.

That shapeless "mass of wretched wealth / Purchased by rapine" is countered by the abundant wool, wheat, apples, hogs, and timber Durrants
pours forth in the "several seasons" of the year (39–46). But Jonson intends
more than an economic contrast. He transforms the bounty of Durrants into
a metaphor or moral innocence (66). That bounty, moreover, becomes the
symbol of God's generous love: "howsoever we may think things sweet, /
He always gives what he knows meet, / Which who can use is happy" (97–
99). Material substance becomes a metaphor for spiritual life, not just an
obstacle to it, and therefore a means of its attainment in imagination.

Jonson converts to metaphor even the trick ending of the Horatian epode,
transforming the language of usury into a language of love. Man is "dearer"
to God than he is to himself (96); God "gives what He knows meet, / Which
who can use is happy" (98–99). God is the lender of life itself, and Wroth can
pay his debt to God by meeting a double obligation: "To do thy country
service, thyself right" (103). Jonson's metaphor honors both Horatian detachment and Christian obligation: "when thy latest sand is spent, / Thou
mayst think life a thing but lent" (105–6). Jonson not only turns satire to
complimentary counsel but goes beyond the Horatian stoicism that takes
personal autonomy as its goal.

II

The first three poems establish the patterns that will be worked out in *The
Forrest* as a whole and indicate some of the different relationships between
the acts of address, imitation, and self-definition. The poems at the heart of
The Forrest seem to abandon the patterns established in the first group of
poems. The first, "Farewell to the World" (*For.* 4), has a woman as its

speaker; the songs (*For.* 5–7, 9) and the satiric epigram "On Sickness" (*For.* 8) take women as their object. These poems are not written in Horatian genres, they do not address the Sidneys, and they cannot be construed as the poet's self-dramatization. By placing these poems immediately after the two Horatian epistles, Jonson forcefully asserts the character of his book as a miscellany. As we shall see, however, in less obvious ways these poems do contribute to the actions that unify this book.

It has been noted by other critics that there are thematic links between these poems and the rest of the collection. Don E. Wayne has remarked on the repetition of the theme of dwelling "at home" common to the Sidney epistles and "Farewell to the World."[25] Jonathan Kamholtz outlines the relationship between marriage (praised in the epistles) and courtship (enacted in the songs) as stages in human love, and argues that these poems point forward to the formulation and enactment of sacred love later in *The Forrest*.[26] It should also be noted that these poems as a group present three different, common approaches to woman as symbolic subject.

I want to propose that these apparently anomalous, disparate poems contribute to the three rhetorical actions I find central to the book. Two of the poems in this group contain hitherto unnoticed Horatian allusions that are crucially important to each poem's tone and action. The Sidneys are not expressly addressed in any of these poems, but several have been linked to the family. According to Drummond, "That Women Are But Men's Shadows" originated as a jest at the Pembroke table, and the satiric epigram "To Sickness" may have been occasioned by Jonson's sympathy for the mother of Sir Philip Sidney, who was scarred by smallpox.[27] Although none of these poems can be called acts of personal self-definition, they do define the range of the poet's voice (including his ability to create a voice wholly other than his own, that of the "gentlewoman"). Moreover, in "To Heaven" (*For.* 15) Jonson will present as his own an act very like that of the gentlewoman's farewell to the world. The connection between these two poems is not the development of theme so much as the congruence of action. What Jonson praises in Wroth and dramatizes in the gentlewoman's monologue, he will finally prove on his own pulse.

The apparently effortless and amply rewarded choices of the Sidneys and Wroth stand in sharp contrast to the decision of a virtuous gentlewoman in her dramatic monologue "To the World" (*For.* 4). She achieves peace not by withdrawing from the world but by recognizing its dangers as the external equivalents of her own weaknesses. Yet part of the action of this poem is the banishing of a certain kind of familiar metaphor-making that prevents useful self-knowledge. The moment when her language changes, moreover, is marked by an allusion to a Horatian text. In this poem, it is the Horatian temper that replaces metaphor with a chastened realism.

Wesley Trimpi has dismissed this poem as "accumulated aphoristic comment," but all its commonplaces further the gentlewoman's dramatic realization of what these ideas can mean for her own life.[28] Moreover, the aphorisms of the poem are concentrated in the first twenty lines, as she recounts what she "knows" about the "false world" and about her own ideal self. The world, she insists, is a "stage," a labyrinth of "subtle ways," a seducer whose gifts are "baits." In her eyes, the world is a whore:

> I know too, though thou strut and paint,
>   Yet art thou both shrunk up and old;
> That only fools make thee a saint,
>   And all thy good is to be sold.
>
> (13–16)

The pun on "good" as virtue and commodity leads to another familiar metaphor, the world as "a shop / Of toys and trifles" (17–18). As whore or toyshop, the world is enticing, deceptive, and for sale. To oppose the world as whore, the gentlewoman adopts an idealized image of woman. She imagines herself a second Virgin Mary, defying the world in the language of the biblical covenant (Gen:3.15):

> Do not once hope that thou canst tempt
>   A spirit so resolved to tread
> Upon thy throat and live exempt
>   From all the nets that thou canst spread.
>
> (5–8)

Whether or not Jonson wrote this poem while he was a Catholic, influenced by vestiges of Mariolatry, is hard to say. Only the Virgin, according to Catholic doctrine, was exempt from human frailty; only for her sake "a miracle was wrought" (58). In any event, Jonson's gentlewoman sees herself and the world in terms of the familiar extremes of woman as whore and woman as virgin.

An allusion to a Horatian satire signals her escape from the restrictive idiom that shaped the first twenty lines of her complaint.[29] Her rhetorical questions—"Having 'scaped, shall I return / And thrust my neck into the noose[?]"; What bird or beast, "tasting air and freedom," will seek a cage? (21–32)—echo word for word those of the slave Davus, who rebukes Horace for being slave to his own passionate desires: "quae belua ruptis, / cum semel effugit, reddit se prava catenis?" (*Sat.* 2.7.70–71). "Who then is free?" Davus asks, and answers his own question: "The wise man, who is lord over himself" [quisnam igitur liber? sapiens, sibi qui imperiosus] (83). The language of classical stoicism enables the gentlewoman to define herself more truly than the extremes of woman as virgin and woman as whore would permit. Freed from metaphoric extremes, she can freely accept both the world and herself: "Else I my state should much mistake, / To harbour a divided thought / From all my kind" (57–59). She does not need the "false relief" promised by the world, nor need she fear it as an image of what she might at her worst become. She can assess her strengths "as they are," not as metaphor would have them be (67). Thus classical Horatian satire has served contemplative Christian resolve.

Jonson's first song to Celia (*For.* 5) surely embodies the seductive world the gentlewoman resists. This remarkable song shifts the audience from morality to eroticism, from complaint to lyric, from the chaste contemplation of the gentlewoman to the self-serving exhortation of Volpone. By juxtaposing "Farewell to the World" and "To Celia," Jonson gives austere complaint and exuberant song equal weight as attitudes toward life. His *Forrest* includes both *contemptus mundi* and hedonism, Christian plain style and lush Catullan lyric.

There is one important point to make about the several songs grouped together in *The Forrest:* their theme and tone are less important than their highly polished art. The leavening of morality (and poetry) by sensual enjoyment—refined by the discipline of poetic craft—is sufficient justification for their presence here. Not love but love song is the substantive achievement they record. Jonson includes the songs to Celia because they can stand alone as perfected songs, not because they are memorable bits from *Volpone.* It has never been noticed that Jonson added several lines from another Horatian satire (*Sat.* 1.2) to the *Forrest* version of this song.[30] The last lines of Jonson's song, "To be taken, to be seen, / These have crimes accounted been," echo a lecher's final comment in a Horatian satire on the risks of adultery: "deprendi miserum est" [To be caught is an unhappy fate] (134). This Horatian allusion restores to the song something of the cynicism that was provided in *Volpone* by the disparity between the lyric song and its lecherous singer.

The perfection of song is nowhere more achieved than in the one song to Celia that was not part of Volpone's repertoire. "Drink to me only with thine eyes," like its wreath of roses sent to Celia, weaves together lines from several poems of Philostratus and turns them into something wholly new. The action of the poem can be quickly summarized: the lover sends Celia a wreath of roses; she returns it; it now reminds him of her, and leads him to want more from her—a look, a kiss. The poem seems to proceed from imagined gifts to a real wreath of roses; only on reflection do we recognize that the sending of the wreath and its return precede the poem. Yet the wreath, by being placed last in the poetic sequence of gifts, becomes the climax as well as the origin of that sequence.

If the inverted sequence of the narrative suggests the force of desire, the syntax testifies to a further complexity of tone and response characteristic of Jonson's best songs. Even the first two lines illustrate the complex shifts of tone that mark this poem. "Drink to me," a robust and sensuous invitation, bespeaks Jonsonian gusto. The addition of "only" confirms the importunity of the lover, who bids insistently for the lady's exclusive attention ("me only"). The rest of the line, "with thine eyes," qualifies the poet's initial direct plea. Turning drink to metaphor in this way, Jonson renders the sensation of idealized desire. At the same time, the qualification goes in the opposite direction, toward a realistic expression of his refusal to accept disappointment. Just a look will do, he pleads, willing to trade "me only" for "only with thine eyes."

The entire lyric sustains this tension between assertion and plea, wish and fact. Each act is explained, every hope qualified. And/Or, But/Not, Not so much/As, Not/But: this syntax governs every line, moving to and fro between the actions of lover and lady, between her gestures and his interpretations. The lyric balances moderation and excess, desire and disapointment. The wreath of roses, initially an emblem of love, becomes an emblem of the lady and, finally, an emblem of Jonson's poem as well, as he intricately weaves together allusion and interpretation, act and feeling.

Taken together, the poem to Wroth, the gentlewoman's meditation, and the songs present an indirect commentary on poetry as the making and unmaking of metaphor, or, rather, on the transformation of one kind of discourse into another, or the alternations between two kinds of language— classical and English, Horatian and Christian, factual and symbolic. Each of these poems creates an act of voice out of these competing languages.

III

The morality, love, and cynicism that Jonson separated into different texts—in the gentlewoman's monologue, the songs to Celia, and the satiric epigram "To Sickness"—he brings into direct confrontation in the "Proludium" and "Epode" (*For.* 10–11). Jonson may have included these two poems in *The Forrest* because they represented a significant episode in his involvement with the Sidney circle and because they constituted another phase of his Horatian imitation. However, his editorial decision to place these early poems two-thirds of the way through *The Forrest* can also be explained in terms of the idea of poetic voice worked out in the collection.

The personal drama of the book seems intertwined with its changing perspectives on love poetry. Jonson had begun the book by refusing to write love poetry. Having paid tribute to the moral idealism of the Sidneys and Sir Robert Wroth, he summed up his vision of moral *contemptus mundi* in the dramatic monologue of the gentlewoman. From her moralistic contempt for the world he turned to the set of love songs based on the poet-lover's contempt for the moralistic world. The erotic songs to Celia expend their logic on a justification of indulgence. "Kiss me sweet" (*For.* 6), in particular, argues for the safety and invulnerability of lovers. The epode offers a reply to such arguments: "Man may securely sin, but safely never." Jonson, in short, follows his elegant love songs with a Neoplatonic moral poetry that can constrain and sublimate the kind of erotic desire that is indulged in the songs.

The epode charts an uncertain course from lust to reverence. The division of the poem into contrasting movements—rather like the strophe, anti-strophe, and stand of an ode—emphasizes sudden modulations from one theme or attitude to a contrasting one. The strophe announces the theme of the guarded self: "'Tis the securest policy we have / To make our sense our slave" (17–18). The antistrophe rejects this posture at once: "But this true course is not embraced by many. / By many? Scarce by any" (19–20). Passions "invade the mind, / And strike our reason blind" (29–30). To escape this impasse of the divided self, the poet invokes the Neoplatonic concept of a higher love, a "golden chain let down from heaven," that subsumes passions into "god-like unity" and "peace" (47–55). Another counterturn of thought serves both to defend this idealism from scepticism and to distinguish it from debased imitations (sexual restraint achieved by mere incapacity or fear). The poem then reaches a second stand in which the higher love is reasserted in the more personal form of the dove, the "divine . . . creature" (102) that both subdues and elevates the passion of her devotee. The conclusion brings together—one might almost say orchestrates—the disparate attitudes that come before. Extreme positions have been defined and rejected in favor of a tempered response. The virtuous mood of devotion to higher love combines with the "weight of guilt" (113) and prudential regard for consequences: "Man may securely sin, but safely, never" (116). Both vigilant self-control and ideal love come together in the attitude of reverence that marks the close.

The argument of the poem lends credence to the theory that the epode (and the other poems of obscure Neoplatonic moralizing by Chapman, Shakespeare, and others originally published with it in *Love's Martyr*) may have been written not only to celebrate a noble wedding, but also to speak obliquely "to deep ears" (*For.* 10.30) about the relationship of Elizabeth and Essex.[31] A narrowly political reading of the poem would interpret it as part of the effort to persuade Elizabeth to restore Essex to favor (a cause endorsed by the Sidneys). In a larger sense, the political-erotic allegory concerns the need to convert self-aggrandisement to loyalty, and to subdue both personal and patriotic ambitions to the less heroic but more fruitful enterprises favored by a queen determined to avoid faction and war. Her restive nobles needed to learn what Essex ultimately failed to learn: to let their "fortunes swim / In the full flood of her admired perfections"; to obey out of a sense of duty and in hopes of royal favor and perferment, rather than to pursue their own political programs. In addition, the aspiring noblemen of Elizabeth's court took pleasure in intricate Neoplatonic formulations that could have political as well as moral implications. Jonson's poem may have been written in the spirit of their intellectual ambition as well as in the service of a campaign to restore Essex to royal favor.

What is most distinctive about the epode is Jonson's explication of Neo-platonic ideas in poems of Horatian form and phrase. The epodes and satires of Horace, composed at approximately the same time, represent two op-posed models for the organization of social poetry. In the satires, attack dominates idealism. The epodes reverse that priority: satire is subordinate to idealism. Jonson adopts this Horatian model and also alludes to a Horatian epistle (*Ep.* 1.16.52–53), in effect marshalling all his Horatian forces to advance his argument. By writing a Neoplatonic poem in a Horatian idiom, Jonson makes the project his own.

He declares his intention to do just that in the proludium, a poem that invites readers to read it as the poet's own utterance. Rejecting Cupid and Venus once again, as he had in "Why I Write not of Love," Jonson declares himself a poet-Phoenix: "I bring / My own true fire. Now my thought takes wing, / And now an *Epode* to deep ears I sing" (28–30). Most readers rightly sense in the proludium and epode a second beginning of *The Forrest*, as the poet returns from fictive speakers to his own voice, affirming his own integrity and praising integrity in others. The epode rehearses in the abstract a range of attitudes toward poetry, love, and self-worth that will be more concretely realized in the epistles and ode that follow (*For.* 12–14). In particular, mutual love of the sort defined in the epode is made to support Lady Aubigny's decision to live apart from the "giddy" world, and dis-tinguishes her from the gentlewoman of *For.* 4 who seems so entirely alone. It is not the development of an abstract theme of love that is important here, but the emergence of the poet's voice, a Horatian blend of idealism and hard-headed realism that informs his poems to the Countess of Rutland, Lady Aubigny, and Sir William Sidney.

The second pair of epistles in *The Forrest*, addressed to the Countess of Rutland in 1601 and to Lady Katherine Aubigny in 1612, testify to Jonson's increasing mastery of that Horatian form. Both poems were written to aristocratic young wives who were anticipating motherhood. These similar circumstances, however, occasion two different methods of poetic imitation and two different arguments for epideictic poetry. The epistle to the Count-ess of Rutland imitates a specific Horatian text, while the epistle to Lady Aubigny emulates the general temper of Horatian art. Praising the Countess of Rutland, Jonson defends poetry as a public act, a "golden pyramid" that can immortalize the poet and his subject. His epistle to Lady Aubigny defends poetry as an intimate act of private praise, a mirror that can show the lady an image of her own moral worth. Jonson seems to discuss the poem with her as she reads it, and thereby draws on the drama of the occasion to explore with her the process and value of praise. In each epistle, the relationship between poet and lady vivifies the general argument about poetry.

By pairing these epistles, Jonson makes something like the commentary on praise effected by his two epigrams to Alphonso Ferrabosco (*Ep.* 130–31). The poems to Ferrabosco present two different perspectives on fame, defending music first as a vehicle for public fame and then as a satisfying private alternative to fame's vicissitudes. The first poem emphasizes Ferrabosco's commitment to music as a public act, the second urges on him the private value of self-sufficiency. The Rutland and Aubigny epistles bring to this contrast the poignancy of Jonson's own experience. When Jonson wrote to the Countess of Rutland he was ambitious to join the Sidney-Bedford circle and to realize Sir Philip Sidney's vision of a new English poetry. By the time Jonson wrote to Lady Aubigny, he had suffered the failures of *Catiline* and *Sejanus,* his experiments in classical verse tragedy, and had taken refuge for several years at the estate of Aubigny, his new patron in the Jacobean court. In a fervent epigram to Aubigny, Jonson admits "How full of want, how swallowed up, how dead / I and this muse had been if thou hadst not / Lent timely succours, and new life begot" (*Ep.* 127). Yet writing to Lady Aubigny, he declares himself less vulnerable to the "arts and practice of the vicious" because he has maintained his integrity in the face of adversity: "I, that have suffered this . . . have not altered yet my look / Or so myself abandoned" (15–17). He encourages Lady Aubigny to adopt the self-sufficiency he took as his own personal goal: "Wisely you decline your life / Far from the maze of custom, error, strife" (59–60). Although he praises her for choosing the solitary country life, he himself was not willing to withdraw entirely from the public world. By editing and publishing the 1616 Folio, he made his definitive bid for literary fame and for self-sufficiency. Indeed, by publishing this epistle Jonson transforms his argument for a poetry of private praise into an act of public poetry.

In their stylistic differences, these two poems exemplify two stages of Jonson's classical poetics. The epistle to the Countess of Rutland epitomizes the late Elizabethan phase of of Jonson's classical imitation. He defines his contemporary role as poet in the context of his classical predecessors. References to Berenice and Ariadne, Homer and Orpheus, arm him against the Countess of Bedford's "verser" (49–78). In the epistle to Lady Katherine Aubigny, written a decade later, he omits such a show of his own learning and grounds his praise entirely in the circumstances of the world she inhabits. The poem is devoid of mythological references, and his allusions to classical texts (Juvenal's sixth satire, a moral epistle of Seneca) are absorbed into personal speech.

The juxtaposition of these two epistles calls attention to their Horatian form, and at first reading they seem alike in their Horatian idiom. The poet blends conversation and declaration, satire and compliment, historical fact and literary allusion, seeking to capture in verse the moral equanimity that can blend ease and dignity. However, these two epistles represent two stages in Jonson's engagement with Horatian poetry: close imitation and loose emulation. The epistle to the Countess of Rutland closely imitates a Horatian ode in defense of public poetry (*Odes* 4.8) and echoes other Horatian texts that assert the poet's power to immortalize himself and his subject. It was Horace who formulated the idea of poetic fame that became a Renaissance commonplace: "Exegi monumentum aere perennius / regalique situ pyramidum altius . . . non omnis moriar" [I have finished a monument more lasting than bronze and loftier than the Pyramid's royal pile . . . I shall not altogether die] (*Odes* 3.30.1–6). Jonson, who echoes this Horatian passage in the Rutland epistle, believed that the learned poet, in particular, had the advantage of being fully appreciated by learned readers. When he vows to write "strange poems, which, as yet, / Had not their form touched by an English wit" (81–82), he does not name Horace as the source of this idea; the allusion will be recognized by those readers who recall Horace's vow to adapt Aeolian song to Italian verse (*Odes* 3.30.13–14) and who know that the new English poetry required such knowledge.

Jonson's epistle to Lady Aubigny is not modeled on a specific Horatian text, nor does the poet rely on a web of Horatian allusions to strengthen his argument. The Rutland epistle, moreover, was marked by definite patterns of assertion and qualification, its complex syntax mediating the competing claims of formality and colloquialism. The epistle to Lady Aubigny seems plain by comparison, yet in temper and method it more truly deserves to be called "Horatian." Emulation has displaced imitation, and Jonson claims a Horatian temper as his own. This epistle, in fact, alludes only once to a specific Horatian text, and then so minimally that it is hard to make the case for any allusion at all. When Jonson refers to himself as a "priest" of the Muses (101), he alludes to a few lines that preface Horace's praise of the simple country life:

> Odi profanum vulgus et arceo;
> favete linguis. carmina non prius
> audita Musarum sacerdos
> virginibus puerisque canto.
>
> (*Odes* 3.1.1–4)

[I hate the uninitiate crowd and keep them far away. Observe a reverent silence! I, the Muses' priest, sing for maids and boys songs not heard before.] In the epistle to Lady Aubigny Jonson enacts what Horace envisions: a private, privileged mode of poetry. It is part of that intimacy to create a voice entirely his own.

The distinctive presence of Horatian allusion in these epistles—pervasive in the first, minimal in the second—shows that Jonson found models for the poetry of public and private praise in the odes and epistles of Horace, not only in their propositional arguments but also in their modes of self-presentation. Jonson makes public his debt to Horace as he argues for an art of public statement. The understated, muted epistle to Lady Aubigny emulates the very different, but equally characteristic, Horatian poetry of privileged intimacy.

The epistle to the Countess of Rutland combines several characteristic Jonsonian actions: the poet distinguishes himself from the rest of her entourage, attacks materialistic society, reflects on the power of poetry, and celebrates the lady as moral exemplar. These diverse actions could have resulted in a loosely discursive epistle, but the poem gains structural unity from the shifting relationship between gold and poetry in the language of the epistle. Gold the poet first condemns as a commodity antithetical to poetry but then transforms into a metaphor of everything he values.

Horace opened his ode in defense of poetry (*Odes* 4.8) with a declaration that he would send rich gifts to his friends if he only could:

> Sed non haec mihi vis, non tibi talium
> res est aut animus deliciarum egens.
> Gaudes carminibus: carmina possumus
> donare et pretium dicere muneri.
>
> (9–12)

[But I have no such store, nor does my condition or thy spirit crave such toys. In songs is thy delight. Songs we can bestow, and can name the worth of such a tribute.] Jonson's version—"whilst gold bears all this sway, / I, that have none to send you, send you verse" (18–19)—not only opposes gold and verse but offers the Countess of Rutland a compliment at his own expense. He may have a bit of gold, but none to send her, and to do so would certainly belie everyone's expectations. Jonson's intimate joke follows his gruff refusal to demean himself (or her) by acting like a "fool . . . who will want and weep / When his proud patron's favours are asleep" (13–14). He acknowledges his dependency even as he asserts his independence. Transforming classical allusion into intimate jest, Jonson elevates his relationship with the Countess of Rutland above the common run of patronage alliances.

After establishing the opposition between gold and verse, Jonson converts gold into a metaphor of value. As commodity, gold destroys grace, fame, friendship, love, integrity. As metaphor, gold provides Jonson with a vocabulary to express their greater good. Satiric synecdoche is the first phase of Jonson's metaphor-making. Men so insecure they judge their own worth "Just to the weight their this day's presents bear" (8) are equated with the coins they covet: these "noble ignorants . . . Turn upon scorned verse their quarter-face" (27–29). Jonson turns his scornful verse to celebration, making gold a metaphor of his poetry. He promises the countess that the "rich and golden pyramid" (83) of his poetry will "show how, to the life, my soul presents / Your form impressed there" (86–87). In these lines Jonson reconciles the competing idioms of purchase and morality by adopting the terminology of Renaissance emblem books. Poetry is not only a golden coin, "impressed" with the image of the lady's virtue, but the "soul," or verbal element, of an *impresa* (the visual element of a moral emblem). Jonson's "soul"—at once his essential self and his poem—will body forth the life of her moral spirit.

Jonson's friendship with the Countess of Rutland gives the authority of personal feeling to his metaphorical argument. He shares with her his professional ambitions and his angry contempt for a world that overvalues gold and undervalues art. He even shares with her his fantasy of being famous:

> Then all that have but done my muse least grace
>   Shall thronging come, and boast the happy place
> They hold in my strange poems. . . .
>
>   (79–81)

He admires the "rage divine" of poets and vows to be one of them, to write of "high and noble matter, such as flies / From brains entranced and filled with ecstasies" (89–90). For Jonson, that "noble matter" will be his poetic apotheosis of the Countess, daughter of "the god-like Sidney" (91).

Despite his vow to apotheosize the Countess, this poem tells us more about poetry than about her. Of the ninety-three lines in the published version of the epistle, only eight compliment the lady—and five of those praise her "love of the Muses." Although Jonson addresses her as subject, audience, and writer of poetry, his ideas about his art finally have little to do with her. His decision to present the Countess of Rutland in this way would later enable him to delete the personal ending of the poem and publish a truncated version in *The Forrest*. The Horatian ode that served as the model for the Rutland epistle ends with a hope that vows have timely issue. In the original text of the epistle, Jonson converted that idea to a description of his poem as "A vow as new and ominous as the year" whose timely issue would be the Rutlands' first child. Both the Countess and her husband were dead by the time Jonson published the poem, and they had never had a child. Jonson omitted the ending of the poem from *The Forrest*, saying only "The rest is lost." That he published the poem at all can best be explained in terms of his poetic agenda in *The Forrest*. Publication of the poem disengaged it from its original function as a New Year's gift to the Countess of Rutland and emphasized its continuing value as a statement about poetry.

The epistle to Lady Katherine Aubigny concerns not poetry in general but this particular poem: his writing of it, her reading of it. His argument for the value of poetry as private compliment is inseparable from his own relationship to the lady. Her acts of choice originate and validate his poem, and there is no defense of poetry to which she is merely bystander. Despite the "danger" that "praised and praisers suffer," Jonson commits himself "to speak true" and urge Lady Aubigny to "Be bold to use this truest glass." He addresses the lady, not the world: "Hear / Yourself but told unto yourself" (23), "Look then, and see yourself" (29). Hearing, seeing, reading herself, she may be conscious of virtues that can be maintained only by the conscious effort to avoid self-abandonment, dissipation, and, for that matter, too nice a regard for others: "For other's ill, ought none their good forget" (6). Even the lady's status as a person receiving this praise is made central to the process of the poem. She is at once hearing this poem and reading it. The poem's immediacy, the new conscience of the lady, and her discomfort are set forth in the idiom of hearing, telling, speaking. In contrast, the language of reading and writing conveys a sense of stillness—permanence and constancy, serene reflection and silence. In their stillness, lady and poem mirror each other. As complementary moral symbols, each attains a meaning beyond the immediacy of experience.

Printing a text reinforces the autonomy already inherent in writing. As an act of speech, the poem is addressed to a particular person on a particular occasion. To move from the immediacy and contingency of speech to the enduring autonomy of a written text is Jonson's literary equivalent of the lady's own attainment of constancy. By exploiting both the immediacy and the permanence of occasional art, Jonson offers Lady Aubigny two perspectives on herself, as an individual person in unique circumstances and as a moral exemplar whose life can have general significance. Unlike John Donne, who defended his *Anniversaries* as the portrayal of "the idea of a lady and not as she was," Jonson contrives a way to praise both the idea of this lady and what she was.[32]

This poem owes its complex structure to the development of a single metaphor, the poem as mirror. Jonson unfolds the implications of that metaphor, using a series of mirroring relationships to dramatize the mutuality of giving and taking.[33] He does not transfer the factual terms of a satiric argument to a metaphorical idiom of compliment, as he had in addressing the Countess of Rutland, but establishes from the very beginning a consistent metaphorical discourse that can define every significant element of the poem.

Jonson organizes the poem as a series of mirroring actions to provide a structural correlative to the moral idea he argues. He sets himself and his poem before her: "See / In my character what your features be" (23–24). His self-portrait in the first half of the poem mirrors his portrait of Lady Aubigny in the second half. He is in danger from "the arts and practice of the vicious," she from the envy of great wives. He is "forsook / Of fortune" (15–

16), the lady blessed by beauty, wealth, ancestry, and rank, but they have in common conscience and integrity. Jonson proudly declares he has "not altered yet my look, / Or so my self abandoned" (16–17); Lady Aubigny has sought the path of virtue, keeping "an even, and unaltered gait" (61). Her life, like Jonson's art, depends on the Pauline virtue of charity, "Without which all the rest were sounds, or lost" (49–50). The poet's mirror not only catalogues her advantages but can "reflect" (38) upon their relative importance, arranging them in a moral hierarchy more important than any arithmetic of power. The numerical discrepancy between the "few" good minds and "the bad, by number . . . fortified" (3) can be redressed by one resolute poet and even more by one virtuous lady willing to persevere "alone, without companions" (61) and then to give herself in the "one" of loving marriage. The epistle begins by postulating an equation between the poet and his poem (it is his "character"), but Jonson gives this image of himself to Lady Aubigny. His poem, which "takes and gives the beauties of the mind" (44), depends on its subject.

Within this basic structure, Jonson traces a complex set of relationships: the contrast between his true speech and the false practice of "the vicious," who "think it fit / For their own capital crimes to indict [his] wit" (13–14); the equation of the poet and his text; the comparable self-sufficiency of Jonson and Lady Aubigny; the loving union of Lady Aubigny and her husband; the contrast between Lady Aubigny and faithless wives who "start forth and seem" (63); the union of Lady Aubigny and her husband once more, imaged in the child to come; and, finally, the congruence of the lady and the poem, its "truest glass" as constant as she. Jonson does not isolate these relationships in separate stanzas, but uses the nonstanzaic form of the epistle to create a single discursive action. There are no easily defined segments, no closed couplets. The negative and positive mirroring relationships in each half of the poem mirror each other, but together they constitute a linear progression, a chain of relationships that shifts inexorably from poet to lady.

What Lady Aubigny gives the poet as subject of his poem she is invited to take as its reader. Contrasting his art to her beauty, wealth, and station—"the gifts of chance" (41)—Jonson reiterates the image of the poem as looking glass: "My mirror is more subtle, clear, refined, / And takes and gives the beauties of the mind" (43–44). The moral mutuality he celebrates in this epistle is grounded in a self-awareness quite opposed to the narcissism usually associated with poetic portraits of a woman at her looking-glass. The intimate reference to "Your soft blush" and the sly reminder that "No lady but, at some time, loves her glass," are clues—if we need them—that Jonson is doing something quite different with the old sonneteer's conceit of the looking glass. Perhaps the best example of the conceit can be found in Sonnet 45 of Spenser's *Amoretti:*

Leave lady in your glass of christall clene,
Your goodly selfe for evermore to vew:
And in my selfe, my inward self I meane,
Most lively lyke behold your semblant trew.
Within my hart, though hardly it can shew
Thing so divine to vew of earthly eye,
The fayre Idea of your celestiall hew,
And every part remaines immortally:
And were it not that through your cruelty,
With sorrow dimmed and deformd it were,
The goodly ymage of your visnomy,
Clearer then christall would therein appere.
But if your selfe in me ye playne will see,
Remove the cause by which your fayre beames darkned be.[34]

Spenser, courting his lady, urges her to repent the "cruelty" which has "deformed" him, and therefore has deformed the "goodly image" of herself she might otherwise find in him. He appeals to her self-love in order to gain her love for himself: seek the image of your (inner) beauty in my love instead of in your glass. Jonson turns this amorous conceit to a new ethical purpose: Seek the image of your inner beauty in my "character" (24)—in my moral commitment and in my poem. Jonson wants Lady Aubigny to appreciate herself, to recognize, value, and thereby sustain her own virtue. Knowing herself, she can securely choose "Right the right way" (68).

Unlike amorous verse, in which the relationship between poet and lady is the exclusive concern, Jonson's epistle celebrates the union of husband and wife, who sustain one another in "chaste love" (96). It is Aubigny's "word" (114), not the poet's, on which Lady Aubigny depends. The poet conquers time by preserving an image of the beautiful; the false world vainly denies time, refusing to see that "vice doth every hour / Eat on her clients and some one devour" (87–88); but a marriage of true minds accepts time and thereby triumphs over it, creating children and maintaining a love that constantly renews itself: "your souls conspire, as they were gone / Into each other, and had now made one" (119–120). In that word "conspire" Jonson appropriates for married love the esoteric, erotic conceit of the interinanimation of souls famous in Donne's "Extasie." Here, however, the conceit does not startle with its own ingenuity; its rareness pays tribute not to the wit of the poet but to the virtue of married lovers, "of whom there are so few." When Jonson ends his poem by advising Lady Aubigny to "Live that one still" (121), he means both the "one" of her integrity and the "one" of marriage, because he defines marriage as a unifying act of mirroring selves. True autonomy permits and gains from relationship. As Jonson declares to Lady Aubigny, her husband will be "the dearer prize / Unto himself, by being dear to you" (116–17). Jonson has offered her a mirror image of her value through the private medium of his poem; in the private world of marriage, she offers her husband an image of his true worth. Her own "conscience" enables her to do for Aubigny what the poet has done for her.

What we can know of Lady Aubigny's life during this period suggests that Jonson both celebrates and protects her in his choice of compliments. By making her conscious of her own worth, Jonson shows her that she need not be vulnerable to the circumstances that threatened to overwhelm her. Jonson wrote this epistle only one year after her marriage, when she was enmeshed in a bitter dispute between her husband and her father. The unpleasant story can be patched together from references in the *Calendar of State Papers, Domestic* and the chatty letters of John Chamberlain.[35] Lady Aubigny's father, Baron Gervase Clifton, won his title by acceding to the royal wish that his daughter and only heir marry Aubigny. Clifton, irascible and ambitious, feared that he would somehow be cheated of his own promised gains after the marriage. Acting too promptly to secure what he thought was his, he was accused of "unjust conduct" and fraudulent land seizure by Aubigny and his brother, the Duke of Lennox. By April, 1612, when the first Aubigny child was born, the family was torn by acrimonious recriminations. Here is Chamberlain's account of the christening day: "This day the King and Prince are to be at a christening in the Blackfriars of a sonne of the Lord Dobegnie by the Lord Cliftons daughter. Her husband and she have been at great warres with her father, and very fowle matters have been opened at the consaile table, wherewith he was so netled, that to spite them he vowed he wold kepe halfe a dozen whoores and yf he gat any of them with child he wold marrie her."[36] Several years after Jonson wrote his epistle to Lady Aubigny, Clifton married Penelope Rich (the daughter of Sidney's "Stella"), but she died childless one year later. Clifton himself would commit suicide in 1618, shortly after his release from the Tower, where he had been confined for threatening the life of Lord Bacon. Chamberlain records that Clifton chose "to stab and mangle himself with a penknife in two or three places, without any other shew of reason or cause, but even *vitae taedio* (as he saide himself) for the suites twixt his daughter and him were ended and all friends, so that he lodged in her house and there made himself away."[37]

Read in the context of the Aubigny/Clifton feud, Jonson's poem seems to offer Lady Aubigny two different kinds of complimentary counsel. First, he suggests that the forthcoming birth may give her an opportunity to reconcile her father and her husband. Her child can be her gift to both men, fulfilling her "pledges of chaste love" to Aubigny and providing her father "a noble stem, to give the fame / To Clifton's blood that is denied their name" (96–98). Even more important (both in terms of Jonson's own ethic and his close friendship with Aubigny), Jonson endorses Lady Aubigny's decision to side with her husband against her father. She is "truly that rare wife / Other great wives may blush at, when they see / What your tried manners are, what theirs should be. / How you love one, and him you should; how still / You are depending on his word and will" (110–14). This conventional tribute to wifely submissiveness conceals his pointed praise of her loyalty to Aubigny.

To reiterate the value of her "tried" and constant self, Jonson returns to the metaphor of the looking glass in the final lines of his poem. The earlier pun on "character" disappears. Jonson's coda places the focus squarely on the poem as a mirror of the lady:

> . . . as long years do pass,
> Madam, be bold to use this truest glass,
> Wherein your form you still the same shall find,
> Because nor it can change, nor such a mind.
>
> (121–24)

The last line of the poem syntactically sums up the complex mirroring relationship of text and lady. The balanced phrases ("nor . . . nor") do not, finally, offer a complete parallelism. The first phrase minimizes the poem (as "it"), but supplies the crucial verb ("can change"). The second ends the poem by reiterating its central subject ("such a mind"). Through this forceful syntax, change is denied, poem and lady affirmed. The poet subordinates poem to lady in the syntax of the last line and also in the generalized language of the final phrase, "such a mind," that at once sets her apart and makes her a type of the few good minds he mentioned in the first lines of the poem.

Any poem of praise necessarily has the effect of making the person who is praised self-conscious. Lady Aubigny's "soft blush" (22) should not surprise us: self-consciousness, or "conscience," may seem more a burden than a "comfort" (68–69). This poem builds on that unavoidable aspect of epideictic art. Lady Aubigny's natural response to praise becomes central to the meaning of the poem, not merely incidental. Jonson does not merely flatter her by confirming what she had already made of herself, but urges her to take comfort in her knowledge of what she is. By making central to the poem feelings that would usually be regarded as incidental, Jonson goes beyond the conventional formulas of praise. He enhances their effect by borrowing from the drama of the poetic situation just as he had borrowed from the drama of the lady's and his own historical situations.

This way of defining the mirroring action of the poem gives the force of revelation to the final lines. We know that the lady can find in the glass of the poem an emblem not only of the poet's moral character, or even her own, but also of the process that makes that image efficacious. As we read this poem, we seem to overhear the poet telling her what kind of poem he intends to write and how to interpret its meaning. The poem makes her own act of reading a mirroring event. Moreover, by publishing this poem in *The*

Forrest, Jonson extends the act of mirroring to include other readers reading. He presents his poem to her as an act of speaking shaped into an act of writing, but for all other readers the poem is an act of writing that creates the illusion of direct speech. If the poet transmutes speech into text, the reader must then transform text into speech, granting the poem the continuing force of utterance "as long years do pass."

This poem is normative of Jonson's moral attitudes and also of his practice in epideictic art. The situation of such poetry is always the same: the poet praises the person he addresses. His difficulties, opportunities, and best effects stem from that situation. The drama of interchange contains the act of description. Jonson brings together the actions of self-dramatization and description in order to celebrate what John Danby has called "the grand human imagery of actual persons in their living relation with him and with the image of man."[38] Individual and image—Lady Aubigny is both, and in the mirror of Jonson's poem is invited to see for herself what the relationship can be between these aspects of herself. Jonson requires every reader to attend to the problems of history and symbol as pressures upon self, and to the capacity of each to counter, but ultimately to enhance, the other. His epideictic art honors both historical fact and eternizing art, and is constituted at once by the intimacy of conversation and the impersonality of publication.

IV

In his poems to the Countess of Rutland and Lady Aubigny, Jonson extends the range of a discursive form to include the more exalted tone typical of ode, "such as flies / From brains entranced and filled with ecstasies" (*For.* 12.89–90). The birthday ole to Sir William Sidney (*For.* 13) reverses the procedure. Jonson uses the stately form of the Pindaric for an occasion that also requires warmth, intimacy, and tactful understatement. Therefore, just as he incorporates allusions for formal Horatian odes in the epistle to the Countess of Rutland, so in the ode to Sir William Sidney Jonson adapts lines from specific Horatian epistles which were also written as avuncular advice to a young man (*Ep.* 1.2, 1.18). Combining forms does not result in blurred distinctions or a new hybrid poem. The epistle remains epistolary, the ode an ode. Jonson modifies generic decorum not to violate it but to achieve a poetic style of mingled ease and formality appropriate to each poetic occasion.

The problem of interpretation presented by the birthday ode lies less in reading the text than in understanding Jonson's decision to include it in *The Forrest*. If Jonson wants this collection to call attention to his relationship to the Sidneys, it seems odd that he would include a poem for the family scapegrace who had died at the age of twenty-two.[39] Formally, it is the most unusual poem in *The Forrest:* the Pindaric ode was one of those strange forms "as yet untouched by an English wit" (*For.* 12). This celebratory form suits the occasion of a young man reaching his majority, and Pindar's heroic ethic, summed up in the motto "Become what you are," constitutes the message of the poem. The import of the poem would have greatly changed, however, between the time of its composition and the date of its publication in *The Forrest.* As a poem of initiation, composed for William Sidney's twenty-first birthday, the ode is the most overtly occasional and the most relentlessly forward-looking poem in *The Forrest.* Yet by the time of its publication the young man was dead. Is it then an elegy? If not for him, then for an era?

Not quite. This curiously abstract poem contains nothing specific to this young man or to the Sidney tradition. Reaching one's majority is a moral occasion common to all men: growth ceases being a natural endowment and becomes a heroic challenge. Jonson urges the young man to become what he is, a Sidney—but only for his own sake. There is no sense that Penshurst, poetry, or Protestantism would be imperiled if he did not, although that kind of poetic strategy was certainly available to Jonson and would have been appropriate to the occasion. Jonson does not even urge the young man to please his parents. Only by remembering that he is a Sidney will Sir William find the strength to become one, but his obligation is only to himself, not to his family heritage.

In most of his complimentary poems, Jonson seeks out someone who exemplifies reason, grace, wisdom, serenity, excellence. This ode is an exception. Sidney was a hot-tempered, spoiled young man who seriously wounded his tutor and was then dismissed from Prince Henry's service. There was little to praise in the young man except the potential implicit in his heritage, but Jonson warns him not to rely on that: "For they that swell / With dust of ancestors, in graves but dwell" (39–40). He tries to make young Sidney stand on his own, not because of any weakness of his family (Jonson loves "the cause and authors of the feast") but because he must prepare for a time "When all the noise / Of these forced joys / Are fled and gone, / And he with his best genius left alone" (17–20).

Sir William Sidney did not live to take Jonson's advice. He died little more than a year after this ode was written. With Sidney dead, the poem exemplifies the memorializing power of poetry and the didactic power of the memorial. The ode carries the burden of preserving the Sidney legacy, since the young man himself cannot. In Sir Philip Sidney's *Apology for Poetry,* the poet is assigned the task of creating exemplary characters as ideal images of virtue so that the reader will be moved to virtuous action. The reader in turn has the obligation to become a living exemplar. Although Jonson endorses the Sidneyan ideal of poetic utility, he writes in a different mode. Other people, the Sidneys among them, provide noble characters in real life and in his poetry; he then draws the moral and names their virtue. He urges virtue directly in his own distinctive voice, rather than indirectly by inventing exemplary characters. On this occasion, Jonson moves from the "forced joys" that required a poem, any poem, to heartfelt counsel; he begins by noticing the customary bonfire at the hearth and ends with the hope that there might come a day when "logs not burn, but men." Published after Sir William Sidney's untimely death, Jonson's poem can only commemorate a moment of hope. In a certain sense, Jonson himself has become the Sidney heir. His poem fulfills the Sidney tradition, its flame kept alive in his "true fire."

To read the ode this way is to emphasize the idea of the poet implicit in the order of Jonson's *Forrest*. He does not arrange his poems chronologically to record the sequence of their composition, or the process of his involvement in Horatian imitation, or the development of his relationship to the Sidneys. The only kind of narrative line in *The Forrest* is the poet's reflection on what it means to be a poet who can burn with "[his] own true fire" (*For.* 11). Yet for the most part Jonson does not emphasize self-portraiture. The epistles either omit his personal ambition and experience (as in the poem to Wroth) or subordinate them to his praise of someone else; and in other poems he assumes the role of singer, satirist, or even gentlewoman. Although he uses the epistle to set forth his theory of poetry and his poetic ambitions, and tests both of these in the ode to Sir William Sidney, only three poems— "Why I Write not of Love" (*For.* 1), "And Must I Sing?" (*For.* 10), and "To Heaven" (*For.* 15)—take the poet's own experience as their primary subject. Jonson arranges his collection to establish his poetic ideal, but nothing in his life suggests that this arc of ideal experience coincides with his actual experience. It is more accurate to say that he could etch this myth because of Horatian art and Sidneyan community, and forms his ideal in tribute to them.

Instead of making that claim explicit, Jonson turns to his own spiritual condition in "To Heaven," the meditative poem that ends the book.[40] There is nothing of Horace in the poem. Nor should there be, according to the Horatian paradigm of imitation Ben Jonson adopts: the writer's goal should be to overgo the model and thereby achieve a new and richer poetic identity. For a Humanist like Jonson, however, the classical concept of imitation is superseded by an Erasmian paradigm that assigns truth only to Christain experience. The first fourteen poems in *The Forrest* dramatize how far Jonson was able to adapt Horatian writing to his own condition and his own poetic ideal. In the last poem, he not only eschews Horatian language and form but sets aside the classical temper of the Horatian poetic voice. The introspection of Christian meditation replaces his classical ethical stance. His place in the human community no longer commands his attention.

Just as the poem contains no reference to Horace, so also it lacks any mention of the Sidneys. The poet turns away from external social occasion as well as literary tradition in order to ponder his own spiritual state. Yet just as this poem can be read as an effective conclusion to a Humanist work of literary imitation, so also the act of spiritual introspection appropriately concludes Jonson's Humanist celebration of virtuous community. Because "To Heaven" affirms the experience basic to such community, the Sidney tradition is not superseded but fulfilled by Jonson's turn to private meditation. The day at Penshurst, we may recall, began and ended in household prayers. If Penshurst has seemed the setting and the analogue of Jonson's book, it finally serves as emblem of his soul as well, where he prays his divine Lord will "dwell" (15).

This poem begins abruptly, at the critical moment of painful question: "Good and great God, can I not think of thee, / But it must straight my melancholy be?" (1–2). The poet's concern is his melancholy, not society's interpretation of his state, and the first twelve lines of the poem show him trapped in that melancholy. He seeks a special relationship with God, turning his memory of his own sins and of consoling religious commonplaces into a personal plea to God: "As thou art all, so be thou all to me" (9). Trapped in self-concern, Jonson can think only of "my melancholy" (2), "my sins" (4). Even God is uniquely his own: "My faith, my hope, my love; and in this state, / My judge, my witness, and my advocate" (11–12).

In the first poem, Love "fled" from Jonson's poetic net; God, by contrast, stoops to him, rescuing him from the fetters of his own self-concern. Jonson had written of love as "a golden chain let down from heaven" in the epode; "To Heaven" tests that idea in the poet's own religious experience. As he dramatizes his own meditative acceptance of divine grace, he depicts the ideal last phase of his poetic voice. As friend, observer, even lover, Jonson always sets himself apart from the envious, the foolish, the greedy. In this poem he at last admits his kinship with the world he had heretofore rejected. Like the gentlewoman of "To the World," Jonson in meditation recognizes that it is not virtue that binds soul to soul but the common fall from grace. The powerful voice of the poet, learned from Horace, raised to honor the Sidneys, and now informed by grace, can finally say "I know my state" (17) and "I feel my griefs" (21). He not only admits his shame, scorn, melancholy, and weariness of life, but submits them to a judgment beyond society's, beyond his own. The poet, like his poetry, is "destined unto judgment, after all" (20). The effect of this acceptance is not isolation and "weariness of life" but unity and "love" (26).[41] As Louis Martz has argued, meditative action permits the soul to be one with itself, with other human beings, with created nature, and with the supernatural.[42]

If Horace, the Sidneys, and Jonson the poet can be described as "authors of the feast" (*For.* 14) that is *The Forrest*, Jonson's readers—the named original readers and the nameless audience of the published book—rewrite it by recognizing its simultaneous diversity and unity. To claim that *The Forrest* is a unified book of poetry, more than a miscellany, and that Jonson arranges these poems to dramatize his debt to Horace, his tribute to the Sidneys, and his ideal of poetry, is not to deny the impression of variety and richness his book conveys. To the contrary, such a reading enhances the variety of meanings and implications for every poem. Some poems may be especially prominent in one phase of Jonson's poetic action, some in another, but all claim an important place. At times it seems that the "rosy wreath" (*For.* 5) he sends to Celia can be interpreted as an emblem of his carefully woven book. At other times it seems that the strands of the argument, as well as men and women, are being described in Jonson's song: "Follow a shadow, it still flies you; / Seem to fly it, it will pursue" (*For.* 7). *The Forrest* remains a cornucopia of Jonson's finest poems, each distinctive in genre, theme, tone, and technique. Perhaps this collection, in all its orderly variety, finds its best emblem in the holiday festivities at Durrants, the estate of Sir Robert Wroth, where "Freedom doth with degree dispense" (*For.* 3, 58). The line can have two meanings: the freedom of holiday does away with hierarchy and degree, or freedom and degree together give forth in a holiday spirit. The effect of freedom and degree, mingled in the great hall of Durrants and in Ben Jonson's concentrated book of poetry, is the same in either case: not turmoil, but community.

Jonson has formed his voice in relation to Horace and the Sidneys, but he finally turns to a poetry generated from within himself: "Good and great God, can I not think of thee, but it must straight my melancholy be?" Unlike the "Proludium," which posited the "true fire" of self as the agent of poetry, "To Heaven" takes self as the subject for poetry. To Ben Jonson, this kind of occasion marks the end of a book. Self, as it turns inward, escapes the interpretive net as surely as Cupid had escaped Jonson's poetic net. Self cannot be trapped, or woven in a wreath, or dispensed. It may be seen only in its shadow, or, by analogy, in the reader's own inward turn. The poet, however, does not end his book by making an explicit appeal for this kind of understanding but turns away from his art to his interior life where no reader can follow. If the poems of *The Forrest* are at once autonomous and part of a coherent book, so also the literary and moral community they celebrate consists of separate, private selves never entirely constituted or determined by that community. In order to "speak true," the poet acknowledges this doubleness in the actions of his book.

6

"So Short You Read My Character": Jonson's Autobiographical Poems of 1623–1624

> Life doth her great actions spell
> By what was done and wrought
> In season.
> *(Und. 70, 59–61)*

In 1623 and 1624, Ben Jonson wrote three of his longest poems, "To the Memory of . . . William Shakespeare" (*U. V.* 26), "An Execration upon Vulcan" (*Und.* 43), and "An Epistle Answering to One that Asked to be Sealed of the Tribe of Ben" (*Und.* 47). Each of them was occasioned by a significant event: the publication of Shakespeare's work in folio, the destruction of Jonson's library, and the end of his collaboration with Inigo Jones. One might expect these poems to reflect and work through the experience of loss, and it would not be surprising if they could be regarded as a sequence on the theme of loss. Such a hypothesis, however, would not hold. The problem is clearest in the case of the tribute to Shakespeare. Shakespeare had been dead for seven years, and the First Folio offers an occasion more for celebration than mourning. In "An Execration upon Vulcan" Jonson mourns the loss of his own work but turns that personal occasion to a general meditation on mutability and survival. Although Jonson seizes the occasion of the Tribe of Ben epistle to confront his resentment of Inigo Jones, the poem bears witness to new work and new friendship. In all three poems, Jonson celebrates a gain as much as he mourns a loss. He explores different modes of poetic action in order to understand "a little" what it means to be a poet. As a group, these poems constitute his comprehensive defense of poetry.

Instead of reducing an argument to one intensive point, Jonson develops an extensive meditation on Shakespeare, or the fire, or his own career. Each of these poems epitomizes a different mode of poetic action. The tribute to Shakespeare commemorates a particular literary achievement set against Jonson's own literary theory; each takes the uneasy measure of the other. "An Execration upon Vulcan" weighs the life of ideas against their embodiment in transitory objects (books, buildings) and probes the relationship between personal loss and the destructive forces always at work in the larger world of history and politics. Just as the poem for Shakespeare ranges widely through literary history, so the "Execration" meditates on the events of political history and the history of Jonson's own career. He tries to master his own vulnerability by generalizing from his loss, citing other catastrophic fires in history, in mythology, in Renaissance London. By contrast, he takes his own political and professional situation as his covert subject in "An Epistle Answering to One that asked to Be Sealed of the Tribe of Ben." If analogues between public and personal life are affirmed by the "Execration," the Tribe of Ben epistle resists and escapes such analogy. Self can stand apart, the poet insists, and shape its own intimate world of trust.

Each of these poems depends on the drama of particular relationships. Through the dyadic relationships of Jonson and Shakespeare, Jonson and Vulcan, Jonson and his new friend, the poet dramatizes his judgment, frustration, and trust. His attitude toward Shakespeare blends respect and rivalry. "Envy" is perhaps the most common term in Jonson's poems for other writers, in which he often exorcises whatever envy he may feel by ascribing it to other, lesser men. The word opens the poem for Shakespeare: "To draw no envy, Shakespeare, on thy name, / Am I thus ample to thy Book and Fame." He disclaims not only any envy of his own, but also any intent to arouse envy in those who might resent the praise he will lavish on Shakespeare. In writing for the First Folio, Jonson seeks a way to praise a friend and rival whose art differed radically from his own. He resolves the problem of loss by seeming to deny it or displace it. Shakespeare lives, in his own book and in Jonson's poem for that book. Jonson could be expected to rage against the loss of his own books in "An Execration upon Vulcan," but he goes further, meditating on aggression—whether elemental, sexual, or political—as a destructive force never fully to be justified or exorcised. When he curses Vulcan, he curses a god who embodies the destructive desire and unpredictable loss endemic to all people throughout history. In addition, by cursing Vulcan Jonson exorcises a force in himself. The fiery Vulcan figures forth those traits the poet most often struggles to control or to banish. "An Epistle Answering to One that Asked to be Sealed of the Tribe of Ben" posits a dyadic relationship between the poet and a new friend that enables Jonson to reveal his reactions to the failure of his friendship with Inigo Jones. The new friend occasions the poem but he is not dramatized in Jonson's text. Although Jonson accepts him "as you have writ yourself," that writing is extrinsic to the epistle. The friend's only role in this poem is to listen. Jonson's memory of Jones, on the other hand, permeates the poem. Its incidents, emotional emphases, even its imagery derive from the dissolution of their friendship and their continued quarrelsome competition. By revealing his feelings about Jones, Jonson enacts with his new friend the intimacy he expects and promises in this new friendship.

The richness of allusion, detail, and incident may mask the structural and figurative unity of these long poems. All three poems depict relationship through an extensive pattern of figuration. In the tribute to Shakespeare, book and performance are not only the matter of Shakespeare's career but also the metaphors of Jonson's praise. "Body" (87) is the master trope of "An Execration upon Vulcan." Jonson organizes the poem around different meanings of the word: his physical self, the *corpus* of his works, the body politic threatened by Vulcanic war, Vulcan himself cursed with the consequences of bodily desire. The concluding pun on *"pax"* and "pox" extends the earlier pun on "body," shifting its focus from the poet himself to his vision of a peaceful body politic and a pox-ridden Vulcan. In the Tribe of Ben epistle, Jonson teases out different meanings of "sealing" to vent his feelings about Jones, to confirm a new friendship, and to affirm his own life and writing. This poem is the most personal of the three texts discussed in this chapter. Instead of limiting himself to the role of critic, or joking and generalizing at his own expense, here Jonson takes a hard, clear look at his own situation. "Character," not "body," is the term he finally chooses to image the equation of self and work. The concept of "character" extends the trope of "sealing" by shifting the focus of the poem away from Jones, and away from the new friend, toward the poet and his poem.

The poet's self-presentation in each of these poems is appropriate to the particular occasion he addresses. The eulogy for Shakespeare is a formal, highly structured introduction to the First Folio. Jonson presents himself as the reader of that work, as a critic, a fellow writer, and a surrogate for the large audience of readers who will take up Shakespeare's book. In the eulogy, Jonson draws on the convention of encomium to speak at different moments to Shakespeare, other playwrights, the audience, himself. He exploits the possibilities of his formal rhetorical stance to make the case for Shakespeare's literary excellence; every shift in the poem seems carefully contrived to advance that argument.

"An Execration upon Vulcan," on the other hand, seems anything but planned. From the initial outburst—"And why to me this, thou lame lord of fire"—we feel we have come in at the middle, never to know what fiery words preceded that "And." We overhear what Jonson presents as direct, unmediated, impassioned speech. Vulcan comes to stand for whatever is inimicable to art, society, and life itself. Yet the catalogues, mythologies, anecdotes, and analogues hurled at Vulcan finally cannot counter the stark inventory of what Jonson lost or the power of Vulcan to destroy human peace. After 85 lines of wishful thinking and self-justification, Jonson at last itemizes his loss, only to turn at once from the "ruins" of his library (105) to his memory of "the world's ruins" when the Globe Theatre burned (137) and finally to his horror of the ruinous battlefields where Vulcan roams free, his "Engines of murder . . . massacring mankind so many ways" (207–8).

A similar illusion of spontaneous speech marks the Tribe of Ben epistle, although its tone is intimate, its progressive associations more and more personal. The poem opens with something of the suddenness of the "Execration." We never hear the friend's request, never know the friend's name. We hear only Jonson's reply, and cannot know how much of that is for the friend, how much an interior monologue for our ears only. Of the three poems under discussion, only this epistle combines introspection with an explicit apology for poetry. Jonson's meditation on his art and his status at court is marked by a shift from dialogue to monologue, from an illusion of speech to a reflection on the poem's "character" as writing. Jonson caps his attack on Jones's visual images in architecture and stage sets with a defense of writing. However vulnerable the "frail pitcher" of his external condition in the world, the "character" of his work can attain a kind of invulnerability, an immortality not possible to Inigo Jones and his ephemeral "Glorious Scenes." In this poem and the other autobiographical poems of 1623–24, Jonson's dramatic defense of poetry will turn on the issue of survival: what kind of art can live, and how.

I

Ben Jonson's poem for the First Folio, "To the Memory of My Beloved, the Author, Mr. William Shakespeare, and What He Hath Left Us" (*Und.* 26), is Jonson's finest poem of praise of another poet. Most readers remember at least two short tags: Shakespeare had "small Latin and less Greek" (31); he was "not of an age, but for all time!" (43). Readers may question the first opinion and applaud the second, and may sense in their juxtaposition a certain tension between censure and praise, possibly resulting from the rivalry between the two very different playwrights. Although cited repeatedly for the biographical evidence it provides about their relationship, the poem as a whole is rarely discussed. Modern readers find it so smoothly written, its arguments so appealing and familiar, that they may not recognize the difficult task Jonson set for himself. He believed it was the office of the true critic to "judge sincerely of the author, and his matter, which is the sign of solid and perfect learning in a man" (*Discoveries*, 2588–90). He performs this office in the eulogy, overcoming difficulties that can be traced to two sources: his own critical and personal concerns and the novelty of the First Folio.

Jonson's eulogy is the cornerstone of a concerted attempt by the makers of the Folio to establish the enduring value of Shakespeare's plays as literature worthy to stand with the drama of classical Greece and Rome. In 1623 it was unusual to publish in folio the popular plays of a London dramatist; the only precedent was Jonson's own *Workes* of 1616. The Shakespeare Folio resembles it in substantive areas; some scholars have detected Jonson's influence in the selection of texts and even in punctuation and lineation.[1] Hemminge and Condell's prefatory letter "To the Great Variety of Readers" is so Jonsonian in concept and style that W. W. Greg proposed Jonson as its author; E. A. J. Honigmann, who regards the epistle as a "composite work," contends that Jonson, Heminge and Condell, Blount and Jaggard "may all have had the opportunity to rephrase the epistle and dedication."[2] At the very least, the makers of the Folio closely followed the only precedent available to them. We can assume that Jonson, whatever the extent of his participation in the enterprise, would have been deeply satisfied to see the literary claims advanced for a fellow playwright that he had audaciously made for himself in 1616. The eulogy, although it echoes *topoi* of praise that Jonson uses in other poems, is far more than a routine commission: it signifies a personal vindication.

That sense of satisfaction would have been just one element in Jonson's complex poem. He struggles to resolve his personal responses to Shakespeare and through that struggle to find a critical method adequate to Shakespeare's art. Jonson's model here, as in so many of his works, is Horace. Richard S. Peterson's commentary on the poem points to its elaborate network of references to Horatian texts and ideas.[3] Jonson adopts a self-consciously Horatian stance in judging his fellow playwright, but Horace also stands as one of the models for Shakespeare. The double use of the Horatian model minimizes the contrast between Jonson and Shakespeare, as would be appropriate for the occasion of the First Folio.

The personal contrast between the two men, however muted, underlies the poem's large design of thematic oppositions and comparisons, and lends special strength to the theoretical reconciliations that justify the final vision of Shakespeare's apotheosis. Jonson's poem brings together for the first time those disparate approaches to Shakespeare that still enliven and bedevil criticism: the dual nature of plays as stage events and as literature, the dramatist's reputation and influence, his relation to contemporary and classical playwrights, the usefulness of different norms—Nature and Art—in evaluating Shakespeare's work. The success of the poem ultimately depends on the presence of both men in the poem; Jonson explores his own principles and methods completely, using Shakespeare and "what he hath left us" to resolve, redefine, or transcend critical dilemmas.

Readers have easily accepted the myth of Shakespeare offered in the poem, but they have not easily admitted Jonson's sincerity.[4] The rivalry between the playwrights is too well known. Most of the evidence for it consists of

Jonson's allusions to Shakespeare in *Discoveries* and in the prologues to *Bartholomew Fair* and *Every Man in His Humour,* and Jonson's comments seem to be at odds with the eulogy. For example, the poem praises Shakespeare's craftsmanship in individual lines, but in *Discoveries* Jonson declares that Shakespeare was too cavalier and hasty in writing them: "Would he had blotted a thousand!" (650). Jonson explains that he directed this remark not against Shakespeare but against the players who chose "that circumstance to commend their friend by, wherein he most faulted. . . . He flowed with that facility, that sometime it was necessary he should be stopped" (652–53, 658–59). Their foolish praise only called attention to Shakespeare's occasional lapses.[5] Jonson rebuked them "to justify [his] own candor" in honoring Shakespeare's memory "on this side idolatry" (653–55). The eulogy opens in a similar vein by deploring those who praise Shakespeare from "blind affection" and "silliest ignorance" (7–9). Jonson's bitter ode of 1629, in which he rages that "a mouldy tale, / Like *Pericles*" too often holds the stage, has also been interpreted as an attack on Shakespeare, but the real target is the English audience, which prefers reruns (twenty-year-old reruns, at that) to new plays.[6]

The Induction to *Bartholomew Fair* castigates plots that violate probability; the Prologue to *Every Man in His Humour* criticizes Shakespeare for violating the "unities" and for relying too heavily on spectacle. Jonsonian drama is based on thorough study of classical authors and derives from them an Aristotelian economy of means alien to the "great, but disproportioned muses" (26) of Elizabethan popular drama, chastening the native English techniques, characters, and plots present in his plays. As Glynne Wickham suggests, Jonson may well have believed that Shakespeare, by perfecting the native Elizabethan mode, actually stood in the way of progress and deliberate art.[7] The wonder of the First Folio poem lies in Jonson's ability to subdue such disapproval and to make his Aristotelian principles into grounds for praising Shakespeare. What he cannot commend (the history plays, for example, or the romances) he does not mention; he searches for a mode of criticism that can justify both his own principles and Shakespeare's dramatic practice.

Near the end of the eulogy, Jonson declares that "to write a living line" a poet must turn himself as well as his words upon the "muse's anvil" (59–62). Before he can write of "my gentle Shakespeare," then, Jonson must become in some sense Shakespeare's Jonson. In the first half of the poem, he subdues his own norms to those of Shakespeare. Later Jonson delights in finding a common meeting ground in their love of language and "designs." He begins by depicting himself as critic, not as rival poet; only later, when he moves from critical evaluation to explication of poetic theory, does he emphasize his role as poet. The shift in emphasis occurs gradually, without sudden leaps or abrupt contrasts. The poet does not choose between his two roles, but finds a way to bring them together in the service of his argument. The careful and comprehensive argument of the eulogy requires a less epigrammatic mode than is customary in Jonson's complimentary poems. Substantive comparisons replace the antithesis and pointed judgment of epigram. Nor does this poem contain the conventional list of flattering adjectives. In the eighty lines of the eulogy, the only adjectives applied to Shakespeare are the inevitable "sweet" and "gentle."[8] Extended evaluation of Shakespeare's literary significance requires more than a catalogue of his virtues.

Opposition and comparison provide the basic material of the poem. Even such formal matters as the recurrence of paired words reflect the large design. The eulogy is divided into four parts, with eight couplets at the beginning and end, and two groups of approximately equal length in the center. Each section exploits an apparent opposition or comparison and resolves it in a different way. The opening sets Jonson apart from lesser critics; he essays their type of praise only to reject it and them. Shakespeare deserves more than they can do. The second section compares Shakespeare to his English and classical predecessors, and assigns him a preeminent place in both traditions. The third section judges Shakespeare's work according to the competing values of Nature and Art; his achievement makes it possible to redefine or clarify their interdependence. The conclusion apotheosizes Shakespeare as "star of poets" (77) and his book as a source of new light. Throughout the poem Jonson as mythmaker tries to free Shakespeare's achievement from the limiting contexts of history and personality. In examining and resolving apparent oppositions, Jonson invariably moves away from the particularities of history toward a general and timeless myth.[9]

This process is exemplified by Jonson's treatment of drama as stage event and as literature. He begins by speaking of Shakespeare's "book" and ends by praising the "volume's light," yet he also acknowledges its origins in those performances "that so did take Eliza, and our James" (74). In order to reconcile the opposition of stage and page Jonson makes performance a metaphor for the creation of literature. The Greek playwrights are summoned to be Shakespeare's audience; he, the writer of comedy and tragedy, is described as one who could "shake a stage" when he wore—as a classical actor would—the sock or buskin (36–37); and the goddess Nature is described as an actor who "joyed to wear the dressing of his lines" (48). The use of theatrical metaphors calls attention to the prominence of similar metaphors in Shakespeare's dramatic style. However, Jonson's emphasis on the plays as literature—an emphasis present in the other prefatory poems and in Hemminge and Condell's letter—serves to elevate Shakespeare from the ephemeral realm of stage history.

Jonson's effort to raise Shakespeare from ephemeral popularity to eternal fame, to transfer his work from one medium to another, necessarily begins in history, with a consideration of the playwright's reputation. Seeking the proper "paths" to praise Shakespeare, Jonson takes special care to consider the most familiar critical comments on Shakespeare up to that time: Robert Greene's attack, William Basse's eulogy, and Francis Meres's commendation in *Palladis Tamia*. Greene enviously attacks Shakespeare for daring to be more than a player: he writes blank verse and thinks himself "the only Shakescene in a country."[10] Jonson uses Greene's pun to show that Shakespeare is indeed more, that he can "shake a stage" not only in Britain but among "all scenes of Europe" (37, 42). He repeats the pun to argue that Shakespeare's works "shake a lance, / As brandished at the eyes of ignorance" (69–70). Greene calls Shakespeare "an upstart crow"; Jonson praises the "sweet swan of Avon" (71). He overgoes William Basse's declaration that Shakespeare is worthy to lie with Chaucer, Spenser, and Beaumont by arguing that Shakespeare's works are "a monument without a tomb" and that he lives on in his book; the three poets can rest in peace (19–24).[11] Jonson echoes Meres's tribute, that "the muses would speak with Shakespeare's fine filed phrase, if they would speak English," by praising the poet's "true-filed lines" (68), and he extends Meres's suggestion that Shakespeare be compared to great classical playwrights.[12]

"Soul of the age," Jonson tells us, marks the real beginning of the poem. He declares his intention to compare Shakespeare to Chaucer and Spenser, the great poets of England, but then proceeds to compare him to writers of the English stage. That comparison is the necessary first step toward claiming literary immortality for Shakespeare. Punning at the expense of the "great, but disproportioned muses" of Elizabethan drama, Jonson marvels "how far thou didst our Lyly outshine, / Or sporting Kyd, or Marlowe's mighty line" (29–30). These men can be compassed in a word; Shakespeare cannot. The spectrum of English playwrights cited in the poem is limited to these three men—not, I think, because they were dead and famous, or because they antedated the War of the Theatres, or even because their names provided irresistible opportunities for puns, but because their practice contributed to Shakespeare's language, themes, and dramaturgy. Omitted are playwrights who wrote in the more Jonsonian modes of satiric city comedy and neoclassical tragedy.

The entire section of the poem moves away from describing Shakespeare in terms of his contemporaries. He is more than the "soul of the age! / The applause! the light! the wonder of our stage!" (17–18); he is "not of an age, but for all time!" (43). Jonson summons forth Aeschylus, Sophocles, and Euripides as Shakespeare's proper audience and only peers. The second step in removing Shakespeare from ephemeral history is to compare him to other playwrights whose works have been accorded the status of literature. Jonson's notorious reference to Shakespeare's "small Latin, and less Greek" (31), perhaps one source of the perennial description of Shakespeare as an unlearned child of nature, probably means only that Shakespeare knew some

Greek and more Latin. However judicious his intent, Jonson succeeds only in shifting the reader's attention to himself. He, not Shakespeare, is the leading exponent of vernacular classicism in England, and the line recalls forcefully the contrast between the two men, which had until this point been subdued. However, Jonson speaks not from personal envy but from personal authority, to affirm that Shakespeare's achievement equals that of the Greek playwrights. Like them, Shakespeare can imitate nature directly and has no need of models. In that sense, he transcends ordinary poets who must remain rooted in literary tradition. Shakespeare so far surpasses the writers of classical comedy that they seem hopelessly confined to history. Their works "antiquated, and deserted lie—as they were not of Nature's family" (53–54).[13]

In order to define Shakespeare's timelessness, Jonson ranges through time himself, shifting from the present tense ("thou art a monument without a tomb") to a visionary present that would make Shakespeare one with "thundering Aeschylus, / Euripides, and Sophocles" (33–36), to an elegaic past tense in which his death is lamented. Britain owes her present glory to Shakespeare and his book: "Triumph, my Britain, thou has one to show / To whom all scenes of Europe homage owe" (41–42). But Britain's loss, evident in the emptiness of her stage, evokes nostalgia for the past:

> He was not of an age, but for all time!
> And all the muses still were in their prime
> When like Apollo he came forth. . . .
>
> (43–45)

The loss is also nature's and reverberates through all time. Her past alliances with Plautus, Terence, and Aristophanes no longer "please"; in her present sorrow she will "vouchsafe no other wit" (50).

The reference to classical playwrights, which occurs in the center of this shifting passage, is the fulcrum of the poem. From this point on, the Shakespeare praised is Jonson's, "my Shakespeare," an exemplar whom a Jonsonian poet can endorse and imitate. Jonson uses changes in tense to alter the balance slowly, so that he does not undermine his initial praise of Shakespeare. One effect of the complex series of tense changes is to blur the apparent contrast between classical playwrights and nature as models for a poet to imitate. The second and third sections of the poem are thereby closely woven together: Shakespeare's art validates both historical and timeless norms, and both testify to his excellence.

The focus on Shakespeare's achievement enables Jonson to explicate in specific terms the proper relationship between two different timeless norms. In the Renaissance, Nature and Art possessed what Edward Tayler has called "the glamour of completeness." They could be and were used habitually, almost without effort, to define or demonstrate almost any relationship: "together these two terms encompass the totality of specifically human experience."[14] Frank Kermode and Hiram Haydn have documented the many ways in which these terms were used to articulate central intellectual conflicts in the Renaissance, while Tayler argues that in "orthodox" Renaissance moral philosophy, Art and Nature are "in fine balance, complementing each other and contributing together to the making of poets and poetry, of men and fine art."[15]

In Jonson's theoretical statements, nature seems to dominate. He associates natural wit with poetic fire, placing imitation in a secondary position: "Arts and precepts avail nothing, except Nature be beneficial in aiding" (*Dis.* 1767). In his own plays and poems he gives pride of place to art or craftsmanship, and his discussion of Shakespeare reflects that predisposition. Art is introduced in the eulogy as subordinate to Shakespeare's natural talent but is finally the subject of Jonson's main statement. The burden of Jonson's argument in *Discoveries* and in the eulogy is not that art or nature is primary. Rather, in a Senecan vein, he insists that nature is the poet's subject and his genius, art his power to give them shape and expression: "though the poet's matter, Nature be, / His art doth give the fashion" (57–58). Jonson's conclusion may be, as Tayler argues, "orthodox," but it is informed with unusual personal intensity. The reconciliation of apparently opposed norms of judgment serves the poet's overall effort to reconcile his own poetic theory and practice to those of Shakespeare. Jonson uses Shakespeare's actual achievement to test his critical theory, rather than vice versa; the First Folio plays effect a reconciliation of art and nature more powerfully than could any abstract formulation. Jonson begins the eulogy by implying that the two norms are in conflict but ends by affirming they are complementary. He also applies them to two different areas of concern: the work in relation to the nature it imitates, replaces, or evaluates and the artist's craftsmanship in relation to his natural talent or genius. In *Discoveries*, Jonson describes the interdependence of poem and subject, craft and sensibility, in a theoretical aphorism: "Without Art Nature can nere bee perfect, & without Nature Art can clayme no being" (2503–4). The external relationship between art and nature is replicated within the poet in the relationship between his craft and talent.

Instead of relying on abstract theoretical statements, Jonson uses a series of common metaphors to describe Shakespeare's art as a closely woven cloth, imagination's flight, the poet's child, a light that promises day. While they all occur elsewhere in his poetry, the cluster of these different and explicit metaphors is unprecedented and may suggest something of the pressure he felt to reconcile his own poetics to Shakespeare's. Usually one metaphor suffices in a Jonsonian complimentary poem, and that one is often subdued in the service of logical argument. Here each is used to full effect and then yields to another; together they define, describe, and echo Shakespeare's metaphorical art.

One metaphor in particular demonstrates Jonson's attempt to accommodate his poetic methods to Shakespeare's. After praising Shakespeare's alliance with nature, Jonson insists on the equal importance of aesthetic discipline: "For a good poet's made, as well as born" (64).[16] Jonson harmonizes the potential opposition of "made" and "born," of art and nature, by combining them in the familiar *topos* of art as a poet's child:

> Look how the father's face
> Lives in his issue: even so, the race
> Of Shakespeare's mind and manners brightly shines
> In his well-turned and true-filed lines.
>
> (65–68)[17]

A good poet may be made as well as born, but through his making he gives birth. This metaphor of art as body, here the infant bodying forth the poet's spirit, recurs throughout Jonson's works, ranging from the positive idealism of this poem to the satiric narrative of Vulcan's bastardy and Jonson's lost "parts" in the "Execration" to the reversal of the metaphor in his heartfelt lament for his son, his "best piece of poetry."

The images in the final section provide a mode of praise that finally frees Shakespeare from historical contexts. Each image describes a way in which the poet achieves immortality through his art. The progression of images serves the upward progress of the poem from praise rooted in history to praise rooted in timeless norms to apotheosis, at which point Shakespeare himself becomes a norm for judging future playwrights.

By the end of the poem, Shakespeare also becomes the norm for critics, looking down from the heavens as a very Jonsonian critic. Jonson has emerged as playwright, thus reversing the roles the two men played as the eulogy began. Shakespeare is asked to judge and inspire those who remain on earth:

> Shine forth, thou star of poets, and with rage
>   Or influence chide or cheer the drooping stage;
> Which, since thy flight from hence, hath mourned like night,
>   And despairs day, but for thy volume's light.
>
> (77–80)[18]

The false critics, whose praise could "ruin, where it seemed to raise" (12), can ultimately be refuted not so much by Jonson's power as critic as by the influence—aesthetic or astral—of Shakespeare's art. Again, and more significantly than in the opening lines, the apparent opposition between true and false criticism has been discarded, transcended by Shakespeare's excellence. The poem returns to where it began, with Shakespeare centering its circle. Although Jonsonian norms increasingly dominate the latter half of the poem, the emphasis remains on the value of Shakespeare's work.

That emphasis can be seen in the use of Shakespeare's name to mark the different sections of the poem. A person's name is often the focal point of praise in Jonson's complimentary poems, but only here does he use the name repeatedly to emphasize the central moments in a developing myth. In the opening line, Jonson announces the subject of his poem by name. He invokes the name of Shakespeare again in line 19 as he begins to remove Shakespeare from the realm of Time and place him in the pantheon of English and classical writers. In line 56, as Jonson pays what for him is the highest compliment, he names Shakespeare as a man whose art gives "fashion" or form to nature. Finally, as the eulogy shifts from the poet to his book, the First Folio is described as the issue of "Shakespeare's mind and manners" (67). Jonson can claim the right to name the poet, even to pun on his name, because he has defined Shakespeare's art, working through a series of conflicting and limiting contexts to forge "true-filed" lines of commendation.

Readers unfamiliar with Jonsonian complimentary poetry, and with Renaissance complimentary poetry in general, may still question Jonson's sincerity. The very use of conventional themes and strategies arouses skepticism in a modern audience. However, in the poems to fellow artists and to the aristocracy Jonson relies heavily on such conventions. Because he can assume intimacy and equality when writing to artists but not when addressing the aristocracy, Jonson uses different conventions in the two situations. Only in the poem for Shakespeare does he combine both methods. The combination suggests that he recognized in Shakespeare the only rival who could be judged his superior.[19]

Jonson wrote many poems to lesser rivals and closer friends. But of all his commendatory poems, the eulogy for Shakespeare is his best. I am not trying to deny the rivalry that Jonson certainly felt but to argue that it is a sign of his greatness and Shakespeare's that Jonson does his own best work in praise of another man's art. He channels rivalry into praise and finds with integrity a perspective that is sympathetic to Shakespeare and that simultaneously justifies his own poetic methods and principles. Shakespeare is of course more than Jonson's myth of him, and Jonson is more than Shakespeare's admiring critic. We can value the eulogy for what we learn of Shakespeare's achievement. We can also find in the poem that blend of assertiveness and deference, rivalry and respect, imposition and generosity, that is the hallmark of true criticism.

II

In the poem for Shakespeare, Jonson affirms his personal ideal of the artist as a kind of Vulcan, turning and polishing his art at the Muses' anvil. But when fire consumed his library later in 1623, Jonson had reason to curse the "lame lord of fire" as the enemy of art, letters, and the entire world. "An Execration upon Vulcan," a comic anathema, ranges from Mt. Olympus to the Bankside, from ancient Troy to the battlefields of modern Europe. This wide-ranging invective, now comic, now serious, exploits myth, literary allusion, contemporary incident, catalogue, analogy, and pun to portray the destructive power of Vulcan and to demonstrate the opposed power of art. Jonson's portrait of Vulcan occasions a dramatic self-portrait far more comprehensive than the idealized poet-critic of the Shakespeare eulogy. In the "Execration" Jonson defends himself as a man of the bankside and the Court as well as the community of Humanist scholars; he is Londoner and loyal servant of the King as well as classicist. In the poem for the First Folio Jonson celebrates Shakespeare's work as a prime example of a poetics at once classical and English. "An Execration upon Vulcan" extends, in very specific ways, Jonson's agenda for English literature—its proper forms, its function in society. Although most readers would agree with J. G. Nichols that the poem is "something more" than a joke and have appreciated the poet's "serio-comic bravery" in the face of a devastating loss, no critic has penetrated the dense mass of allusion and detail to consider the argument of the poem.[20] It has merely been mined for evidence about Jonson's lost works. By emphasizing the portraits of Vulcan and Jonson that emerge in the poem, I hope to describe the method and meaning of Jonson's argument.

The poet sets up a chiastic relationship between himself and Vulcan, shifting from self-defense to curse as the burden of guilt shifts from the poet to the god of fire. At first Jonson presents himself as a man of classical literature, Vulcan a classical god. He declares his own values through comic indirection, protesting that he, unlike gods and other poets, has done no harm to Vulcan. Moreover, Jonson seems to endorse Vulcan's right to destroy literature when he catalogues specific books and popular literary "follies" that deserve to be burned. But after he describes the burning of the Globe and surveys in comic dialogue the efforts of the Puritan brethren to justify Vulcan as an agent of divine retribution, the poet steps forth as a man of the Bankside and the Revels, loyal even to the watermen and the whores of the Winchestrian liberty. He brands Vulcan, not the players and prostitutes, as the outlaw. To buttress his case Jonson cites the fire that destroyed the Six Clerks Record Office, which not even the most rabid Puritan could describe as a pleasure palace. Speaking with the vigor of a London burgher, Jonson calls on the six "Good Men" to levy harsh sentence on Vulcan: confine him to suburban breweries, brick kilns, or iron mills; reduce him to the hearth fire in a "vile tavern" or the candle end in a bellman's lantern. Vulcan, far from being a classical force or God's avenging angel, is allied with Satan as a servant of evil. Whatever the Puritan brethren may think, Vulcan is responsible for many "divine" losses: St. Paul's spire, the Temple of Diana at Ephesus, the library of sacred books at Alexandria. Even worse, Vulcan the armorer is linked with the medieval legend of Berthold Schwartz, the necromantic friar "Who from the Devil's Arse did guns beget" (202), and with the classical myth of Pandora's box, source of all the evils in the world. Vulcan has done more than destroy manuscripts and buildings; he is the force in men that fosters their desire to destroy other men with ever-stronger "Engines of murder" (207).

Jonson's attack on Vulcan culminates in the "civil curse" that ends the poem: "Pox on your flameship, Vulcan" (191), and "therefore once again / Pox on thee, Vulcan" (213). The poet has moved from lament for his private loss to vehement protest against the arms race of his day: "We ask your absence here, we all love peace, / And pray the fruits thereof and the increase" (209–10). Suddenly Jonson reverts to humor, now darkly sardonic: "So doth the king, and most of the king's men / That have good places" (211–12). They only value war who would use it to advance their own fortunes. Such men are as foolish as the watermen who "made a Vulcan of a sheaf of reeds" (126), trusting it "to dress, not burn, their boats" (128), and who instead occasioned the burning of the Globe, "though it were the fort of the whole parish" (133).

Although the poem alternates between myth and realism, each segment features a different argument against Vulcan. The first segment is the kind of negative opening argument characteristic of Jonsonian poetry. He sets himself apart, in this case from the classical gods who goaded or victimized Vulcan. He summarizes the mythic grievance of Vulcan, absolving himself from any crime of poetic usurpation (1–14). Nor, if Vulcan is the agent of social justice, can he charge Jonson with crimes against Crown, Church, Gown, State, "the times" in general, or even against the poet's self-interest by "some self-boasting rhymes" (23–26).

Still seeking the "cause" of Vulcan's attack—"why this fire?" (27–28)—Jonson goes on the offensive, enumerating literary works and forms that would have given Vulcan ample "colour" (reason, choler) for his flames. A list of contemporary bestsellers and literary "trifles" replaces the mythical crimes of Venus, Jupiter, Mars, and Jove. Jonson, dismissing romances as "the learned library of Don Quixote" (31), alludes to the moment in Cervantes' novel when the Priest and the Barber find themselves unwilling to burn any of Don Quixote's 'dangerous' books (I,vi). Jonson's list of incendiary romances follows that in *Don Quixote*, from *Amadis de Gaul* to *Palmerin of England*. Of this last the Priest exclaims, "that palm of England, let it be kept and treasured as a rarity."[21] Apparently oblivious to the ironic wit of *Don Quixote*, Jonson misreads Cervantes' web of indirection in order to weave his own indirect self-defense, and perhaps to hint at a wish that something might have dissuaded Vulcan from burning his own "learned library."

Jonson often uses the image of the body, especially his own, to make a moral or philosophical point. In this poem, he plays on the metaphoric equation of his own works—his *corpus*—and his body. This poet's not for burning. He has committed none of the verbal crimes for which one is customarily burned: "treason . . . heresy, / Imposture, witchcraft, charms, or blasphemy" (15–16). Although he grudgingly admits that "some parcel of a play" might be "Fitter to see the fire-light than the day" (42–43), he would prefer to be burned by public opinion or even to die "piece by piece" at the kitchen hearth, each sheet of his work lining a roasting pan or pie tin. Jonson's culinary vision of his *corpus* and Vulcan's rage "To make consumption" (58) coalesce in his fantasy of "a feast of fire, / Especially in paper . . . for Vulcan to lick up" (59–84). Jonson's menu reflects his own religious, literary, and political bias: he lumps together the Talmud, the Koran, "the whole sum / Of errant knighthood," broadside pamphlets, news gazettes, and the eccentric prophecies of madmen.

Only after he envisions Vulcan gorging on literary junk food does Jonson return to his own factual situation to inventory the works that were actually consumed by the fire. They can scarcely be called a *corpus:* "I dare not say a body, but some parts / There were of search, and mastry in the Arts" (87–88). At last he can itemize his loss—a translation of Horace, an English grammar, a travel book of his journey to Scotland, a translation of a political allegorical romance, a history of Henry V, books lent him by scholarly friends, notes on his readings in biblical exegesis and theology.

The act of compiling this list seems to require that he begin all over again. He returns to the language of myth to ponder the origin of Vulcan's rage and the language of fact to survey its effects. No longer is the human body a metaphor to describe the poet's work. Instead, Jonson mourns all the human bodies destroyed by the voracious appetite of Vulcan. "All soot and embers," "Son of the wind," begotten in lust and flung away by his own mother, Vulcan is possessed by a lust to destroy (106–14). Anyone foolish enough to embrace this god may "Lose his eyes with gunpowder" shooting off holiday fireworks (121), or suffer the loss of arms, legs, and life in martial combat. The "Engines of war . . . Massacring mankind so many ways" (207–8) not only maim and kill the bodies of the King's loyal soldiers but also signal the corruption of the body politic by those who prefer power to peace, who have been corrupted by the desires this god embodies.

The narrative in this poem responds to Vulcan using the same alternation between myth and fact, catalogue and anecdote, description and dramatization, that Jonson used to figure Penshurst. The language of fact punctuates the narrative of the "Execration," bursting the balloons of Jonsonian fantasy, but also occasioning further fantasy. For example, Jonson's factual list of his books ends with a final reckoning of his loss: "How in these ruins, Vulcan, thou dost lurk, / All soot and embers, odious as thy work!" (105–6). The cherished specificity of each book has been reduced to a shapeless heap, "All soot and embers." Yet the phrase syntactically defines Vulcan as well as the books that are now his "work" and leads into a mythic account of Vulcan's origin, his parents' detestation of him, his early life with "the clowns of Lemnos" (107–17). From that myth of the Olympian past, Jonson turns to the clowns of Jacobean London, "the wise men . . . on the Bankside, / My friends, the watermen" (123–24), whose foolish "trust" in a benign Vulcan perversely occasions the fire god's "cruel stratagem" against the Globe (130). This fantasy of Vulcan's psychology—the battered child turned criminal— comes to an abrupt halt with Jonson's eyewitness account of the fire that destroyed the Globe, "with two poor chambers taken in / And razed, ere thought could urge, This might have been!" (133–34). The fact of Vulcan's fiery appetite destroys the world of fantasy that was the Globe, and turns wit, too late, toward the requirements of fact: "See the world's ruins, nothing but the piles / Left! and wit since to cover it with tiles" (137–38).

At this point, Jonson interpolates the voices of other interpreters to ponder how "wit" tries to justify catastrophe. He dramatizes the scene after the fire: puzzled citizens argue, a Puritan harangues the crowd. His sermon parodies Puritan attacks on the stage and other popular pleasures, echoing not only the rhythms of such diatribes but also their reliance on sign and example. The imaginary preacher interprets the fire, for example, as a visible sign of the dangerous fires of passion loosed in the Bankside brothels, or of the violence in bear-baiting arenas like Paris Garden: God has turned their own "sparkle" against them (141–47). To the rumor that the notorious whore, Kate Arden, set the fire, one realist protests that "No fool would his own harvest spoil or burn" (150). He is shouted down at once: "O no, cried all" (153). Everyone agrees that Vulcan's justice has nothing to do with his own self-interest: "*Fortune*, for being a whore, / Scaped not his justice any jot the more" (153–54). (Jonson here gets in a dig at the management of the Fortune Theatre, which had burned to the ground in 1621.) Any haunt of players or even of dancers, though it be the King's own banqueting house, could expect divine retribution.

The Puritan ends his tirade with a mythic example, the burning of Troy— and at that point Jonson steps in to reply to Puritan and Vulcan alike. The interpolated dramatization ends and the poet's direct attack on Vulcan resumes. The transition is especially comic because it is difficult to tell precisely where the poet shifts his address from the Puritan to Vulcan:

> Fool, wilt thou let that in example come?
> Did not she save from thence to build a Rome?

> And what hast thou done in these petty spites,
> >   More than advanced the houses and their rites?
> I will not argue thee, from those, of guilt,
> >   For they were burnt, but to be better built.
> 'Tis true that in thy wish they were destroyed,
> >   Which thou hast only vented, not enjoyed.
>
> (161–68)

Jonson equates the hot breath of Vulcan and the hot air of the Puritan, so that in speaking to one he addresses the other as well. Both, he argues, engage in efforts that are, finally, futile, but Jonson's syntactic puns in the last of these couplets especially skewer the Puritan, who has neither destroyed nor enjoyed the theatres he hotly attacks and just as hotly imagines.

Since Jonson will not admit "guilt" as the cause of any of the fires in the Puritan's list, he cites a new example of his own to prove that it is Vulcan who is guilty and unjust. The question then becomes how to punish him: reduce him to base uses; extinguish him once and for all; or turn his own myth against him. Jonson revives the myth of Venus and Vulcan that he hinted at in the opening lines of the "Execration" and that the Puritan "sermon" connected to the houses of Venus on the Bankside. The last lines of the poem cite the myth of Pandora's box, a tale of unforeseen consequences, of evil released on a hapless world, and turns it against Vulcan, creator of the box:

> Pox on thee, Vulcan, thy Pandora's pox,
> >   And all the evils that flew out of her box
> Light on thee; or if those plagues will not do,
> >   Thy wife's pox on thee, and Bess Broughton's too.
>
> (213–216)

Venus, Vulcan, and Mars have long been an allegory of the relationship between erotic desire, betrayal, and violence. In the last lines of the poem, Jonson joins the myths of Pandora and Venus to the fact of Bess Broughton, cursing Vulcan with the discord and suffering emblemized by the fires of Venus. The "pox" of disease and degradation stands finally against the "pax," or peace, Jonson seeks for himself and his country.

The clash between Vulcan and Jonson in this poem is particularly powerful because Vulcan so accurately depicts the grim underside of Jonson's own character. The volcanic Jonson is quick to erupt, a man of passion and insatiable appetite. It is the Vulcan in Jonson that so often denies him peace and confirms him in self-destructive anger. Yet in the "Execration" Jonson never acknowledges Vulcan as an image of whatever is worst in himself, nor does he use the fire as an occasion for introspection. Instead, he treats his personal loss as the basis for a larger, impersonal argument about the volcanic forces of destruction and desire in the political world. Instead of seeking stability and peace within, he trusts to the King and "most of the King's men" (211).

III

Jonson directly confronts himself—his prospects, values, "carcass" and "character"—in the great autobiographical poem of 1624, "An Epistle Answering to One that Asked to be Sealed of the Tribe of Ben." The epistle has the complications of dramatic monologue: the mind of the poet works by association, vignette, image, catalogue, proverb, precept, and vivid detail. He veers from generality to memory, from metaphor to fact, from commonplace to unique personal feeling. He brings to this occasion of new friendship all he has read, and wished for, and known. "To speake myself" (6), the act at the core of the poem, seems on close inspection to mark every line. Unlike "An Execration upon Vulcan," in which Jonson evades self-analysis and introspection, this poem keeps the focus on the poet. But another pattern of this poem is its recurrent action of going out from and returning to the poet's self, a "self" redefined through each repetition of the pattern. Each segment of the poem extends and deepens his self-portrait. Tracing the intricate networks of elaboration, negation, allusion, qualification, contrast, and repetition, we can "read [his] character" (73) in the characters of his writing.

Jonson, however, does not present his poem only as an introspective meditation. The epistle is occasioned by an opportunity for a new friendship, and the poem enacts an initiation. He addresses an unnamed "Sir" and initiates him into friendship. The poem could even be described as three stages of that initiation. First, as is often the case in such Jonsonian poetry, the poet sets himself and his friend apart from the crowd of gossip-mongers and social climbers who cannot meet any test of integrity or generosity. He then describes himself: his values, his liabilities, his resolute integrity. Finally, after pushing through the welter of political circumstance and painful personal memory, Jonson goes beyond self-defense to define and celebrate the friendship that now begins. According to this way of patterning the poem, portraits of false friends and a definition of true friendship frame Jonson's self-revelation. The language of economics—appropriate to the portrayal of friendships based on financial gain—is replaced by the language of gift giving. The image of "sealing," corrupted by economic meaning in the public sphere, is restored by the personal, private ending of the poem to the spiritual signification of the title and the opening lines. Embrace and service replace test. Jonson's self-revelation dramatizes the "safe and sure" trust in self that he had declared, in the opening generalization, essential to all friendship.

Most critics have read this poem as only one of its two actions, initiation and introspection.[22] Yet both actions are crucial to the poem. They are bound together through the development of a metaphorical argument and a drama that turns from address to introspective self-analysis and finally returns to a direct address to the new friend. The two actions of the poem do not undo or contradict each other but are brought into relation as the text unfolds. If we read this poem as an act of friendship, then we can be expected to realize that self-esteem is the necessary precondition to friendship.[23] But it is also possible to consider the situation of friendship as the necessary precondition to introspection. Jonson can express himself more fully in the context of intimacy than when he stands entirely alone. Because he can use the other person as a stable, still point of reference, he can address his fear that his career has peaked and his anger at Inigo Jones, and can incorporate those powerful feelings into a coherent self-affirmation.

Like "On Inviting a Friend to Supper" (*Ep.* 101), this poem enacts the friendship it promises. The poet jokes at his own expense, and, at the other extreme, proudly incorporates phrases from his earlier poetry to excoriate false friendship. The situation of safety and trust anchors the poet's meditation on his world and his career, and keeps him from despair. For example, after a long series of vignettes of false friends that reaches its climax in a repulsive image of "flies and worms" feeding on the dead, Jonson breaks off his diatribe to reaffirm the value of one true friendship: "I study other friendships, and more one / Than these can ever be; or else wish none" (29–30). The real utility of friendship lies in the achievement of "one," a new union of selves, a word that defines both the number and the character of the bond he would "study." Secure in that oneness, the poet can freely outline his own political and patriotic values, can admit that Jones has superseded him at court, can confide his strategy for survival. He can even play, sharing with his friend the pleasure of making metaphors that enable him to master, at least in imagination, his insecure position at court. Finally, Jonson turns from rueful survey and playful imaginings to the initial occasion of the poem, and straightforwardly confirms his new friendship. The new friend now knows what to expect; Jonson has tested the capacity of their friendship to absorb and affirm the whole range of his "character." In the course of the poem, the occasion of friendship will be transformed from a test to a gift: "First give me faith, who know myself / A little. I will take you so, / As you have writ yourself" (75–77). Friendship consists of free exchange and mutuality.

The metaphor of writing and reading that ends the Tribe of Ben epistle ends a progression of exploratory metaphors, all derived from the image of "sealing" announced in the title. Each of these subsidiary metaphors— spiritual, economic, alchemical, theatrical, literary—is developed for its own sake and also related, with more or less directness, to the others, so that each of them extends, repeats, and reinforces the main action of the poem.

The title, with its biblical allusion to the Tribe of Ben, implies a religious test, but the opening lines add a Christian reference and an economic implication to the initial image of the sealing: the spiritual integrity of martyrs and the economic integrity of gold together define the virtuous, self-sufficient man. Both emblems are also subject to distortion: a self-serving man may too easily depict himself as a beleaguered martyr, or value a friend only because he can "seal" or guarantee a loan. It is no accident that the terms used in these lines are alchemical jargon as well: true and false gold are the metaphorical problem of the poem.

The title, rich in implications of affiliation and initiation, leads a reader to expect a searching examination—a kind of Last Judgment—of the new friend. The moral maxim that opens the poem seems to lay the groundwork for such a test, be it religious, economic, or alchemical:

> Men that are safe and sure in all they do,
>   Care not what trials they are put unto;
> They meet the fire, the test, as martyrs would,
>   And though opinion stamp them not are gold.
>
> $\qquad\qquad\qquad\qquad\qquad\qquad\qquad\qquad$ (1–4)

Jonson, however, surprises us. The applicant will be tested mainly in his capacity to listen well. The poet has already decided to "seal" their new friendship, and uses the poem to consider just what his own new commitment will entail. He, not the friend, will be tested:

> I could say more of such, but that I fly
>   To speak myself out too ambitiously,
> And showing so weak an act to vulgar eyes,
>   Put conscience and my right to compromise.
>
> $\qquad\qquad\qquad\qquad\qquad\qquad\qquad\qquad$ (5–8)

Because a man who describes himself in these terms makes himself vulnerable, Jonson quickly denies any intent to say what he has in fact said. Despite his disclaimer, Jonson has declared his own worth. The rest of the poem will progress in the same pattern of assertion and qualification, as the poet tries to "speak [him]self" truly, and at the same time to counter the "mere talk" and "rhymes" of gadflies and gossips.

Jonson's reluctance to seem ambitious reflects a central sociopolitical theme of English Renaissance life. Arthur Marotti, discussing the sudden profusion of sonnet sequences in England during the last ten years of Elizabeth's reign, argues that the language of power was converted to a language of love.[24] "Ambition" and "envy," terms of political life, were converted to "hope" and "jealousy," terms of a private relationship. As a Jacobean poet, Ben Jonson led the development of a new metaphoric language of power, the language of friendship. To King James and his Court this relationship, primarily between man and man, was far more important than romantic love between man and woman. In Ben Jonson, James found a poet with a complementary natural disposition toward friendship, but free of the dangerous eroticism of his own relationship with court favorites.

Friendship in the political sphere, although unmarked by overt eroticism, was characterized by ambivalent goals. On the one hand, friends could advance one another's careers and interests. However much men might acknowledge Aristotle's contempt for such friendship in his *Nicomachean Ethics*, power in Jacobean public life was synonymous with "friendship." As Francis Bacon, in his essay "Of Followers and Factions," remarks with a sigh, "There is little friendship in the worlde, and least of all between equals; which was wont to bee magnified. That that is, is betweene superiour and inferiour, whose fortunes may comprehend the one the other."[25] Yet the success of such friendship depended in part on denying its utility. Affection and service, not ambition, were the putative basis of court friendships. What was true for the court was true for the city and the professions as well. Jonson's own "Tribe of Ben" designated not just an informal group of friends but the locus of literary power in Stuart London. On the other hand, friendship was also cherished as a private refuge antithetical to the rivalry and the jockeying for power that marked public life. Although few people might admit it, most of them would want to have had it both ways. Jonson probably thought he had such a friendship and collaboration with Jones, and suffered a double loss when their friendship dissolved into name-calling and bitter competition.[26]

Although Jones and Jonson would occasionally collaborate on court entertainments after this poem was written, Jonson's self-evaluation in the epistle makes it clear that there could be no friendship between the two men. Deciding to risk attempting with a new friend the trust and loyalty that had been so rudely shattered in his past experience with Inigo Jones, Jonson reflects on the inadequacies of most men and on his own ways of reacting to them. It is a sign of his honesty that he brings into this poem the political consequences of his falling out with Jones and that he shies away from any attempt to base his future career on the utility of a new friendship. Instead, he comes to regard friendship only as a refuge. Integrity, not dependency, will be the basis of both his private friendships and his public career.

By rejecting ambition as a motive or beneficiary of friendship, Jonson tries to distinguish between blameworthy pride and integrity. To make that distinction, he makes use of negation, a device characteristic of his satires, to describe what he and his new friend are not. He derides men who would question, because they could not pass, any test of integrity. He fleshes out "Opinion," creating a world of men who "merely talk and never think" (9), who joke about other (absent) people, or feed "Like flies or worms" on the "corrupt parts" of a dead man's character (18). Adopting a strategy typical of his other epistles, Jonson moves from a real to an imagined occasion. The imaginary men embody what he wants to avoid; they write libellous "rhymes" (26) he abhors and reject the values he cherishes. They would mock the friendship he seeks.

The technique of negation is but one of the satiric devices Jonson adapts to his nonsatiric act of introspection in this epistle. In many of his satiric poems, for example, Jonson makes an absolute statement and then qualifies it so as to unfold his satiric intent. For example, in "An Execration upon Vulcan," Jonson declares that "we all love peace," including "the King and most of the King's men / That have good places" (209–12). Jonson's straight-foward nonsatiric claim sidles into satire with the word "most" and doubles that move in the wry qualification "That have good places." The progressive qualification of Jonson's initial statement sets up a clear contrast between selfless patriotism and the self-serving politics of the court. In the Tribe of Ben epistle, Jonson uses this technique of statement and qualification both for satire and for serious self-revelation. He heaps contempt on men of "opinion" who "never yet did friend or friendship seek" (14), only to add a damning exception in the next line: "But for a sealing" (15). He adopts the same strategy for his serious affirmation of friendship: "I study other friend-ships, and more one / Than these can ever be; or else wish none" (29–30). This is the arithmetic of friendship: better one than all these; better none than all these. He also returns to the "One" of the title, to the real occasion, the fact of the poem.

Yet the particularities of the venal world overwhelm him, as he itemizes the "deal of news" that the "covey of wits" bring "to strew out the long meal." The catalogue of news is not arbitrary. Every item concerns Spain: the Spanish-French struggle for Valtellina; the Spanish-Dutch struggle for the West Indian shipping lanes, the Spanish-English negotiations for a mar-riage of Prince Charles and the Infanta. These references to Spain point to Jonson's bitter memory of the circumstances that led to his final break with Jones, an event antithetical to the occasion of this epistle. Jones had been commissioned to plan the festivities that would have honored the Spanish Infanta had she come to England as the bride of Prince Charles. Jonson was entirely excluded from those plans.

The poet's attitude here is surprisingly complex. He seems, on the one hand, to take a stand above it all. He considers the circumstances only at the level of public policy, and even then refuses to be drawn into the debate about the desirability of the marriage. He does not condemn the ill-fated enterprise of the Prince and Buckingham, nor does he lament its failure. "I wish all well," he declares tactfully, and emphasizes his willingness to serve the King as a soldier, whatever his status as court poet: he will "live, or fall a carcass in the cause" (42), should James go to war with Spain.

Jonson's versified account of the tense political situation with Spain shows that his "ignorance" is no greater, and demonstrably far less, than that of the gossips and newsmongers he mocks, although he couches his knowledge of politics in the idiom of disclaimer and indifference. Only after he protests his indifference to politics and proclaims his unquestioning loyalty to the King does Jonson slip in, again in the idiom of disclaimer, his own grievance against Inigo Jones. Jonson's deft political stance—"I wish all well"—anchors his self-defense and his firm resolve to rise above Jones's neglect:

> I'll be well,
> Though I do neither hear these news, nor tell
> Of Spain or France, or were not pricked down one
> Of the late mystery of reception,
> Although my fame to his not under-hears,
> That guides the Motions and directs the bears.
>
> (45–50)

The rhetoric of this resolution deserves special attention. After his clear plain statement, Jonson then disclaims/admits his disadvantages. The first ("Though I do neither hear these news, nor tell / Of Spain or France") seems disingenuous, even dishonest; Jonson's satiric attacks on political gossips make it clear that this is one disadvantage he would not care to correct. The confident satire of the first admission shifts to personal anger in the second, that he "[was] not pricked down one / Of the late mystery of reception." Jonson's anger comes through in his refusal to name Inigo Jones, and in his use of a slang verb for "writing" that sexualizes and trivializes Jones's insulting omission. Even the use of the vague, impersonal "one" to refer to Jonson and to those Jones did select ironically echoes the antithetical act that is this poem: Jonson's sealing of "one" new friend. Jonson's anger changes to self-assertion when he contrasts himself to Inigo Jones. The image of "hearing" centers the contrast: Jonson may not hear the news, but other people hear about him. However, the awkward neologism, "under-hears," hints at the strain and the anger that still underlie his self-assertion.

Denying that he has been damaged and declaring that he can survive both continental war and court infighting, Jonson finally admits that Jones's decision has hurt him:

> But that's a blow by which in time I may
> Lose all my credit with my Christmas clay
> And animated porcelain of the court;
> Aye, and for this neglect, the coarser sort
> Of earthen jars there may molest me too.
>
> (51–55)

This is the low point of the poem, as Jonson vacillates between propping himself up and admitting he has been sorely wounded. To imagine what will happen he uses the indirect idiom of metaphorical fantasy to dehumanize his fickle noble patrons. The fantasy has a double effect: Jonson satirizes the brittle aristocracy and the "coarser earthen jars" that fill out the Court, and he also shares with his friend a fantasy, that most intimate and private form of thought. The making of fantastic metaphor constitutes a new language for the poem, replacing the dramatic vignettes of false friends and the factual catalogue of "news." Yet here, as in those earlier sections, Jonson uses that language to set himself apart from those he describes. Characterizing himself as a "frail pitcher" (55), Jonson puts himself in the imagined world of figurines and jars and vows to protect himself from being "jostled, cracked, made nought, or less" (59).

In the confines of his fantasy, Jonson offers a rather grandiose vision of his own regal power to determine his fate: "what to do / I have decreed" (56–57). However, he turns from fantasy to faith, from pride to "reverence," from "credit" at court to the "gifts" of Heaven:

> Live to that point I will, for which I am man,
>   And dwell as in my centre as I can,
> Still looking to, and ever looking, heaven;
> With reverence using all the gifts thence given.
>
> (59–62)

The language of direct moral statement provides Jonson with an idiom to define the ideal of human friendship and its basis in Humanist faith. This is the language of "conscience and my right" that had been silenced early in the poem because Jonson was unwilling to seem "weak" to "vulgar eyes" (6–7). The language of conscience can finally be restored when he acts on his own terms, no longer worried about being looked at by the world, but "Still looking to, and ever loving, heaven" (61). Jonson had used metaphorical fantasy to distance himself from the court. He now revises his own perception of himself—becoming an active subject, not a passive object—to detach himself from court language and values, resolving to consider only himself and his God.

Jonson does not end with this resolution to keep well sealed the spiritual vessel of his soul, but addresses once more the crisis in his professional career. He does so by developing yet another set of meanings possible to the trope of "sealing." His bitter experience with Jones equipped him with a set of vivid metaphors for false friendships. Like the sets of a masque, such friendships are constructed only of "canvas, paper, and false lights," soon deformed into "Oily expansions, or shrunk dirty folds" (65–68). Against that mocking metaphor, Jonson sets his own masquelike vision of friendship: "All so clear and led by reason's flame / As but to stumble in her sight were shame" (69–70). If false friendships are as flimsy as masque sets, true friendships are "square, well-tagged, and permanent" (64–68). The word "well-tagged" links the metaphor of masque sets to the metaphor of sealing, "Tag" can mean "to fasten, stitch, or tack together; to join" (OED), and so compares the act of sealing a friendship to the act of stitching or building a set. "Tag" can also mean "a strip of parchment bearing a seal" (OED), and so recalls the economic and contractual language developed throughout the poem—especially the contrast between a true friend and a man who wants only a guarantor for his debts.

Set against the contractual or economic language of the "sealing" is a new foundation for that sealing, the language of conscience, faith and trust. Jonson replaces the image and idea of masque with a straightforward declaration of commitment to true friends: "These I will honour, love, embrace, and serve, / And free it from all question to preserve" (71–72). This is the kind of language Jonson adopted in his earlier prayerful reliance on God; the love and faith there affirmed he now transfers to friendship. In the closing lines of the poem, Jonson returns to the religious values implicit in the title and the opening lines of his poem, grounding friendship in the religious bond of the human and the divine.

Many different actions are evident in his final act of accepting friendship and life: remembering, judging, wishing, defying, resolving. He has sought analogies and example. He does so painfully, proudly, angrily, hopefully, and at last can accept life and all its uncertainties. In Jonson's earlier epigram, "On Inviting a Friend to Supper," the poet sought the "fair acceptance" of a "grave sir," and spun a pleasing web of promise and wish to secure it; now he himself is invited to begin a new friendship, but knows it must rest on an acceptance of painful fact as well as anticipated pleasure. He equates his act of deciding with his writing of the poem. My reading of the poem centers on this last analogy, expressed as a contrast in the last lines:

> So short you read my character, and theirs
>   I would call mine, to which not many stairs
> Are asked to climb. First give me faith, who know
>   Myself a little. I will take you so,
> As you have writ yourself. Now stand, and then,
>   Sir, you are sealed of the Tribe of Ben.
>
> (73–78)

What he has written is not a static catalogue of his traits but a set of actions and modes of action, as he imagines how to address the world. Turning from that imaginary action to the friend before him, he presents a crafted version of himself, with the implicit promise of more to come. The poet defines himself as his action: he writes himself. Writing is finally the act to be interpreted, and to interpret the poem is to know the poet. But the poet turns from writing and reading to a performative speech act: "Sir, you are sealed of the Tribe of Ben."

In the opening lines, Jonson seemed to disregard the poem as poem, as privileged and crafted utterance. As in so many of his poems, he presents the text as unmediated statement: "I could say more of such"; "I fly to speak myself out too ambitiously" (5,6). The words "say" and "speak," familiar poetic conventions, at once disclaim the act of writing and emphasize writing as a special kind of speech. In the last lines of the poem, when he refers to the action of friendship as the writing and reading of character, Jonson does more than move from speech to poetry. He makes the poem itself a metaphor for the action it describes. This poem is not "about" poetry, any more than Jonson's plays are "about" the theatre, but awareness of the poem is incorporated in the poet's action, thereby unfolding and enriching its meanings.

The sober confidence and commitment of the last line, and of the entire poem, are evident when the last line is read aloud. Friends, once accepted, are subject to no further test or question. The final sealing is not a carefully qualified contract but an initiation. The metaphor of "sealing" has been finally purged of economic implications; letter replaces number. The *Oxford English Dictionary* first defines "character" as "mark, stamp, sign": seal. Seal as letter, as the written language that is the poem, becomes the sign of the poet. The punning metaphor is a commonplace: the second major set of definitions of "character" derives from its figurative denotation of the moral qualities and traits of a person. Jonson has written a poem; he has also written himself. Yet it is crucial to the act of mutual faith in this poem that the reader not presume to know the entire being of the poet, who confesses only to "know [him]self / A little." When Jonson makes this qualification, he shares with us his belief that self exceeds, in possibility if not in fact, our particular knowledge of self. The littleness of even the most thorough and capacious writing must be compensated for by the large generosity of the reader.

The progressive unfolding or enhancement of the metaphor of "sealing" and the mode of address in this poem combine to implicate the reader in the act of the poem. When we "read [his] character," we write our own. Jonson appropriates the situation of the poem as the concluding element of his defense of poetry: because he does not name his new friends, every reader is invited to fill that role. The Tribe of Ben epistle concludes with Jonson's willingness to share with his reader the authority to determine both the meaning and value of his poetic action. Indeed, the survival of Jonson's writing depends on the reader's decision to be sealed of the Tribe of Ben. The Tribe of Ben epistle, therefore, honors not only the initial occasion of its writing but also the perennial occasion of its reading.

In defense of poetry, the three autobiographical poems of 1623–24 insist on the endurance of art despite death, loss, or failure. Even more important is their definition of the requirement for endurance: not aesthetic idealism or ethical judgment but reciprocity and generous exchange. In these poems, the metaphors of book, body, and character define three different versions of the relationship between the poet and his text. The fourth figure that can define the text is the act of friendship that occasions the Tribe of Ben epistle. Friendship can serve as a model for the relationship between a text and literary tradition, between a text and its occasion, between a text and its book, between a text as speech and a text as writing. In perceiving these relationships, we also are initiated into reading as a freely chosen act of friendship. Friendship is not only the action in the poem, but the action of the poem; the actor is not only the poet but the reader as well. As a reader of Shakespeare, Jonson subsumed his aggression and admiration into a poetics of respect, peace, and pleasure. He offers us this poetics as our own.

7

"Acts of Grace": Notes toward a Reading of *Under-wood*

> I hate such measured, give me mettled! fire,
>   That trembles in the blaze, but then mounts higher,
> A quick and dazzling motion! When a pair
>   Of bodies meet like rarefied air!
>
> *(Und.* 59)

With age and straitened circumstances, and with the increasing political crises of Caroline England, came a new valuing of the single dazzling moment when poetry and history could intersect, when interpretation could occur. At the time of his death in 1637, Jonson was preparing *Under-wood* for the press; Sir Kenelm Digby, his patron and literary executor, completed the editorial work and published the collection of poems in 1640. Both individual poems and the collection as a whole are congruent with Jonson's earlier work in *Epigrammes* and *The Forrest*. He reiterates the poetic actions of description and self-dramatization so prominent in the 1616 Folio. For example, the epigram for the Earl of Newcastle, that provides the epigraph to this chapter depends on the dramatic wit of relationship central to the poems in *Epigrammes*: the poet's definition of valor applies equally to Newcastle's heritage and Jonson's art *(Und.* 59). However, what Jonson had once assumed as established foundations for poetic action he has come to regard as fragile, fleeting opportunities. *Under-wood* documents the difficulty, as well as the pleasure, of his ongoing attempt to enact a "true relation" with his literary predecessors, his friends, and his aristocratic patrons. The book as a whole provides a retrospective summary of his poetic career subsequent to the 1616 Folio: his political relationships and friendships, his experiments with literary form and language, and his assessment of his own prospects and worth. The collection is marked by experimentation as well as reiteration: Jonson attempts a poetry of greater scope, using networks of metaphor, relationship, and self-representation to advance his arguments.

Although the arrangement of *Under-wood* may reflect some of Digby's own choices and values, Jonson was organizing the collection along the lines he had first attempted in *The Forrest*. His preface to *Under-wood* establishes the connection between the two books: "I am bold to entitle these lesser poems of later growth by this of *Underwood*, out of the analogy they hold to *The Forrest* in my former book, and no otherwise."[1] This disclaimer can be read as a statement that *Under-wood* was planned as a book analogous to *The Forrest* in its multiple actions and types of poetry. The chronological pattern of composition loosely orders the collection, but its dramatic pattern of action consists of a meditation on the nature and functions of poetry as public statement, private meditation, and intimate conversation, each mediating the claims of community and personal autonomy in the "rarefied air" of art.[2]

Like the poems in *The Forrest*, the lyrics of *Under-wood* derive their meaning from their original occasion, but that meaning is often augmented by circumstances that obtained at the time *Under-wood* was edited for publication. Annabel Patterson, the only critic to consider *Under-wood* as a cohesive collection, cites three typical examples of the way the occasion of publication can supplement the original occasion of composition: Jonson's commendatory epigram for Ralegh's *History of the World* has become an epitaph for Ralegh (*Und.* 24); complimentary epigrams for Sir Edward Coke and Francis Bacon, two public figures subsequently discredited (*Und.* 46, 51), retell "the old story of fortune's slippery wheel, updated to fit the new social mobility of the seventeenth century."[3] Jonson's editorial work sets each poem in tension with two historical contexts: the occasion of its writing and the occasion of its inclusion in *Under-wood*.

The aesthetic context of the book adds a third dimension of meaning to each of the poems. Because his poems are preserved in a collection divorced from past and present circumstance, the poet's voice can veer from one to the other, taking on the added character of nostalgia, commemoration, and prophecy. John Lemly reads Jonson's late poems as personal nostalgia, psychological portraits of melancholy and self-contempt, while Anne Barton finds in Jonson's Caroline works a political nostalgia for the Golden Age of Elizabeth.[4] Annabel Patterson takes a rather grim view of the politics in *Under-wood*, emphasizing its "ironic economy" and its "half-light" of understatement, indirection, and subversive whispers.[5] I find another mood dominant in the book. Jonson wants to affirm the past—both his world and his work—and to accept a diminished present, "these lesser poems of later growth." *Under-wood* portrays a society that had outlived the priviliged moments celebrated in *The Forrest*. The poet does not have the choice available to the Infant of Saguntum (*Und.* 70), who could refuse to enter the world, but must find a way to look back in elegiac praise and forward in hope and grace.

Although *Under-wood* follows roughly chronological order, the first and last set of poems violate chronology in order to inscribe the arc of Jonson's poetic action. The book begins with three "Poems of Devotion" and ends with five translations of classical poems defining the happy life; the religious poems were probably written late in Jonson's life, the translations much earlier.[6] Whether Jonson or Digby chose this arrangement, the rest of the poems in *Under-wood* are thereby framed by Christian and classical values. In the first devotional lyric, Jonson vows to perform "acts of grace," and the word "grace" will reverberate through *Under-wood*, used at least thirty times to celebrate grace of speech, style, political authority, and personal spirit.[7] The term epitomizes Jonson's ideal of art and life, and gains its spiritual meaning from Christian theology, its ethical import from classical literature.

The investigation of poetry as an act of grace is central to the three major sections of *Under-wood:* poems dating from 1616 to 1620, following publication of the 1616 Folio (*Und.* 2–29); poems of the late Jacobean years, 1620–25 (*Und.* 30–52); and the Caroline poems of Jonson's last years (*Und.* 53–84). The book as a whole defines the possibilities and limits of poetry as Jonson knew them during the late Jacobean and Caroline years. In the first section, Jonson relies on poetry as a way to address society; he adapts to hostile circumstance by seeking a sympathetic audience. The second section radiates outward from "An Execration upon Vulcan" and the Tribe of Ben epistle. In this section, Jonson defends poetry as a personal act defining his literary *"corpus"* and his "character." In the third section a new visionary concept of poetry appears for the first time, as Jonson contrasts poetry to the other arts as well as to history. Poetry offers the poet a way to celebrate and transcend circumstance; he finds an emblem of poetry in the "bright asterism" of a heavenly constellation (*Und.* 70).

The religious poems that introduce *Under-wood* are followed by a set of Petrarchan lyrics dramatizing private play and desire (*Und.* 2–11). These poems, as I have argued in discussing "A Celebration of Charis" and "My Picture Left in Scotland," dramatize Jonson's mastery and dismissal of Petrarchan poetry.[8] His own choice of a different poetic mode is clear in the social poems that immediately follow the lyrics (*Und.* 12–18). These epitaphs and epistles assert the poet's integrity in the face of social decadence, public disdain, breach of trust, and death. Sustained by friends like Sackville and Selden, and inspired by their achievements, he trusts in his own future: "All is not barren land doth fallow lie" (*Und.* 17). Even when he returns to poems of desire and satire (*Und.* 18–22), he writes about the failure of sympathy: husbands do not value their wives, women seem incapable of friendship with men. He finally rebukes himself for trying to please a large public audience and angrily resolves to address only a coterie, so that he can sing "Safe from the wolf's black jaw and the dull ass's hoof" (*Und.* 23).[9]

Jonson ranks first among those English poets who have dared make art of anger. Satiric distribe offered him one conventional avenue for a poetry of anger, and his many poems in that mode set the standard by which later English satirists still are judged. More rare, and more risky, are his poems of personal anger—the odes to himself, the attacks on Inigo Jones (*U. V.* 34–35). In an ode to himself (*Und.* 23), Jonson effectively crafts a poetics of anger. He not only attacks the boorish crowd but rebukes himself for being implicated by his silence in the decay of taste he despises. That rebuke becomes the foundation for his renewed resolve to speak. He does not suppress his rage but enlists it in the service of his renewed commitment to poetry.

This private poem, a kind of dramatic monologue, prepares the way for a set of public odes and memorial verses, after which he reaffirms his poetic amibition (*Und.* 24–29). He struggles to be adequate to public occasion (*Und.* 25) and private affection (*Und.* 27), stimulated by the requirements of history (*Und.* 24), friendship (*Und.* 26), and example (*Und.* 28). Buoyed by a renewed faith in his audience and himself, he can mock the hollow molds of Petrarchan poetry, especially the rhyme "That expresseth but by fits / True conceit" (*Und.* 29, 2–3). The outdated mode of Petrarchan poetry will not enable him to address the audience he seeks. The remedy is not an attack on poetic form, however, but a confident mastery of it. This segment of *Under-wood* ends with a comic triumph of form against form, as the poet trans-forms the "fetters" of rhyme into "true measure" (11, 45). Anger has been displaced by laughter.

Jonson submits this personal affirmation to challenge and redefinition in the second large segment of *Under-wood*. This section, which begins with a set of Jacobean complimentary epigrams (*Und.* 30–33) and ends with a comparison between painting and poetry (*Und.* 52), testifies to the range of Jonsonian poetry during the early 1620s: a satire on smallpox, an epitaph for a child, a love song, elegies, epistles, complimentary epigrams. These poems, in all their variety, support the two major statements in defense of poetry, "An Execration upon Vulcan" (*Und.* 43) and the Tribe of Ben epistle (*Und.* 47), that stand at the center of *Under-wood*. The "Execration" affirms the possibility of good resulting from loss, creation from destruction. The Tribe of Ben epistle acknowledges limitation as a foundation for personal and poetic renewal: "I know myself / A little," Jonson declares, and that must suffice.

These personal statements themselves frame three political poems: a Horatian satire on the aristocratic "carcasses of honour" who evade public service (*Und.* 44), and two brief tributes to friendship and merit. Jonson's poem to Sir Arthur Squib sets forth the importance and process of friendship in general terms: "First weigh a friend, then touch, and try him too" (*Und.* 45). Praising the authority, eloquence, and learning of Sir Edward Coke (*Und.* 46), Jonson calls attention in the title of his poem to Coke's fall from power in 1616. The conditions of friendship and the vicissitudes of power are, of course, the subjects of Jonson's Tribe of Ben epistle, in which he establishes a new friendship and assesses his dwindling authority at court.

The four poems that follow the Tribe of Ben epistle document Jonson's different reactions to the waning of his own professional star. He dedicates the King's wine cellar in a delightful *jeu d'esprit* (*Und.* 48); bitterly attacks the "Court Pucelle," one of the "animated porc'lain" ladies whose favor had shifted away from him (*Und.* 49); praises a virtuous widow who shuns "the vices of the time" (*Und.* 50); and willfully preserves an earlier poem honoring the discredited Sir Francis Bacon (*Und.* 51). Jonson may have included this poem to comment on the fickleness of Fortune, to insist on his own enduring admiration for Bacon, or even to assert the power of art to triumph over changing circumstance.[10] We cannot know for certain. However, by grouping these four poems together, Jonson dramatizes the range of his own response to Jacobean court life.

Jonson takes the contrast between poetry and painting as his new theme in his "reply" to the painter, Sir William Burlase (*Und.* 52). At first, the poet seems to defer to the painter, joking that an artist's pen needs neither form nor language, but only ink, to do justice to him: "With one great blot, you had formed me as I am" (12).[11] With grace and generosity, he then envisions a language that can address the qualities of Burlase beyond physical appearance:

> Yet when of friendship I would draw the face,
> A lettered mind and a large heart would place
> To all posterity: I will write *Burlase*.
>
> (82–84)

To "write *Burlase*" means to enact in language the relationship between these two friends, for language joins the writer to his subject—and his subject to "posterity." The pun on "lettered mind" epitomizes Jonson's idea of this poetry of relationship. Burlase is well-read; Jonson's letters can capture in poetry the quality of his mind and convey that quality to future readers. These lines ring yet another variation on a theme introduced in Jonson's epigrams to Sir Henry Goodyere and the Countess of Bedford and developed most extensively in the Tribe of Ben epistle. Jonson adds to that theme the primacy of poetry in the hierarchy of arts. Poetry is not confined to verisimilitude or externals, but can offer an interpretive vision that transcends the materiality of its ostensible subject. As Jonson writes in *Discoveries*, quoting Plutarch: "*Poetry*, and *Picture*, are Arts of a like nature . . .

For they both invent, faine, and devise many things, and accommodate all they invent to the use, and service of nature. Yet of the two, the Pen is more noble, then the Pencill. For that can speake to the Understanding; the other, but to the Sense" (1509–16). Jonson goes on to meditate on the history of painting and the variety of its achievement, admitting that sometimes "it doth so enter, and penetrate the inmost affection (being done by an excellent Artificer) as sometimes it orecomes the power of speech" (1526–28). Still, the very method and purpose of painting, its "faining," Jonson attributes to poetry (1549). In these lines from *Discoveries*, Jonson suggests four possible relationships between painting and poetry: similarity, contrast, contest, and influence. These are aspects of relationship often dramatized in his social poetry; now they become aspects of his meditation on his own work.

The third and largest segment of *Under-wood* extends the idea of poetry as a visionary act of reading and writing, and develops the contrast between poetry and painting introduced in the poem to Burlase. This anthology of Jonson's Caroline poetry begins with a set of complimentary poems for his friends, patrons, and the royal family (*Und.* 54–69), including two poems that suggest his own straitened financial circumstances (*Und.* 57, 68). The last poem in this group, "Epigram to a Friend, and Son" (*Und.* 69), reiterates the critique of painting implicit in the poem to Burlase and puts it to explicit satirical use. Jonson lashes out at the flattery that dominates life at the Caroline court, where "All is but web and painting" (24). What emerges in these poems is the poet's increasing sense of his own isolation, made worse by the condition of financial strain. It is ironic, given the contrast between painting and poetry developed in these poems, that Jonson had a portrait painted in which he holds up a copy of his appeal for prompt payment of the pension due him from the Exchequer (*Und.* 57).[12]

The Cary-Morison ode (*Und.* 70) testifies to Jonson's triumph over the conditions of loss and diminution, a triumph that can admit the forceful reality of those conditions. The poem has recently received a good deal of critical attention, and is now widely regarded as Jonson's major Caroline achievement.[13] The last in a series of similar but lesser poems for James Desmond (*Und.* 25) and Sir William Sidney (*For.* 14) offering counsel, trust, and praise in a context of misfortune, doubt, and death, the Cary-Morison ode at once celebrates "harvest" and mourns loss, taking the measure of a short, full life, "the lily of the day," against a life "long, not liv'd." Jonson's cadenced stanzas combine a sense of intimacy with majestic formality and poetic virtuosity.

The placement of this poem in *Under-wood* not only ends a series of celebratory odes but also parallels and counters the action of bitter with-drawal in the "Ode. To Himself" (*Und.* 23). The Cary-Morison ode is a work possible only to an assured artist able to take risks—ranging from the startling opening image of the Saguntum infant to the poet's use of his own name, "Ben / Jonson" (84–85), to join two stanzas as his poem joins two friends. In his double capacity as man and poet, represented by the division of his name in the text, Jonson can address the double claims of private grief and public honor and can bring them together in the act of poetic speech.

The arresting description of the "Brave Infant of Saguntum" (1–10) recalls the surprising openings of Pindar's odes, but its meaning comes clear only when the poem itself is recognized as a celebration of the union of man and man, humanity and nature, art and life. The infant's "unnatural" return to the womb, an immediate and total withdrawal from life, is a "natural" reaction to the unnatural violence and evil rife in the world. When Jonson questions the child's reason for withdrawing, the answer is a familiar elegaic theme: who, foreseeing "Life's miseries," would want to live? He turns from this rhetorical question, which seems to offer a defense of the infant, to a narrative portrait of the "stirrer," the man of long but purposeless life: "He stooped in all men's sight / To sordid flatteries, acts of strife" (38–39). These portraits, the first developed from a brief note in Pliny and the second from Jonson's own satiric poetry, are not allowed to define the possibilities for life. Instead, they yield to a celebration of Morison, who died young but lived a full life. With the description of Morison, the ode moves from indirect consolation to a direct confrontation with loss. No longer is the infant the summed circle "Of deepest lore" (10); Morison is now the "sphere" of human excellence (52).

The poet's self-presentation becomes a crucial element of this confrontation with loss. Jonson addresses not the infant but himself in lines that seem almost a private exhortation within this public poem, as he rejects his own beginning and attempts a more appropriate form of praise. Berating himself—"he never fell, thou fall'st, my tongue" (44)—Jonson replaces the infant and the stirrer as a foil for Morison:

> Go now, and tell out days summed up with fears;
> And make them years;
> Produce thy mass of miseries on the stage,
> To swell thine age;
> Repeat of things a throng,
> To show thou hast been long,
> Not lived.
>
> (53–59)

In this ironic exhortation, Jonson attributes to himself the fears of the infant and the useless age of the stirrer.[14] He reformulates the contrast between their lives as a contrast between a false art that merely sums up the artist's "mass of miseries" and the true art of Life, who "does her great actions spell / By what was done and wrought / In season" (59–61).

It remains to the poet to overcome his own melancholy and "taste a part of that full joy he meant / To have expressed / In this bright asterism" (87–89). The "asterism" emblemizes not only the friendship of Cary and Morison, but also the bright ode which celebrates that friendship. Just as the poet splits his name to join two stanzas ("Ben / Jonson"), so he splits the metaphor of the friends as stars ("twi / Lights") in order to acknowledge their separation (one is dead, while the other lives) and to unite them in a single image (92–93). The separated word is a carefully contrived poetic imitation of the "design" (95) of nature, which the poet's art can only amend in imagination. The ode also imitates the Humanist virtue of Cary and Morison, the "simple love of greatness and of good / That knits brave minds and manners more than blood" (105–6). The word "brave" now has none of the irony inherent in Jonson's account of the "Brave infant." Language, like time, has been redeemed by the memory and the vision of these two friends.

The poet pulls back in the last stanza to a realistic recognition that not all men will follow the example of Cary and Morison. The poet, who had already moved from direct reference to himself ("my tongue") to the distancing of the third person ("Ben / Jonson"), finally joins the anonymous throng of observers:

> And such a force the fair example had,
> As they that saw
> The good and durst not practise it, were glad
> That such a law
> Was left yet to mankind;
> Where they might read and find
> Friendship in deed was written, not in words;
> And with the heart, not pen,
> Of two so early men
> Whose lines her rolls were, and records.
> Who, ere the first down bloomed on the chin,
> Had sowed these fruits, and got the harvest in.
>
> (117–28)

Of the many images brought forward in this poem, that of life as an example of art, as itself the greatest work of art, prevails in the final stanza. Jonson praises "two so early men" whose deeds overgo the art that celebrates them. Yet this ambitious poem also enacts the poet's own personal recovery. He remakes himself by taking poetic risks that give new life to the poetry of imitation, exhortation, and social occasion. In the early poems, so rigorously limited in form, language, and image, Jonson sowed the seeds of Humanist poetic and social ideals; in this ode, he too, however belatedly, "got the harvest in."

The ode is surrounded by the lesser realities of Caroline circumstance: routine compliments, petitions, commemorations. After the ode, the poet's emphasis shifts disturbingly away from intimate sustaining friendship toward the exigencies of finance. The next eleven poems are addressed mainly to Jerome Weston, the Royal Treasurer.[15] Even in the few poems written directly to King Charles as "gifts," Jonson's hope for royal largesse in return lurks in the background.[16]

These harsh realities are not only ignored but countered and surmounted by two elegies, for Lady Jane Paulet and Lady Venetia Digby (*Und.* 83–84). Like *The Forrest*, *Under-wood* features a pair of major epistles for men near the beginning of the collection and a comparable pair of poems for women near the end. Moreover, like the epistle to the Countess of Rutland, the elegy for Lady Jane Paulet can best be read as an introduction to "Eupheme," the poem for Lady Venetia Digby that follows it. In accordance with Jonson's customary practice, the first poem anticipates and is superseded by the second. The theme and action of language is announced in the elegy for Lady Jane Paulet. The poet laments his own inadequacy: he could not name her soul "Had I a thousand mouths, as many tongues, / And voice to raise them from my brazen lungs" (22–24). She, on the other hand, "Speaks heaven's language, and discourseth free / To every order, every hierarchy" (71–72). This contrast is developed further in "Eupheme," where the lady's "voice so sweet [and] words so fair . . . Still left an echo in the sense" (*Und.* 84.4.37–40). The poet seeks a language adequate to her excellence and his own grief, contrasting his voice to hers, the power of painting to that of poetry, even the life-giving language of God to the limited language of the human mourner.

As a sequence of lyrics, "Eupheme" invites comparison with "A Celebration of Charis" (*Und.* 2), the playful poems at the beginning of *Under-wood*. To compare these sequences is to see how far Jonson had come in the direction of complex baroque lyric and symbolic argument. The drama of social relationship has been replaced by an attempt to place the lady's meaning in the vast scale of being, ranging from earth to heaven, from her infancy and ancestry to her death and descendants.

"Eupheme" represents Jonson's most ambitious attempt to write in the symbolic mode of the baroque lyric most notably undertaken by John Donne in the *Anniversaries*. As an investigation of the symbolic capacity of language, "Eupheme" constitutes Jonson's final defense of poetry as a visionary act superior to the visual arts. That defense of poetry may have been occasioned by the specific circumstances surrounding the death of Lady Venetia Digby. Artists close to her grief-stricken husband hastened to commemorate her in poetry, painting, and sculpture.

In the third lyric, "The Picture of the Body," Jonson imagines the likeness a painter might produce: a commemorative portrait heavy in its materiality, thick with laces, velvets, jewels. Jonson then offers to the mind of his reader a drama of vision and an act of celebration. His version of an ideal portrait is ironically reminiscent of the masque sets of Inigo Jones, his old colleague and enemy: clouds parting to reveal first her face, then the universe itself. Jonson's vision of "beauty's world" rises to heaven and stoops to earth, his imagination soaring from clay to cloud. He throws down the gauntlet to the painter, challenging him to portray her spiritual perfection.

Jonson may have had a particular artist in mind: Sir Anthony Van Dyck, who painted two posthumous portraits of Lady Digby (the first immediately after she died, the second within the year). Van Dyck had found favor at the Caroline court even as Jonson found himself shunted aside. Norman Farmer has suggested that there may have been a contest between them—if only on Jonson's part—for the favor of the bereaved husband.[17] If Van Dyck knew of Jonson's challenge to the painter in "Eupheme," he did not respond on its terms in either of the two portraits. It may be that neither man knew of the other's commission (though it seems likely they did); it may be that Van Dyck chose to ignore Jonson's poem, following instead his own impulse or Digby's instructions; it may even be that Jonson wrote after one or both of the portraits had been completed, and that he intended his poem to advance the claims of poetry at the expense of Van Dyck's work.

Van Dyck's paintings explore two modes of portraiture: intimate sketch and public allegorical statement. The first portrait, of Lady Digby on her deathbed, is unlike anything else he ever painted. Sir Kenelm Digby, greatly pleased, sent a detailed description of the portrait to his brother in a letter dated 19 June 1633:

> It is the Masterpeece of all the excellent ones that ever Sir Antony Vandike made, who drew her the second day after she was dead; and hath expressed with admirable art every little circumstance about her, as well as for the exact manner of her lying, as for the likeness of her face; and hath altered or added nothing about it, excepting onely a rose lying upon the hemme of the sheete, whose leaves are being pulled from the stalke in the full beauty of it, and seeming to wither apace, even when you looke upon it, is a fitt Embleme to express the state her bodie then was in.[18]

Digby seems pleased both by the realism of the portrait ("every little circumstance") and the painter's choice of one apt emblem, the full-blown rose. Other paintings for similar occasions are set pieces, their emblematic messages more ritualistic and didactic.[19] Van Dyck's intense portrait depicts only her face on the pillow and a rose on the counterpane. The image is entirely personal, intended for Digby alone.

The second painting, an allegorical portrait of Lady Digby as "Prudentia," takes many of its details from the emblem of married chastity in Cesare Ripa's *Iconologia*.[20] Christopher Brown, after quoting Digby's detailed explication of the portrait, speculates that Van Dyck may have been following Dibgy's own instructions.[21] Lady Venetia Digby had acquired a reputation for loose behavior before she married Digby, and this painting may have been designed as a public statement testifying to her marital virtue.[22] This style, too, was not typical of Van Dyck. He made at least one copy of the painting, perhaps to record his work in this elaborate allegorical mode.[23]

As Van Dyck's portraits illustrate two types of art, so Jonson's lyrics to the painter (*Und.* 84.3–4) define two possibilities for poetry. The first poem—elaborate instructions to the painter so that he can "work with my fancy his own hand"—envisions a collaboration of poet and painter, the portrait executing the poet's idea. The painter is banished from the second lyric, as Jonson calls on Lady Venetia Digby to "speak yourself" through his lines. He then ranges high and low to seek a place suited to the loveliness of her mind: heaven, paradise, "a nest of odorous spice and gums," a "field of flowers." Finally, the only *locus amoenus* for her mind is her own body. In the union of her body and soul, she signifies the ideal human harmony that would be the subject of Digby's own treatise on body and soul (written in 1642).[24] Moreover, in the union of her body and soul, she epitomizes the ideal union of human and divine. Jonson's lyrics include his genuine regard for Lady Digby and his sense of personal loss when she died, his distrust of the visual arts, and his accommodation to the Cavalier mysticism of Sir Kenelm Digby. Above all, the lyrics of "Eupheme" seek a language adequate to the occasion of her death. In the last poem of the sequence (*Und.* 84.9), Jonson moves from despair at the loss of his muse ("life of all I said, / The spirit that I wrote with") to a reliance on God as the supreme author and reader of human life: "[He] can trace / Each line, as it were graphic, in the face. / And best he knew her noble character, / For 'twas himself who formed and gave it her" (153–56). Jonson's final appeal to the reader combines grief at his own loss and trust in her immortality: "Who reads, will pardon my intelligence, / That thus have ventured these true strains upon, / To publish her a saint. My muse is gone" (226–28). Jonson writes as a poet, not a mystic. He submits his imagination and his language to the particularities of occasion.

By placing "Eupheme" near the end of *Under-wood*, Jonson (or Digby) preserves the chronological order of the book. At the same time, the sequence of lyrics sums up the major themes and poetic strategies that mark Jonson's entire career. It is a sequence that depends on human relationships: Jonson's own bond with Lady Venetia Digby, his sympathy with her husband and children, his alliance with subsequent readers. To forge those relationships, Jonson ranges from the minutiae of daily life—even the corals, whistles, painted masks, and paper boats of a child's playroom (*Und.* 84.1)—to formulas of genealogy and the visionary analogies between human beauty and divine perfection. Only the visionary mode is new, and may reflect Jonson's sympathy with Digby's Catholic aesthetic or Jonson's own eagerness, even at the end of his life, to experiment with new poetic forms in order to address a significant occasion.

If "Eupheme" sums up Jonson's claim to preeminence as a Cavalier poet in the elaborate baroque mode, the close translations of poems by Horace, 'Petronius Arbiter,' and Martial set last in *Under-wood*—whether placed there by Jonson or Digby—emphasize the enduring power of classical ideals among the Cavaliers. These poems epitomize Cavalier social values: the good life of ease and pleasure, embraced despite the repressive pressures of morality; the sadness of pleasure and the sweet pleasure of sorrow; sensation and imagination indulged with brilliant display; and personal style asserted against the implacable forces of history.[25] Keep "endless holiday" (*Und.* 88). "With Syrian oil let shine / Thy locks, and rosy garlands crown thy head; / Dark thy clear glass with old Falernian wine" (*Und.* 89). Such is the pleasing darkness of life in contrast to the fearsome darkness of death. The pleasures of life range from ideals to pragmatic comforts, from "substance got with ease" and "a continual fire" to "A quiet mind" and "wise simplicity" (*Und.* 90). He who can possess and enjoy such advantages "Makes his life longer than 'twas given him, much" (*Und.* 89). Jonson's last poems in *Under-wood* submit his own voice to the words of Martial, and keep Roman poetry alive in order to argue the value of life itself, even in the "darkest hours" of travail and certain death: "Will to be what thou art, and nothing more; / Nor fear thy latest day, nor wish therefore" (*Und.* 90). This classical ideal of the graceful life—at once Stoic and Epicurean—Jonson asserts with "quick and dazzling motion" (*Und.* 59) despite harsh political reality, the personal strain of ill health and professional eclipse, and the bittersweet memory of a time when decay and defeat had seemed impossibly remote. This ideal was Jonson's legacy to the Sons of Ben. It sustained him, and would sustain them in the last days of Caroline England. The actions of poetry would finally be the crucial actions of life itself.

Notes

Chapter 1. The Poem as Action

1. Ben Jonson, *Poems*, ed. Ian Donaldson (Oxford: Oxford University Press, 1975). All citations of Jonson's poetry are to this edition and are incorporated in the text. Donaldson has modernized the text established in the Herford and Simpson edition of Jonson's works. I shall use the following abbreviations in citing Jonson's poems: *Ep. (Epigrammes), For. (The Forrest), Und. (Under-wood)*, and *U.V.* (ungathered verse).

2. *Ben Jonson*, ed. C. H. Herford and Percy and Evelyn Simpson, 11 vols. (Oxford: Clarendon Press, 1925–52), 8:621. All references to *Discoveries* are to this edition and are incorporated in the text. My debt to these editors is incalculable.

3. Because Jonson creates a powerful illusion of his own presence in his poetry, we seem to know him through his art. Yet he has proved remarkably difficult to define. Critics who try to do so often describe him by charting dichotomies: Jonson as generous friend and severe critic, confident professional and insecure outsider, severe moralist and bawdy jester, exuberant English realist and restrained classicist. He is by turns magisterial and vindictive, tender and savage, collegial and solitary. He distrusts authority, yet claims it for himself. These extremes led Edmund Wilson to label Jonson an "anal erotic" personality in "Morose Ben Jonson," *The Triple Thinkers* (New York: Oxford University Press, 1948), 213–32. Wilson fails to distinguish Jonson from the dramatic characters he creates, attributing to Jonson, for example, opinions expressed by Volpone. Arthur Marotti defines Jonson's character as "Apollonian" and "Diony-sian" in "All About Jonson's Poetry," *ELH* 39 (1972): 208–37. He describes Jonson as an "artistic schizophrenic" who rebels against the poetic order he struggles so hard to create. George Parfitt, in *Ben Jonson: Public Poet and Private Man* (New York: Barnes and Noble, 1977), argues that Jonson's private anguish belies his public authority. Richard Newton, in " 'Ben. / Jonson': The Poet in the Poems," *Two Renaissance Mythmakers: Christopher Marlowe and Ben Jonson*, ed. Alvin B. Kernan (Baltimore: The Johns Hopkins University Press, 1977), 165–95, posits a "fierce repression" at the core of Jonson's art (193). Annabel Patterson makes use of Gromscian ideas of the problematic social role of the intellectual in her discussion of Jonson's covert protests against authority, "Lyric and Society in Jonson's *Under-wood*," in *Lyric Poetry: Beyond New Criticism*, ed. Chaviva Hŏsek and Patricia Parker (Ithaca: Cornell University Press, 1985), 148–63. Rather than set the "conscious" and the "unconscious" of the poet against each other, I prefer to argue that a text is constituted by simultaneous conscious actions of the poet. These deliberate actions can serve different, even contradictory, purposes. For example, a complimentary poem may serve to establish a bond between poet and patron and at the same time establish the poet's moral independence of such bonds. A poem can be at

once an act addressing literary tradition, social circumstance, and private psychic need. My understanding of action as multiple in purpose and effect owes a great deal to Roy Schafer's revisions of psychoanalytic concepts; following Schafer's lead, I have avoided using the language of psychoanalytic metapsychology. See especially his collection of essays, *A New Language for Psychoanalysis* (New Haven: Yale University Press, 1976). Schafer summarizes his theory of action in "Conflict as Paradoxical Actions," *The Psychoanalytic Attitude* (New York: Basic Books, 1983), 82–95. See also the classic essay by Robert Waelder, "The Principle of Multiple Function," *Psychoanalytic Quarterly* 15 (1936): 45–62. The contemporary philosophical debate about the nature of "action" and the pertinence of that debate for literary criticism are discussed by Charles Altieri in *Act and Value: A Theory of Literary Meaning and Humanistic Understanding* (Amherst: University of Massachusetts Press, 1981), esp. 97–159. Although I do not use the terminology of speech act theorists, I am indebted to their work, especially J. L. Austin, *How to Do Things with Words* (New York: Oxford University Press, 1962) and Mary Louise Pratt, *Toward a Speech Act Theory of Literary Discourse* (Bloomington: Indiana University Press, 1977).

4. A classic essay on Jonsonian poetic form remains F. R. Leavis, "The Line of Wit," in *Revaluation: Tradition and Development in English Poetry* (London: George W. Stewart, 1947; reprinted New York: Norton, 1963). Judith Kegan Gardiner, *Craftsmanship in Context: The Development of Ben Jonson's Poetry* (The Hague: Mouton, 1975), traces Jonson's increasing mastery of poetic form during the course of his career.

5. Noteworthy attempts to discuss the Jonsonian stance include T. S. Eliot, "Ben Jonson," *Essays on Elizabethan Drama* (New York: Harcourt Brace, 1956), 65–82; and Geoffrey A. Walton, *Metaphysical to Augustan: Studies in Tone and Sensibility in the Seventeenth Century* (London: Bowes & Bowes, 1955).

6. Thomas Greene describes the "ethics of receptivity" that underlie Jonsonian poetic action in "Accommodations of Mobility in the Poetry of Ben Jonson," *The Light in Troy: Imitation and Discovery in Renaissance Poetry* (New Haven: Yale University Press, 1982), 264–93.

7. Felix Schelling, "Ben Jonson and the Classical School," *PMLA* 13 (1898): 221–49, and Kathryn McEuen, *Classical Influences on the Tribe of Ben* (Cedar Rapids, Iowa: Torch Press, 1939) remain significant. Recent studies of Jonson's classicism include Richard Peterson, *Imitation and Praise in the Poems of Ben Jonson* (New Haven: Yale University Press, 1981), and Katharine Maus, *Ben Jonson and the Roman Frame of Mind* (Princeton: Princeton University Press, 1984). On the theory and practice of imitation, see G. W. Pigman III, "Versions of Imitation in the Renaissance," *Renaissance Quarterly* 33 (1980): 1–32; Mary I. Oates, "Jonson's 'Ode Pindarick' and the Doctrine of Imitation," *Papers on Language and Literature* 11 (1975): 126–48; Ira Clark, "Ben Jonson's Imitation," *Criticism* 20 (1978): 107–27; and Gordon Braden, *The Classics and English Renaissance Poetry* (New Haven: Yale University Press, 1978).

8. See H. A. Mason, *Humanism and Poetry in the Early Tudor Period* (London: Routledge and Kegan Paul, 1959, reprinted 1980). This pioneering study of Humanism as a context for Jonson's poetry remains a useful essay. Jonson's affinities with Erasmus are discussed by Graham Bradshaw, "Three Poems Ben Jonson Did Not Write: A Note on Jonson's Christian Humanism," *ELH* 47 (1980): 484–99.

9. Daniel Woolf, "Erudition and the Idea of History in Early Modern England." Paper presented at the 1985 Pacific Northwest Renaissance Conference, Vancouver, British Columbia.

10. For an outstanding discussion of Jonson's idea of the poetic book, see Richard Newton, "Ben Jonson and the (Re)invention of the Book," in *Classic and Cavalier*, ed. Claude J. Summers and Ted-Larry Pebworth (Pittsburgh: University of Pittsburgh Press, 1982), 31–58.

11. Noteworthy thematic criticism includes Hugh Maclean, "Ben Jonson's Poems: Notes on the Ordered Society," *Essays in English Literature from the Renaissance to the Victorian Age, Presented to A. S. P. Woodhouse, 1964*, ed. Millar Maclure and F. W. Watt (Toronto: University of Toronto Press, 1964), 43–68, and Thomas Greene, "Ben Jonson and the Centered Self,"

Studies in English Literature 10 (1970): 325–48. Critics who discuss the thematic unity of *Epigrammes* include Gardiner, 12–53; Edward Partridge, "Jonson's *Epigrammes:* The Named and the Nameless," *Studies in the Literary Imagination* 6 (1973): 153–98; Bruce Smith, "Ben Jonson's *Epigrammes:* Portrait-Gallery, Theater, Commonwealth," *Studies in English Literature* 14 (1974): 91–110; and David Wykes, "Ben Jonson's 'Chast Booke,'—The *Epigrammes*," *Renaissance and Modern Studies* 13 (1969): 76–87. The only critic to consider *The Forrest* as a unified work is Jonathan Kamholtz, "Ben Jonson's Green World: Structure and Imaginative Unity in *The Forrest*," *Studies in Philology* 78 (1981): 170–93. Richard P. Dutton begins to make a case for regarding the entire 1616 folio edition of Jonson's *Workes* as a unified text in *Ben Jonson: To the First Folio* (Cambridge: Cambridge University Press, 1983), but confines his argument to the description of a few recurrent themes and clusters of related poems.

12. On the satirist as naive observer, see Maynard Mack, "The Muse of Satire," *Yale Review* 41 (1951–52): 80–92.

13. Stanley Fish offers a similar reading of this poem, but to a quite different purpose, in "Authors-Readers: Jonson's Community of the Same," *Representations* 7 (1984): 26–58, esp. 46–47. Fish argues that the double action of Jonsonian poetry often consists of doing and undoing the work of praise, so that the poet simultaneously serves and protests against the system of patronage in which he worked. For a similar argument, see Don E. Wayne, *Penshurst: The Semiotics of Place and the Poetics of History* (Madison: University of Wisconsin Press, 1984), 129–73.

14. George Puttenham, *The Arte of English Poesie*, ed. Baxter Hathaway (Kent, Ohio: Kent State University Press, 1970), 213.

15. See D. P. Walker, "Musical Humanism in the Sixteenth and Early Seventeenth Centuries," *Music Review* 2 (1941): 1–13, 111–21, 220–27, 288–308; 3 (1942): 55–71; J. A. Westrup, "Foreign Musicians in Stuart England," *Musical Quarterly* 27 (1941): 70–89; James A. Winn, *Unsuspected Eloquence: A History of the Relations between Poetry and Music* (New Haven: Yale University Press, 1981), 163–79; Elise Jorgens, *The Well-Tun'd Word: Musical Interpretations of English Poetry 1597–1651* (Minneapolis: University of Minnesota Press, 1982), 175.

16. Herford and Simpson, 5:432.

17. Stephen Greenblatt, *Renaissance Self-Fashioning* (Chicago: University of Chicago Press, 1980). This influential study of the generation of identity in the Renaissance argues that "fashioning oneself and being fashioned by cultural institutions" were actions "inseparably intertwined" (256), but that Renaissance males nonetheless clung to the belief that the human self could be freely fashioned (257). It is not my purpose to deny that Jonson shared this belief in self and self-fashioning, but to argue that he would have regarded self as larger than its particular fictions. Thomas Carew articulates a rather sardonic version of this latter idea at the end of his poem "To Ben Jonson": "The wiser world doth greater Thee confesse / Then all men else, then Thy selfe onely less." These lines suggest the discrepancy between an action of the self and the idea of selfhood that exceeds any particular act.

18. Richard Sennett, *The Fall of Public Man* (New York: Alfred A. Knopf, 1977), 49–51. Courtesy books codified the differential development of public identity. See Frank Whigham, *Ambition and Privilege: The Social Tropes of Elizabethan Courtesy Theory* (Berkeley: University of California Press, 1984). Susan Wells, "Jacobean City Comedy and the Ideology of the City," *ELH* 48 (1981): 37–60, describes city comedy as a genre that reflected contradictory assumptions about the city as at once an ideal place that enabled self-fashioning and a real place that suppressed and devalued the individual person.

19. Frank Manley, ed., *John Donne: The Anniversaries* (Baltimore: The Johns Hopkins University Press, 1963), 73–74.

20. Michel Foucault, *The Order of Things* (New York: Random House, 1970), 24–25.

21. *Conv. Dr.* 649–79. See also Herford and Simpson, 1:177–78. Jennifer Brady argues that Jonson visited Scotland in order to reevaluate his career and distance himself from the Jacobean

court. She does not discuss these poems, but Jonson's acerbic comments on Petrarchan poetry may have reflected his political discomfort with courtly conventions and values. See "Jonson's 'To King James': Plain Speaking in the *Epigrammes* and the *Conversations*," *Studies in Philology* 82 (1985): 380–90.

22. *Conv. Dr.* 660.

23. *Conv. Dr.* 680–89. Thom Gunn offers a sympathetic, astute reading of this poem in his introduction to *Ben Jonson* (Baltimore: Penguin, 1974), 20–21. His introduction deserves to be ranked among the finest short essays on Jonson's poetry. It is reprinted in Thom Gunn, *The Occasions of Poetry* (San Francisco: North Point Press, 1985), 106–17.

24. In *Poetaster* 4.3.110–11, Captain Tucca remarks of Horace that "he wil sooner lose his best friend than his least jest." Horace is usually interpreted as a surrogate for Jonson in the play. See Herford and Simpson, 1:178.

25. A "performative" or "declarative" speech act brings about the condition it refers to (e.g., blessing, marrying). See Mary Louise Pratt, *Toward a Speech Act Theory of Literary Discourse* (Bloomington: Indiana University Press, 1977), 80–88. See also J. L. Austin, *How to Do Things with Words* (New York: Oxford University Press, 1962).

26. Jacques Derrida, "Differance," *Speech and Phenomena and Other Essays on Husserl's Theory of Signs*, trans. David B. Allison (Evanston, Ill.: Northwestern University Press, 1973), 129–60.

Chapter 2. "Fair Acceptance": Jonson's Poetry of Love and Friendship

1. The most useful discussions of Jonson's Humanism are those of H. A. Mason, *Humanism and Poetry in the Early Tudor Period* (London: Routledge and Kegan Paul, 1959), and Thomas Greene, *The Light in Troy* (New Haven: Yale University Press, 1982), 264–93. See also W. D. Kay, "Jonson's Urbane Gallants: Humanistic Contexts for *Epicoene*," *Huntington Library Quarterly* 39 (1975–76): 251–66, and "*Bartholomew Fair*: Ben Jonson in Praise of Folly," *English Literary Renaissance* 6 (1976): 115–26. Katherine Maus asserts that Jonson shares the "distinctive, complex humanist view of the classics, contradictory in theory but powerful in practice" (3–4), but her discussion is more concerned with direct connections between Jonson and major Roman authors.

2. Daniel Javitch, *Poetry and Courtliness in Renaissance England* (Princeton: Princeton University Press, 1978), contends that Spenser initiated the idea of the poet as a replacement of the courtier, but that Ben Jonson gave it currency (160–61).

3. James Tracey, *Erasmus: The Growth of a Mind* (Geneva: Droz, 1972). I am indebted to this study of *libertas* and *simplicitas* as central concepts in the work of Erasmus. On the survival of Erasmian ideas in England, see H. R. Trevor-Roper, *Religion, the Reformation and Social Change* (London, 1967), and J. K. McConica, *English Humanists and Reformation Politics* (Oxford: Oxford University Press, 1965). Douglas Duncan, *Ben Jonson and the Lucianic Tradition* (Cambridge: Cambridge University Press, 1979), argues that the *lusus* common to Erasmus and Jonson can be traced to Lucian but confines his discussion to Jonsonian drama.

4. Richard Lanham, *The Motives of Eloquence* (Berkeley: University of California Press, 1976), 6.

5. Lanham, 8.

6. Each position was defined by relating language to philosophy, history, and what we now would call psychology. See Nancy Struever, "Humanities and Humanists," *Humanities in Society* 1, no. 1 (1978): 25–34. Of the many studies of Renaissance Humanism, I would note the following: Paul O. Kristeller, *Renaissance Thought II: Papers on Humanism and the Arts* (New York: Harper and Row, 1965); George K. Hunter, *John Lyly: The Humanist as Courtier* (Cambridge, Mass.: Harvard University Press, 1962); George M. Logan, "Substance and Form

in Renaissance Humanism" *Journal of Medieval and Renaissance Studies* 7 (1977): 1–34; and Hanna Gray, "Renaissance Humanism: The Pursuit of Eloquence," in *Renaissance Essays*, ed. Paul O. Kristeller and Philip Wiener (New York: Harper and Row, 1968), 199–216.

7. Thomas Greene, "The Flexibility of the Self in Renaissance Literature," in *The Disciplines of Criticism*, ed. Peter Demetz, Thomas Greene, and Lowry Nelson, Jr. (New Haven: Yale University Press, 1968), 248.

8. Greene, 246.

9. Herford and Simpson, 11:246.

10. Sir Philip Sidney, *An Apologie for Poetrie*, in *Elizabethan Critical Essays*, vol. 1, ed. G. Gregory Smith (Oxford: Oxford University Press, 1904), 166.

11. John Danby, *Elizabethan and Jacobean Poets* (London: Faber and Faber, 1965), 41–45. This book was first published in 1952 as *Poets on Fortune's Hill*.

12. On the contrasting personalities of Erasmus and Jonson, see Duncan, 234–35.

13. This point was made by my colleague, Alan Fisher, in "Jonson's Jokes," a lecture presented at the 1984 Pacific Northwest Renaissance Conference.

14. Herford and Simpson, 2:392–93.

15. For expression as a value in rhetorical and musical humanism, see James A. Winn, *Unsuspected Eloquence: A History of the Relations between Poetry and Music* (New Haven: Yale University Press, 1981), 122–93.

16. Petrarch, *Le Familiari*, ed. Vittorio Rossi (Florence: Sansoni, 1934). See also Barry Weller, "The Rhetoric of Friendship in Montaigne's *Essais*," *New Literary History* 9 (1977–78): 504.

17. Petrarch, *Secretum: Petrarch's Secret*, trans. W. H. Draper (London, 1911), 72. Quoted by Hiram Haydn, *The Counter-Renaissance* (New York: Harcourt, Brace and World, 1956), 52.

18. Sidney, *Astrophil and Stella*, Sonnet 1, in *Selected Poetry and Prose*, ed. David Kalstone (New York: New American Library, 1970), 123.

19. Anne Ferry, *All in War with Time: Love Poetry of Shakespeare, Donne, Jonson, Marvell* (Cambridge, Mass.: Harvard University Press, 1975), 147.

20. Ferry, 137.

21. For a comprehensive account of Jonson's attitudes toward Petrarchan poetry, see Lawrence Venuti, "Why Jonson Wrote not of Love," *Journal of Medieval and Renaissance Studies* 12 (1982): 195–220. Critics who consider "A Celebration of Charis" anti-Petrarchan satire include Paul Cubeta, " 'A Celebration of Charis': An Evaluation of Poetic Strategy," *ELH* 4 (1958): 163–80; G. J. Weinberger, "Jonson's Mock-encomiastic 'Celebration of Charis,' " *Genre* 4 (1971): 305–28; Arthur Marotti, "All About Jonson's Poetry," *ELH* 39 (1972): 208–37, esp. 230–35; and S. P. Zitner, "The Revenge on Charis," *The Elizabethan Theatre IV*, ed. G. R. Hibbard (Hamden, Conn.: Shoe String Press, 1974), 127–42. For readings sympathetic to Ben and Charis, see Wesley Trimpi, *Ben Jonson's Poems* (Stanford, Calif.: Stanford University Press, 1962), 209–28; T. J. Kelly, "Jonson's 'Celebration of Charis,' " *Critical Review* (Melbourne) 17 (1974): 120–26; Richard S. Peterson, "Virtue Reconciled to Pleasure: Jonson's 'A Celebration of Charis,' " *Studies in the Literary Imagination* 6 (1973): 219–68; R. V. Leclercq, "The Reciprocal Harmony of Jonson's 'A Celebration of Charis,' " *Texas Studies in Language and Literature* 16 (1975): 626–50; and Raymond P. Waddington, " 'A Celebration of Charis': Socratic Lover and Silenic Speaker," *Classic and Cavalier: Essays on Jonson and the Sons of Ben*, ed. Claude J. Summers and Ted-Larry Pebworth (Pittsburgh: University of Pittsburgh Press, 1982), 121–38. Despite different grounds for the argument, many of these essays agree that the lyric sequence is written in a "mixed" poetic style and tone.

22. Trimpi, 8–10 ff.

23. All references to Demetrius are to the Loeb edition of *On Style*, trans W. Rhys Roberts (Cambridge, Mass.: Harvard University Press, 1953), and are cited in the text by section

number. Bernard Weinberg, "Translations and Commentaries of Demetrius, *On Style* to 1600," *Philological Quarterly* 30 (1951): 353–79, lists 26 complete editions available in Jonson's time, beginning with the Aldine edition of 1608.

24. G. M. A. Grube, *A Greek Critic: Demetrius on Style, The Phoenix,* supplementary volume 4 (Toronto: University of Toronto Press, 1961), 31 and 91 n.

25. Grube's translation of section 28 (p. 91).

26. Edward Tayler suggested this idea to me.

27. Jonson's synthesis of quantity and stress and his alternations of tempo in this lyric are discussed by Lester A. Beaurline, "The Selective Principle in Jonson's Shorter Poems," *Criticism* 8 (1966): 73–74.

28. Trimpi provides a subtle account of the way Jonson combined rhythms and images from many different sources into this deceptively simple lyric. Among the sources of "Her Triumph" Trimpi cites Jonson's *The Devil is an Ass* (2.6.94–113) and *The Haddington Masque;* Spenser's *Fowre Hymnes;* Ovid's *Metamorphoses* 10 and 15, and *Amores* 1.2.23–42; Martial 5.37.4–6; Ficino's commentary on Plato's *Symposium;* and Elizabethan songbooks and ballads (Trimpi, 218–20, 233–34, 284 n).

29. William Spanos, "The Real Toad in the Jonsonian Garden: Resonance in the Nondramatic Poetry," *Journal of English and Germanic Philology* 68 (1969): 1–23. Roger Sale, *Literary Inheritance* (Amherst: University of Massachusetts Press, 1984), comments that a "sense of the observable" here "consorts in perfect ease with the conventional or traditional" (16).

30. There is a hitherto unrecorded fourth stanza of this song in the Tobias Alston commonplace book, now part of the James L. and Marie-Louise Osborn Collection at the Beinecke Library, Yale University:

> Have you seene but ye diamond rocks
> > When a purlinge waue hath dasht them
> Or Auroras golden locks,
> > When a may Morning hath wash't them,
> > > Did you ever softly steale
> > > To heare sweet Philomele;
> Have you smelt the breath of a fish
> > Or a mayd when she kisse
> Or have you tasted the Cythian tree
> O so fayre, o so soft, o so sweet is shee,
> > o so sweete is shee.

There is no irrefutable evidence that Jonson composed this stanza, but the Alston manuscript does contain authoritative texts of major poems by Jonson, Donne, Herrick, and many other poets. Like the canonical fourth stanza, this version appeals to sensations scarcely imaginable. It differs in omitting a specific reference to touch (although the wave dashing against the "diamond rocks" could be regarded as both tactile and visual), and in referring to nature in terms of classical mythology (Aurora, Philomele, the Cythian tree). Sensation and literary convention are not so well harmonized in this newly discovered version, nor can a progression be traced from classical to English pastoral images. The images of beaver, swansdown, and bee, moreover, are more immediately appealing than the "breath of a fish." In sum, I prefer to think that Jonson did not compose this version of the fourth stanza. Whoever did was not alone in trying to overgo Jonson's original: Herford and Simpson record many different versions of this song.

31. Trimpi compares her to the comic heroines of Molière (218).

32. Johan Huizinga. *Homo Ludens: A Study of the Play-Element in Culture* (Boston: Beacon, 1960), 180.

33. Huizinga, 8.

34. Huizinga argues that "the whole mental attitude of the Renaissance was one of play. This striving, at once sophisticated and spontaneous, for beauty and nobility of form is an instance of culture at play" (180). However, the ending of Sidney's sonnet sequence challenges the value of play: because Stella refuses to leave the play-world of courtship for the real world of commitment and vulnerability, Astrophil is trapped in now meaningless poetic formulas. Shakespearean comedies seem most artificial in the first and last scenes, when the action occurs at the threshold of the play-world. The intense and highly structured playfulness of the final scenes (Rosalind's conjuring, Prospero's magic circle) facilitates a renunciation of playing. See Kent T. van den Berg, "Theatrical Fiction and the Reality of Love in *As You Like It*," *PMLA* 90 (1975): 885–93. Jonson does not reject the play-world of Ben and Charis, but protects it by not composing their reply to the other woman's crude joke.

35. Quoted by Hiram Haydn, *The Counter-Renaissance* (New York: Scribners, 1950), xii.

36. Haydn, 41.

37. On the idea of play in Erasmus and Jonson, see Duncan, 26–51, 234–35.

38. *A Concordance to the Poems of Ben Jonson*, ed. Steven L. Bates and Sidney D. Orr (Athens: Ohio University Press, 1978), 278–80.

39. For an account of Aristotelian ideas of friendship in Jonson's poems, see Maclean, 43–68. See also Earl Miner, *The Cavalier Mode from Jonson to Cotton* (Princeton: Princeton University Press, 1971), 250–304, and Laurens Mills, *One Soul in Bodies Twain: Friendship in Tudor Literature and Stuart Drama* (Bloomington: University of Indiana Press, 1937).

40. Horace, *Satires, Epistles, and Ars Poetica*, trans. H. R. Fairclough (Cambridge, Mass.: Harvard University Press, 1929), and *Odes and Epodes*, trans. C. E. Bennett (Cambridge, Mass.: Harvard University Press, 1927). All citations to these Loeb editions are incorporated in the text.

41. Gordon Williams, *Tradition and Originality in Roman Poetry* (Oxford: Clarendon Press, 1968), 104–5.

42. Martial, *Epigrams*, trans. W. C. A. Ker, 2 vols. (New York: G. P. Putnam's Sons, 1920), 2:193. All citations of Martial are to this edition and are incorporated in the text.

43. Mason, 281.

44. Wesley Trimpi, comparing this epigram to Jonson's *Leges conviviales*, suggests that the poem defines a friend rather than a dinner and that the tone of the poem and the character of a friend share the same traits: "*eruditi, urbani, hilares,* and *honesti*" (188).

45. David McPherson, "Ben Jonson's Library and Marginalia: An Annotated Catalogue," *Studies in Philology, Texts and Studies 1974*, 71, no. 5 (December 1974), records Jonson's copy of Erasmus's *Familiarum colloquiorum opus* (p. 43, no. 58).

46. Erasmus's attempt to formulate a Christian ethic of pleasure was part of an ongoing debate begun by Ficino, Pico della Mirandola, and Lorenzo Valla. See Craig Thompson, ed., *The Colloquies of Erasmus* (Chicago: University of Chicago Press, 1965), 536–37. All quotations of Erasmus will be taken from this translation.

47. Edward Surtz, S. J., *The Praise of Pleasure* (Cambridge, Mass.: Harvard University Press, 1957), 9–35.

48. Thompson, 49.

49. M. P. Tilley, *A Dictionary of Proverbs in England in the Sixteenth and Seventeenth Centuries* (Ann Arbor: University of Michigan Press, 1950), H440.

50. Lawrence Ryan, "Art and Artifice in Erasmus' *Convivium Profanum*," *Renaissance Quarterly* 31 (1978): 3. I am deeply indebted to Ryan's discussion of the festive colloquies. Another helpful account of the "festive morality" of the *Colloquies* is provided by Douglas Duncan, 26–51.

51. Gardiner interprets this poem as an act of judgment which "involves distinctions based on balancing, weighing, and ranking several different positive goods" (27). She and Trimpi remark the balance of assertion and concession, positive and negative, in the language and syntax of the

poem; Trimpi notes as well the balance of metrical control and swift narrative movement (185–90).

52. See Kenneth Schellhase, *Tacitus in Renaissance Political Thought* (Chicago: University of Chicago Press, 1976). The English Humanists' interest in Tacitus can be traced at least as far back as More's *Richard III*.

53. Mark Eccles, "Ben Jonson and the Spies," *Review of English Studies* 13 (1937): 385–97.

54. Maclean, 47–52.

55. Jonas Barish, "Feasting and Judgment in Jonsonian Drama," *Renaissance Drama*, n.s., 5 (1972): 35. See also Peter Carlson, "Judging Spectators," *ELH* 44 (1977): 443–57.

Chapter 3. "Times and Occasions": History as Subject and Context of Poetry

1. F. J. Levy, *Tudor Historical Thought* (San Marino, Calif.: The Huntington Library, 1967), esp. 237–86. My account of the Tudor idea of history has been greatly influenced by Levy's work.

2. Critics who discuss the relationship between Jonson's occasional poetry and Baconian empiricism include Achsah Guibbory, "The Poet as Mythmaker: Ben Jonson's Poetry of Praise," *Clio* 5 (1976): 322–39, and Richard Newton, " 'Ben./Jonson': The Poet in the Poems," *Two Renaissance Mythmakers: Christopher Marlowe and Ben Jonson*, ed. Alvin B. Kernan (Baltimore: The Johns Hopkins University Press, 1977), 165–95.

3. Cicero, *De Oratore* 2.9.36.

4. Stephen Greenblatt, *Renaissance Self-Fashioning;* Richard Helgerson, *Self-Crowned Laureates: Spenser, Jonson, Milton, and the Literary System* (Berkeley: University of California Press, 1983); Leah Marcus, " 'Present Occasions' and the Shaping of Ben Jonson's Masques," *ELH* 45 (1978): 201–25. I have found the work of Leah Marcus especially useful.

5. Clifford Geertz, *The Interpretation of Cultures* (New York: Basic Books, 1973), 3–33, 361–67, 404–11.

6. Levy, 251.

7. See Guibbory, 322–39, and Newton, " 'Ben. / Jonson': The Poet in the Poems," 176–84.

8. Smith, 91–110. Another model for the dramatic organization of *Epigrammes* may be the Jonsonian masque, which contains in its order the indulged disorder of the antimasque. See John Lemly, "Masks and Self-Portraits in Jonson's Late Poetry," *ELH* 44 (1977): 251.

9. Thomas Greene, "Ben Jonson and the Centered Self," *Studies in English Literature* 10 (1970): 325–48.

10. William E. Cain argues that this poem reveals Jonson's ambivalence about his role in society. See "The Place of the Poet in 'To Penshurst' and 'To My Muse,' " *Criticism* 21 (1979): 34–48. For a discussion of the epigrams to Salisbury that immediately precede "To My Muse," see Fish, 41–45.

11. B. N. De Luna has argued that Jonson served Salisbury during the days following the Gunpowder Plot. See *Jonson's Romish Plot: A Study of 'Catiline' and Its Historical Context* (London: Oxford University Press, 1967). De Luna bases her case in part on data refuted by Alvaro Ribeiro, "Sir John Roe: Ben Jonson's Friend," *Review of English Studies* n.s. 24 (1973): 153–64.

12. See also *Conv. Dr.* 353–54: "Salisbury never cared for any man longer nor he could make use of him."

13. Herford and Simpson, 1:190–97.

14. For an analysis of Jonson's use of passages from Pliny in the epigram to Camden, see Peterson, 56–61. Jonson echoes Pliny's tribute to his counselor, Corellius Rufus (*Epistles* 4.17.4), and his tribute to Titius Aristo (1.22.2–3). See also W. H. Herendeen, " 'Like a Circle

Bounded in Itself': Johnson, Camden, and the Strategies of Praise," *Journal of Medieval and Renaissance Studies* 11 (1981): 137–67, and Jennifer Brady, " 'Beware the Poet': Authority and Judgment in Jonson's *Epigrammes*," *Studies in English Literature* 23 (1983): 95–112.

15. Herford and Simpson, 11:24.

16. J. H. Williamson, *The Myth of the Conqueror: Prince Henry Stuart, A Study in 17th Century Personation* (New York: AMS Press, 1978); Norman Council, "Ben Jonson, Inigo Jones, and the Transformation of Tudor Chivalry," *ELH* 47 (1980): 259–75.

17. Stephen Greenblatt, *Sir Walter Ralegh: The Renaissance Man and His Role* (New Haven: Yale University Press, 1973).

18. Margery Corbett and R. W. Lightbown, *The Comely Frontispiece* (London: Routledge and Kegan Paul, 1979), 129–36.

19. See especially John J. Major, "A Reading of Jonson's 'Epitaph on Elizabeth, L. H.,' " *Studies in Philology* 73 (1976): 62–86, and Howard Babb, "The 'Epitaph on Elizabeth, L. H.' and Ben Johson's Style," *Journal of English and Germanic Philology* 62 (1963): 738–44. Babb, after admitting the possible importance of historical questions, offers a rhetorical interpretation that does not require the lady be identified. To make the poem's meaning contingent on "some odd surname now lost to us," he insists, would make the epitaph "a private joke" (739n) grounded in "trivial wordplay" (740). Other readings of the poem include Robert B. White, Jr., "A Reading of Jonson's 'Epitaph on Elizabeth, L. H.,' " *Notre Dame English Journal* 9 (1973–74): 9–14; G. N. Murphy and William C. Slattery, "Meaning and Structure in Jonson's 'Epitaph on Elizabeth, L. H.,' " *Re: Arts and Letters* 2 (1969): 1–3; O. B. Hardison, *The Enduring Monument* (Chapel Hill: University of North Carolina Press, 1962), 124–26; Ossi Ihalainen, "The Problem of Unity in Ben Jonson's 'Epitaph on Elizabeth, L. H.,' " *Neuphilologische Mitteilungen* 80 (1979): 238–44; and Jack Winner, "The Public and Private Dimensions of Jonson's Epitaphs," *Classic and Cavalier: Essays on Jonson and the Sons of Ben*, ed. Claude J. Summers and Ted-Larry Pebworth (Pittsburgh: University of Pittsburgh Press, 1982), 107–19. On the significance of the name "Elizabeth," see Nathaniel Strout, "Jonson's Use of a Name in 'Epitaph on Elizabeth, L. H.' " *English Language Notes* 17 (1979): 30–33. George Williamson, *The Proper Wit of Poetry* (Chicago: University of Chicago Press, 1961), praises the poem as a "riddling elegiac epigram" (77–78).

20. David Wykes, "Ben Jonson's 'Chast Booke'—The *Epigrammes*," *Renaissance and Modern Studies* 13 (1969): 77. For the philosophical background of Jonson's ideas about naming, see Martin Elsky, "Words, Things, and Names: Jonson's Poetry and Philosophical Grammar," *Classic and Cavalier: Essays on Jonson and the Sons of Ben*, ed. Claude J. Summers and Ted-Larry Pebworth (Pittsburgh: University of Pittsburgh Press, 1982), 91–104.

21. White, 10–11; Major, 78–86.

22. Major, 74–77. Although Major assumes that *Epigrammes* was completed by 1612, he suggests that 1616, the date of publication, be used as the *terminus ad quem*. It is possible that at least a few epigrams were added after 1612 (e.g., *Ep.* 67 to Suffolk, which may have been written in 1608 when he was named Lord Chamberlain or to praise his appointment as Lord Treasurer in 1614; see Donaldson, 37n).

23. None of the other women proposed as "Elizabeth, L. H."—Lady Huntington, Lady Hunsdon, Lady Hatton, Cecilia Bulstrode, the Countess of Rutland, even Queen Elizabeth—is an appropriate or probable subject of Jonson's poem. Lady Huntington and Lady Hatton had not yet died; Lady Hunsdon, although her husband supported Jonson's company, had no known association with Ben Jonson; Cecilia Bulstrode and the Countess of Rutland had the wrong initials. It is unlikely that Jonson would write an epitaph consigning the name of Queen Elizabeth to oblivion. See Major, 63–78.

24. For a full biography, see Maude Rawson, *Bess of Hardwick and Her Circle* (New York: John Lane Co., 1910), and David Durant, *Bess of Hardwick: Portrait of an Elizabethan Dynast* (London: Weidenfeld and Nicolson, 1977). Both are sympathetic to Bess, unlike Edmund

Lodge, whose harsh opinion of her as "proud, furious, selfish, and unfeeling" is cited approvingly in the *Dictionary of National Biography*. See also the useful bibliography in E. Carleton Williams, *Bess of Hardwick* (London: Longmans Green, 1969).

25. Guibbory uses this phrase to describe all of Jonson's occasional poetry (323).

26. Lucius Cary, Lord Falkland, "An Eglogue on the Death of BEN. IOHNSON, between Melaybaeus and Hylas," *Jonsonus Virbius*, Herford and Simpson, 11:434.

27. It is certain that she would not have been formally addressed as "Elizabeth, Lady Hardwick." She habitually signed herself "Elizabeth Shrewsbury," placed the stone initials "E. S." atop Hardwick Hall, and is mentioned in other documents and correspondence as "Lady Shrewsbury." See the Cavendish-Talbot Manucripts, Folger Shakespeare Library MS. Several are printed in Joseph Hunter, *History of Hallamshire* (Sheffield, 1869). See also the Rutland and Salisbury papers published by the Great Britain Historical Manuscripts Commission, and Basil Stallybrass, "Bess of Hardwick's Buildings and Building Accounts," *Archaeologia* 64 (1913): 347–98.

28. That Bess was referred to as "Elizabeth Hardwick" may be indicated by a portrait in the Duke of Portland's collection at Welbeck, a copy of a portrait at Hardwick Hall, inscribed, "ELIZ. HARDWICK. Daughter and Coheir of John Hardwick of Hardwick. . . . She settled her 3d. Son Charles Cavendishe at Welbeck in the County of Nottingham." The inscription, however, may be intended only to specify her place in the history of Welbeck and to record her parentage. More certain is the currency of her nickname, "Bess of Hardwick." I have been able to trace it back to 1621, when Augustine Vincent of the College of Heralds described "Bess of Hardwycke" in his MS. *Visitation of Darbyshire*. It is not likely that he would coin a nickname. See Rev. Francis Brodhurst, "Elizabeth Hardwycke, Countess of Shrewsbury," *Derbyshire Archaeological Society Journal* 30 (n.d.), 231–60.

29. It is fulfilled in a variant text of the poem: "Underneath this stone doth lye / As much beautie, as could dye: / Which in life did harbour giue / Unto beautie that doth liue" (Herford and Simpson 8:79n).

30. Herford and Simpson state that Jonson was recusant from 1598 until 1610 (9:578).

31. Durant, 66.

32. Geoffrey Hartman, "Wordsworth, Inscriptions, and Romantic Nature Poetry," *From Sensibility to Romanticism: Essays Presented to Frederick A. Pottle*, ed. Frederick W. Hilles (New Haven: Yale University Press, 1965), 394.

33. Trimpi discusses Jonson's epitaphs, but not this particular poem (180–83).

34. Geoffrey Hartman, " 'The Nymph Complaining for the Death of Her Faun': A Brief Allegory," *Beyond Formalism* (New Haven: Yale University Press, 1970), 178–79.

35. Hugh Maclean, " 'A More Secret Cause': The Wit of Jonson's Poetry," *A Celebration of Ben Jonson*, ed. William Blissett, Julian Patrick, and R. W. Van Fossen (Toronto: University of Toronto Press, 1973), 143.

36. Hardison, 126.

37. Winner, 108. Winner's essay moves backward through the collection, from the impersonal "Epitaph on Elizabeth, L. H." to Jonson's personal epitaphs for his associates and his children. However, as editor of *Epigrammes*, Jonson guides our understanding of his art in precisely the opposite direction.

Chapter 4. "The Whole Piece": Epigram and *Epigrammes*

1. Ira Clark, "Ben Jonson's Imitation," *Criticism* 20 (1978): 107–27; Jackson Cope, *The Theatre and the Dream: From Metaphor to Form in Renaissance Drama* (Baltimore: The Johns Hopkins University Press, 1973), 231; R. V. Young, Jr., "Jonson, Crashaw, and the Development of the English Epigram," *Genre* 12 (1979): 137–52.

2. John Weever, *Epigrammes in the Newest Cut and Oldest Fashion,* ed. Ronald B. McKerrow (Stratford-upon-Avon: at the Shakespeare Head, 1922), 13.

3. For a brief survey of the epigrammatic tradition, see Hoyt Hudson, *The Epigram in the English Renaissance* (Princeton: Princeton University Press, 1947). On Jonsonian epigram, see T. K. Whipple, *Martial and the English Epigram from Sir Thomas Wyatt to Ben Jonson* (1925; reprinted New York: Phaeton Press, 1970); Rufus Putney, " 'This So Subtile Sport': Some Aspects of Jonson's Epigrams," *University of Colorado Studies.* Series in Language and Literature 10 (Boulder: University of Colorado Press, 1966), 40–58; R. V. Young, Jr., "Style and Structure in Ben Jonson's Epigrams," *Criticism* 17 (1975): 201–22; Wykes, 76–87. Although markedly different from my own argument about the role of 'occasion' in Jonsonian epigram, the most stimulating reading of this collection is Jonathan Kamholtz, "Ben Jonson's *Epigrammes* and Poetic Occasions," *Studies in English Literature* 23 (1983): 77–94.

4. Smith, 91–110, and Partridge, 153–98. The theme of naming is traced to Plato's *Cratylus* by Ernst Curtius, *European Literature and the Latin Middle Ages,* trans. Willard Trask (New York: Harper and Row, 1953), 495–98. Jonson likely shared the idea of naming expressed by William Camden in *Remaines of a Greater Worke Concerning Britain* (London: G. E. for Simon Waterson, 1605): "The greatest Philosopher *Plato* might seeme, not without cause, to advise men to be carefull in giving faire and happie names: as the *Pythagoreans* affirmed the mindes, actions, and successes of men to be according to their *Fate, Genius,* and *Name.* One also well observeth that these seven things: Virtue, good Parentage, Wealth, Dignity or Office, good Presence, a good Christian name, with a gratious Surname, and seemely attire, doe especially grace and adorne a man" (31). Martin Elsky also relates Jonson's poetic naming to Camden's theory of names in "Words, Things, and Names: Jonson's Poetry and Philosophical Grammar," *Classic and Cavalier: Essays on Jonson and the Sons of Ben,* ed. Claude J. Summers and Ted-Larry Pebworth (Pittsburgh: University of Pittsburgh Press, 1982), 96–97.

5. Geoffrey Hartman, "Monsieur Texte," *Saving the Text: Literature/Derrida/Philosophy* (Baltimore: The Johns Hopkins University Press, 1981), 1–32.

6. Richard Newton, "Ben Jonson and the (Re)invention of the Book," *Classic and Cavalier: Essays on Jonson and the Sons of Ben,* ed. Claude J. Summers and Ted-Larry Pebworth (Pittsburgh: University of Pittsburgh Press, 1982), 31–55.

7. Hartman, "Monsieur Texte," 16.

8. This argument finds a curious validation in the action of anthologizers, who assume that a Jonsonian poem can be read and understood without regard to its original occasion. They further assume that a poem is meaningful in the context of other poems chosen according to their own categories (e.g., other Renaissance poems, or poems similar in genre, technique, or theme).

9. For examples of other clusters of related poems in *Epigrammes,* see Dutton, 75–93, and Fish, 40–46.

10. Lester A. Beaurline, "Ben Jonson and the Illusion of Completeness," *PMLA* 84 (1969): 51–59.

11. Weever, 13.

12. Jonson's heavily annotated copy of Martial's poetry, now at the Folger Shakespeare Library, could not have been the book Jonson used in writing his epigrams. The book was not published until 1619, three years after the publication of *Epigrammes.* The extensive annotations testify to Jonson's ongoing interest in Martial. For a description of Jonson's copy of Martial, see David McPherson, 68–70, item 121. The Folger Library also owns a copy of Thomas Farnaby's edition of Martial (1615) that Jonson presented to Richard Briggs. See McPherson, 67–68, item 119.

13. M. P. Tilley, *A Dictionary of Proverbs in England in the Sixteenth and Seventeenth Centuries* (Ann Arbor: University of Michigan Press, 1950), C608.

14. Herford and Simpson gloss "humanitie" as "culture" (Latin: *humanitas,* 11:1). The Latin

term carries this meaning in Aulus Gellius, *The Attic Nights,* trans. John C. Rolfe, 3 vols. (London: William Heinemann, 1927) 12.17 (2:457). I am indebted to Lawrence Ryan for this reference. See also Trimpi, 113–14; Charles Trinkaus, *In Our Image and Likeness: Humanity and Divinity in Renaissance Thought,* 2 vols. (Chicago: University of Chicago Press, 1970); and Jerrold Siegel, *Rhetoric and Philosophy in Renaissance Humanism* (Princeton: Princeton University Press, 1968), 63–98.

15. Wykes, 76.

16. "Icon" refers to a certain kind of sign, in which the signifier closely resembles the signified. Victor Turner notes that iconicity resides in the name and qualities of a thing, and in its being fashioned by human activity. See his discussion of Dante's mode of depicting character in "African Ritual and Western Literature: Is a Comparative Symbology Possible?", in *The Literature of Fact,* ed. Angus Fletcher (New York: Columbia University Press, 1976), 45–82, esp. 57–58. On Jonsonian signification, see Barbara Kiefer Lewalski, *Donne's "Anniversaries" and the Poetry of Praise* (Princeton: Princeton University Press, 1973), 24.

17. Mack, 88–91. See also Richard Newton, " 'Goe, quit 'hem all': Ben Jonson and Formal Verse Satire," *Studies in English Literature* 18 (1977): 105–16.

18. Herford and Simpson, 11:377. Beaumont's poems in praise of *Volpone* and *Catiline* are reprinted in Herford and Simpson, 11:319–20, 325.

19. Herford and Simpson, 11:378.

20. Jonas Barish, *Ben Jonson and the Language of Prose Comedy* (Cambridge, Mass.: Harvard University Press, 1969).

21. I am indebted for this point to my student, Hilary Horder.

22. See also Spanos, 12, and Young, "Jonson, Crashaw, and the Development of the English Epigram," 137–52.

23. Dutton, 75–92.

24. For other readings of this poem, see Lester A. Beaurline, "The Selective Principle in Jonson's Shorter Poems," *Criticism* 8 (1966): 64–73; Francis Fike, "Ben Jonson's 'On My First Sonne,' " *The Gordon Review* 11 (1969): 205–20; W. David Kay, "The Christian Wisdom of Ben Jonson's 'On My First Sonne,' " *Studies in English Literature* 11 (1971): 125–36; R. W. French, "Reading Jonson: *Epigrammes* 22 and 45," *Concerning Poetry* 10 (1977): 5–11; Judith Kronenfeld, "The Father Found: Consolation Achieved Through Love in Ben Jonson's 'On My First Sonne,' " *Studies in Philology* 75 (1978): 64–83; and William Cain, "Self and Others in Two Poems by Ben Jonson," *Studies in Philology* 80 (1983): 163–82. Barbara Herrnstein Smith, in *Poetic Closure* (Chicago: University of Chicago Press, 1968), notes that the understated conclusion of the epitaph "yields emotion, which is not stable, over to wisdom, which is" (204). On the epitaphs as a group, see Jack D. Winner, "The Public and Private Dimensions of Jonson's Epitaphs," *Classic and Cavalier: Essays on Jonson and the Sons of Ben,* ed. Claude J. Summers and Ted-Larry Pebworth (Pittsburgh: University of Pittsburgh Press, 1982), 107–19.

25. O. B. Hardison, Jr., *The Enduring Monument* (Chapel Hill: University of North Carolina Press, 1962), 125–26.

26. Jonson's poems to false and true readers echo many of the ideas and phrases of the epistles he prefixed to the published texts of his plays. Jonson's attitudes toward his audience as playgoers and readers are discussed by John Gordon Sweeney III, *Jonson and the Psychology of Public Theater* (Princeton: Princeton University Press, 1985). See also Carlson, 443–57, and E. Pearlman, "Ben Jonson: An Anatomy," *English Literary Renaissance* 9 (1979): 364–93.

27. Peter Medine, "Object and Intent in Jonson's 'Famous Voyage,' " *Studies in English Literature* 15 (1975): 97–110. Medine identifies the two noble voyagers as Thomas Shelton, the translator of Cervantes's *Don Quixote,* and Christopher Heydon, author of *A defence of Judiciall Astrologie* (1603). Medine convincingly shows the extent to which "the age itself" is the object of Jonson's satire. C. H. Herford dismisses the poem as "hideous and unsavoury burlesque" (Herford and Simpson, 2:339). George B. Johnston, *Ben Jonson, Poet* (New York:

Columbia University Press, 1945), argues that the poem was written "purely for amusement" (29). Following Edmund Wilson's suggestion that Jonson was an "anal erotic" personality, two critics attribute the decision to end *Epigrammes* with mock-epic to "eruptive or disruptive energy" that compels Jonson to destroy his own hard-won fictions of order. See Spanos, 9 ff., and Marotti, 208–37. J. G. Nichols, *The Poetry of Ben Jonson* (London: Routledge and Kegan Paul, 1969), like Peter Medine, centers on the topical satire of the poem (105–13). Trimpi notes Jonson's parody of the high style, 97–99. See also Edward Partridge, "Jonson's Large and Unique View of Life," *The Elizabethan Theatre IV* (1975), 156. Reuben Brower, *Mirror on Mirror: Translation, Imitation, Parody* (Cambridge, Mass.: Harvard University Press, 1974), describes the relationship between translation and parody, noting their common origin and common limitations. See also G. D. Kiremidjian, "The Aesthetics of Parody," *Journal of Aesthetics and Art Criticism* 28 (1969): 231–42.

28. Jonas Barish, "Feasting and Judgment in Jonsonian Drama," 3–35, argues that the "poetic justice" that ends so many Jonsonian works "fosters our festive responses as well as our judicial approval; it enables us to relish the follies of the fools and the peculations of the knaves without making us feel that we are endorsing the inadmissible" (35). "On the Famous Voyage" parodies the typical Jonsonian "courtroom scene." A soap boiler, an alehouse keeper, and a purblind fletcher—the Rhadamanthus, Aeacus, and Minos of Fleet Ditch—are drafted to "witness" the noble deed of the voyagers. It should be noted that Jonson did not consider laughter at the merely grotesque or obscene a sufficient goal of comic literature. He regarded laughter as "a fault in Comedie," and an appeal to laughter without thought as "dishonesty, and foolish" (*Dis.* 2634–54).

29. *Conv. Dr.* 29–32: "[He said] that Silvesters translation of Du Bartas was not well done, and that he wrote his Verses befor it err he understood to conferr."

30. It could be argued that Jonson wrote the poem to mock Sir John Harrington, a rival epigrammatist whose *Metamorphosis of Ajax* (1596), a mock treatise on the flushable toilet, is alluded to in the last line of the poem. See Medine, 110. Although Jonson certainly jokes at Harrington's expense, the poem as a whole attempts a much more complex humor.

31. Jonathan Culler, *Structuralist Poetics* (Ithaca: Cornell University Press, 1975), 152.

32. See J. Gerald Kennedy, "Parody as Exorcism," *Genre* 13 (1980): 161–70.

33. *The Complete Poetry of Robert Herrick*, ed. J. Max Patrick (New York: Doubleday, 1963), 443.

Chapter 5. "Authors of the Feast": Horace, the Sidneys, and the Poet of Jonson's *Forrest*

1. Jonson's Preface to *Underwoods*, Donaldson, 23.

2. See Alistair Fowler, "The Silva Tradition in Jonson's *The Forest*," in *Poetic Traditions of the English Renaissance*, ed. Maynard Mack and George deForest Lord (New Haven: Yale University Press, 1982), 163–80.

3. I find especially valuable the essay by Jonathan Kamholtz, "Ben Jonson's Green World: Structure and Imaginative Unity in *The Forrest*," *Studies in Philology* 39 (1981): 170–93.

4. M. L. Rosenthal and Sally M. Gall's study of poetic organization, *The Modern Poetic Sequence* (Oxford: Oxford University Press, 1983), aside from a passing reference to Shakespeare's sonnets, does not consider any poetry written before the nineteenth century. Richard Newton's important essay, "Ben Jonson and the (Re)invention of the Book," suggests Jonson's role in establishing the new genre of the coherent book of short poems. See *Classic and Cavalier: Essays on Jonson and the Sons of Ben*, ed. Claude J. Summers and Ted-Larry Pebworth (Pittsburgh: University of Pittsburgh Press, 1982), 31–55.

5. In *The Anxiety of Influence* (New York: Oxford University Press, 1973), Harold Bloom

expressly excludes pre-Miltonic poets from the pattern of a struggle against predecessors he finds common in post-Miltonic literature: "Shakespeare [and, presumably, Jonson] belongs to the giant age before the flood, before the anxiety of influence became central to poetic consciousness" (11).

6. Roger Sale, *Literary Inheritance* (Amherst: University of Massachusetts Press, 1984), 2–54, argues *contra* Bloom that poets can find the work of strong predecessors an enabling influence and takes Thomas Carew's response to Ben Jonson as an example.

7. For a general survey of Jonson's literary debt to Horace, see Robert B. Pierce, "Ben Jonson's Horace and Horace's Ben Jonson," *Studies in Philology* 39 (1981), 20–31.

8. Helgerson suggests that "Why I Write not of Love" imitates the first poem of Ovid's *Amores* but admits that the two poems present opposite situations (110–11). A stronger case can be made for a Horatian model: Jonson's poem closely parallels the first epistle of Horace in situation and tone.

9. The large number of poems addressed to the Sidneys is mentioned by Bradshaw, 496.

10. *Conv. Dr.* 204–32, 350–72. Since Jonson's comments are organized under headings invented by Drummond, there is no indication that Jonson made these comments at one time, but only that he had a good deal to say about the Sidneys. It also is clear that Drummond questioned Jonson about issues important to the Sidney literary circle.

11. For a full description of Rawlinson MS. 31 see Herford and Simpson, 9:8.

12. Baldesar Castiglione, *The Book of the Courtier*, trans. Charles S. Singleton (Garden City, N.Y.: Anchor Books, 1959), 1.

13. See also Helgerson, 166.

14. Sir Philip Sidney, "An Apologie for Poetrie," *Elizabethan Critical Essays*, ed. G. Gregory Smith (Oxford: Oxford University Press, 1904), I, 195. See also Helgerson, 15–16.

15. For a discussion of the invitation poems of Martial and Horace as predecessors of this poem, see Mason, 273–86. See also G. R. Hibbard, "The Country House Poem in the Seventeenth Century," *Journal of the Warburg and Courtauld Institutes* 19 (1956): 159–74. I am indebted to Gordon Williams's comments on the invitational poetry of Horace in *Tradition and Originality in Roman Poetry* (Oxford: Clarendon Press, 1968), 104–5.

16. Raymond Williams, *The Country and the City* (New York: Oxford University Press, 1973), argues that the poet as guest identifies with the social position of the Sidneys, and only that stance enables him to posit a moral economy at Penshurst opposed to the mercantilism and greed of Jacobean capitalism (27–34). For another attempt to place the poem in the context of social circumstance, see Charles Molesworth, " 'To Penshurst' and Jonson's Historical Imagination," *Clio* 1, no. 2 (1972): 5–13.

17. Wayne, 15–80, reads the poem as a reflection of contradictory Jacobean ideologies. Critics who interpret the poem as an uncompromising idealist statement include Paul Cubeta, "A Jonsonian Ideal: 'To Penshurst,' " *Philogical Quarterly* 42 (1964): 14–24; Gayle E. Wilson, "Jonson's Use of the Bible and the Great Chain of Being in 'To Penshurst,' " *Studies in English Literature* 8 (1968): 77–89; and Heather Dubrow, "The Country-House Poem: A Study in Generic Development," *Genre* 12 (1979): 53–80.

18. *Cf.* Martial 3.60. See also Jonson's account of Salisbury's poor hospitality in *Conv. Dr.* 317–21.

19. Harris Friedberg, "Ben Jonson's Poetry: Pastoral, Epigram, Georgic," *English Literary Renaissance* 4 (1974): 111–36. Friedberg argues that the poem moves from satire to pastoral, georgic, and personal epigram, as Jonson seeks a poetic style to "express the values he finds in Penshurst without compromising its *locus* in the world of fact" (127).

20. Wayne, 129–73, and Fish, 26–58.

21. J. C. A. Rathmell, "Jonson, Lord Lisle, and Penshurst," *English Literary Renaissance* 1 (1971): 250–60, surveys the Lisle correspondence and finds that many details in Jonson's poem reflect specific crises in the family. See also Anthony Esler, *The Aspiring Mind of the Eliz-*

abethan Younger Generation (Durham, N.C.: Duke University Press, 1966), 51–86; Millicent V. Hay, *The Life of Robert Sidney, Earl of Leicester (1563–1626)* (Washington: The Folger Shakespeare Library, 1984); and *The Poems of Robert Sidney*, ed. P. J. Croft (Oxford: Oxford University Press, 1984).

22. See Leah Marcus, " 'Present Occasions' and the Shaping of Ben Jonson's Masques," *ELH* 45 (1978): 204–5. See also Lawrence Stone, *The Crisis of the Aristocracy, 1558–1641* (Oxford: Clarendon Press, 1965): 387–93, and William McClung, *The Country House in English Renaissance Poetry* (Berkeley: University of California Press, 1977): 28–35.

23. Josephine A. Roberts, ed., *The Poems of Lady Mary Wroth* (Baton Rouge: Louisiana State University Press, 1983), 10. This introduction contains useful information about the Sidney and Wroth families.

24. *Conv. Dr.* 355–56. See also Roberts, 3–40.

25. Wayne, 166–69.

26. Kamholtz, "Ben Jonson's Green World," 172.

27. Donaldson, 99 n.

28. Trimpi, 118–19.

29. Although the questions are the same, the tone and situation of these poems are entirely opposed. Davus berates Horace; the lady admonishes the world and declares her own resolve.

30. The pragmatic calculation of the lecher at the end of the Horatian satire seems quite alien to the spirit of Catullus's *Vivamus mea Lesbia*.

31. During the 1590s, the Sidney circle supported Essex and urged Queen Elizabeth to restore him to favor. Jonson contributed three poems to *Love's Martyr* (1601), a book designed to advance the cause of Essex. One of these poems, "O splendor more than mortal," may have been composed for the Countess of Bedford and adapted to a political use in *Love's Martyr*. The text of the poem in Rawlinson MS 31 is inscribed to her. By including the other two poems, "Proludium" and "Epode," in *The Forrest*, Jonson removes them from their original political context. His knowledgeable readers, however, could be expected to remember the original occasion. William Matchett makes a convincing case for the political argument of these poems in *The Phoenix and the Turtle: Shakespeare's Poem and Chester's "Love's Martyr"* (The Hague: Mouton, 1965).

32. *Conv. Dr.* 46–48.

33. See James Garrison, "Time and Value in Jonson's 'Epistle to Elizabeth, Countesse of Rutland,' " *Concerning Poetry* 8 (1975): 53–58. See also William Cain, "Mirrors, Intentions, and Texts in Ben Jonson," *Essays in Literature* (Macomb, Ill.) 8 (1981): 11–23. Cain's discussion concerns the mirror as a moral theme rather than a basic structural device.

34. *The Poems of Edmund Spenser*, ed. J. C. Smith and E. De Selincourt (London: Oxford University Press, 1912), 570.

35. *Calendar of State Papers, Domestic, 1611–1618*, 12 June 1611, records a letter to King James from Clifton, affirming that he "bestowed his daughter in marriage according to His Majesty's command. Prays that it may not be to his destruction, in consequence of the fraudulent proceedings of the Duke [of Lenox] and Lord Aubigny, which are detailed" (42). See also *C. S. P. D., 1611–1618*, 127, 505, 511, 517, 584, 585, 596, and *The Letters of John Chamberlain*, ed. Norman E. McClure, 2 vols. (Philadelphia: The American Philosophical Society, 1939).

36. McClure, 1:345–46.

37. McClure, 2:170.

38. John Danby, *Elizabethan and Jacobean Poets* (London: Faber and Faber, 1965), 44.

39. For information about Sir William Sidney, see Lisle C. John, "Ben Jonson's 'To Sir William Sidney, on his Birthday,' " *Modern Language Review* 52 (1957): 168–76.

40. See Louis Martz, *The Poetry of Meditation* (New Haven: Yale University Press, 1962). Trimpi refers to the poem as a meditation (130–31). Paul M. Cubeta describes it as a colloquy

with God in "Ben Jonson's Religious Lyrics," *Journal of English and Germanic Philology* 62 (1963): 101–2. See also Gardiner, 72–83.

41. William Kerrigan, "Ben Jonson Full of Shame and Scorn," *Studies in the Literary Imagination* 6 (1973): 199–217, argues that this poem is written in "querulous despair": "For either Jonson knows himself and God is unjustly absent, or Jonson does not know himself and God is justly absent" (208).

42. Martz, 322.

Chapter 6. "So Short You Read My Character": Jonson's Autobiographical Poems of 1623–1624

1. See A. C. Partridge, *Orthography in Shakespeare and Elizabethan Drama* (Lincoln: University of Nebraska Press, 1955), 130–40. Partridge notes that the careful, heavy, logical pointing of the First Folio, so different from the light pointing of the Quartos, is anticipated only by the Jonson Folio of 1616. T. J. B. Spencer notes other signs of Jonsonian editorial policy. See "Ben Jonson on his beloved, The Author Mr. William Shakespeare," *The Elizabethan Theatre IV* (Hamden, Conn.: Shoe String Press, 1974), 22–40. Ralph Crane, who transcribed the texts of five comedies for the First Folio, followed several Jonsonian practices. According to T. H. Howard-Hill, "Jonson's 1616 Folio must have been influential when Crane considered the best means to make his transcripts attractive to patrons and clients." See *Ralph Crane and Some Shakespeare First Folio Comedies* (Charlottesville: Bibliographical Society of the University of Virginia, University Press of Virginia, 1972), 144. Jonson's influence on Crane's transcription of *The Tempest* is asserted by John Jowett, "New Created Creatures: Ralph Crane and the Stage Directions in *The Tempest*," *Shakespeare Survey* 36 (1983): 107–20. The issue is further complicated by the vexed issue of the working methods of the several compositors. See Paul Werstine, "Folio Editors, Folio Compositors, and the Folio Text of *King Lear*," *The Division of the Kingdoms: Shakespeare's Two Versions of 'King Lear'*, ed. Gary Taylor and Michael Warren (Oxford: Clarendon Press, 1983), 247–312. Jonson's only indisputable role remains his contribution of the major commendatory poem introducing the Folio. Franklin B. Williams, Jr., "Commendatory Verses: The Rise of the Art of Puffing," *Studies in Bibliography* 19 (1966): 1–14, shows that the practice of writing commendatory verses was begun by Italian Humanists and was common among English Humanists. Jonson wrote verses commending thirty books, and in turn received thirty for his seven books; the first English play printed with such prefatory material was his own *Sejanus* (4–5).

2. This proposal, originally made by George Steevens, was dismissed by Pollard and Lee only to be revived by W. W. Greg in "The First Folio and Its Publishers," *Studies in the First Folio*, Shakespeare Association Studies (London: Oxford University Press, 1924), 151–52. He cites echoes of the Induction to *Bartholomew Fair*, the Dedication of *The Alchemist*, *Discoveries*, and Jonson's epigram to his bookseller. See also W. W. Greg, *The Shakespeare First Folio* (Oxford: Clarendon Press, 1955). Greg's proposal is endorsed, at least in part, by E. A. J. Honigmann, *The Stability of Shakespeare's Text* (Lincoln: University of Nebraska Press, 1965), 34.

3. Richard S. Peterson, *Imitation and Praise in the Poems of Ben Jonson* (New Haven: Yale University Press, 1981), 158–94 passim.

4. Samuel Schoenbaum, surveying the history of interpretation of this poem, argues that shifts in criticism reflect shifts in opinion about the relationship between Jonson and Shakespeare. See "Shakespeare and Jonson: Fact and Myth," *Elizabethan Theatre II*, ed. David Galloway (London: Macmillan, 1970), 1–19. See also Miner, 137–43, and Peterson, 158–94. Lawrence Lipking offers an interpretation of the poem congruent with my own, although

different in detail, in *The Life of the Poet: Beginning and Ending Poetic Careers* (Chicago: University of Chicago Press, 1981), 138–46.

5. John Dover Wilson, "Ben Johnson and *Julius Caesar*," *Shakespeare Survey* 2 (1949): 36–43, discusses the line Jonson quotes in *Discoveries:* "Caesar did never wrong, but with just cause." Wilson surmises that the line was amended in the Folio in deference to Jonson's strictures against it. The Folio reading, which makes more sense but leaves a broken line, is: "Know, *Caesar* doth not wrong, nor without cause / Will he be satisfied." Shakespeare's defenders have traced the original version of the line to Cicero.

6. The exclusion of *Pericles* from the First Folio may reflect Jonson's aesthetic judgment, if in fact he played a strong editorial role in the project; more probably, the editors may have been unable to secure a satisfactory text of the play. F. D. Hoeniger surveys the possible reasons for its exclusion in his introduction to the Arden edition of *Pericles* (London: Methuen, 1963), xxv.

7. Glynne Wickham contrasts Jonson's program for drama and Shakespeare's dramatic practice in "Shakespeare's 'Small Latine and less Greeke,'" *Shakespeare's Dramatic Heritage* (New York: Barnes and Noble, 1969), 84–112. Wickham regards Jonson's poem as a sincere tribute, and argues that the "strictures on Shakespeare . . . spring not so much from malice, as from frustration, the words of a man whose vision of the future makes him impatient of the present" (87).

8. Friedberg discusses the prevalence of triple nouns and adjectives in Jonson's complimentary poetry (115–16).

9. Guibbory argues that this poem reflects an ambivalent attitude toward history (324–27).

10. *A Groats-worth of Wit*, cited in *The Shakespere Allusion-Book*, ed. John Munro (London: Oxford University Press, 1932), 2.

11. William Basse's eulogy (1622) begins:

> Renowned Spenser lye a thought more nye
> To learned Chaucer, and rare Beaumont lye
> A little nearer Spenser, to make roome
> For Shakespeare in your threefold, fowerfold Tombe.

Cited in *The Shakespere Allusion-Book*, 286.

12. *Palladis Tamia* (1598), cited in *The Shakespere Allusion-Book*, 46–48.

13. Jonson praises Sir Francis Bacon in similar language: he "hath fill'd up all numbers; and perform'd that in our tongue, which may be compar'd or preferr'd, either to insolent *Greece*, or haughty *Rome*. In short, within his view, and about his times, were all the wits borne, that could honour a language, or helpe study. Now things daily fall: wits grow downe-ward, and *Eloquence* growes back-ward: so that hee may be nam'd, and stand as the marke, and acme of our language" (*Dis.* 916–23). The reference to Shakespeare's natural wit, his "small Latin and less Greek," can be properly understood if we refer to Beaumont's epistle to Jonson:

> Heere would I let slippe
> (If I had any in mee) schollershippe,
> And from all Learninge keepe these lines as cleere
> as Shakespeares best are, which our heires shall heare
> Preachers apte to their auditors to show
> how farr sometimes a mortall man may goe
> by the dimme light of Nature . . .
>
>   (Herford and Simpson, 11:319–20)

Beaumont does not praise Shakespeare for ignorance, but for perfecting his natural gifts and avoiding ostentatious pedantry.

14. Edward W. Tayler, *Nature and Art in Renaissance Literature* (New York: Columbia University Press, 1964), 211.

15. Tayler, 21; Hiram Haydn, *The Counter-Renaissance* (New York: Scribners, 1950), 1–74; Frank Kermode's introduction to *The Tempest* (London: Methuen, 1964), xliii–lix.

16. On the history of this commonplace, see John Freehafer, "Leonard Digges, Ben Jonson, and the Beginning of Shakespeare Idolatry," *Shakespeare Quarterly* 21 (1970): 63–75.

17. Jonson reverses this *topos* in the epitaph "On My First Sonne" (*Ep.* 45).

18. "Rage" and "influence" suggest oppositions astrological, poetic, and emotional. Much as Jonson uses metaphor to reconcile opposed modes, he here exploits grammar and syntax. Both rage and influence can "chide, or cheer" the stage. Shakespeare's rage can chide—and he becomes a Jonsonian critic. His influence can cheer—and as playwright he becomes a Jonsonian exemplar. That he was possessed by poetic frenzy or "rage" may cheer those who follow him, while his influence may chide their inept work.

19. For a less sympathetic reading of this poem, see Trimpi, 148–52. Trimpi argues that Jonson uncomfortably and unsuccessfully tries to praise Shakespeare in inappropriate Jonsonian terms. T. J. B. Spencer argues that Jonson "turned Shakespeare into a kind of sparring partner, whom he could make use of in order to justify his own rather solemn and laborious critical position" (39–40). Spencer concludes that the poem "is not intended to impress us as being well-considered" (39). Although I find Spencer's comments on individual lines apt and useful, I cannot agree with his conclusion. Jonson was personally and professionally engaged by this unique opportunity to consider the central issues of his aesthetic theory in the context of the achievements of his only worthy rival.

20. Few critics have paid any attention to this poem. See, however, Johnston, 16–29, and Nichols, 111–16. Charlotte Winzeler, "Curse upon a God," *Brigham Young University Studies* 5 (1964): 87–94, argues that Jonson uses the formal structure of Christian prayer and the techniques of classical satire to curse Vulcan. Chapman's response to the poem is the subject of an essay by Robert Sharpe, "Jonson's 'Execration' and Chapman's 'Invective': Their Place in Their Authors' Rivalry," *Studies in Philology* 42 (1945): 555–63. Herford acknowledges Jonson's "serio-comic bravery" (Herford and Simpson, 2:357).

21. Miguel de Cervantes, *Don Quixote*, trans. J. M. Cohen (Baltimore: Penguin, 1950), 59. See also Donaldson, 194n. Annabel Patterson argues that Jonson "goes well beyond Cervantes as an antiromancer," but that he had translated and published as political allegory a popular romance, Barclay's *Argenis*, in 1623, "the very same year as his *Execration*." See *Censorship and Interpretation: The Conditions of Writing and Reading in Early Modern England* (Madison: University of Wisconsin Press, 1984), 166, 180–85.

22. Miner, 46–47, 57–58; Peterson, 112–57. Peterson also argues that this poem constructs an argument from metaphor, and he thoroughly examines the classical origins of the major images in the poem. He does not, however, discuss the metaphor of writing and reading, which I regard as the last link in a chain of meanings of "sealing."

23. Hugh Maclean emphasizes the relationship of this poem and Aristotle's definition of friendship in the *Ethics* (8–9). See "Ben Jonson's Poems: Notes on the Ordered Society," 47–51.

24. Arthur Marotti, " 'Love Is Not Love': Elizabethan Sonnet Sequences and the Social Order," *ELH* 49 (1982): 396–428. See also William Kerrigan, "The Articulation of the Ego in the Renaissance," *The Literary Freud: Mechanisms of Defense and the Poetic Will*, ed. Joseph H. Smith, *Psychiatry and the Humanities* 4 (New Haven: Yale University Press, 1980), 261–308.

25. Bacon, "Of Followers and Friends," *Francis Bacon: A Selection of his Works*, ed. Sidney Warhaft (New York: Odyssey Press, 1965), 172.

26. D. J. Gordon describes the differences between Jonson and Jones in "Poet and Architect: The Intellectual Setting of the Quarrel between Ben Jonson and Inigo Jones," *Journal of the Warburg and Courtauld Institutes* 12 (1949): 152–78. The essay has been reprinted in *The Renaissance Imagination*, ed. Stephen Orgel (Berkeley: University of California Press, 1975), 77–101.

Chapter 7. "Acts of Grace": Notes toward a Reading of *Under-wood*

1. Preface to *Under-wood, Poems*, ed. Ian Donaldson (Oxford: Oxford University Press, 1975), 123.

2. Annabel Patterson, *Censorship and Interpretation: The Conditions of Writing and Reading in Early Modern England* (Madison: University of Wisconsin Press, 1984), 126–43.

3. Patterson, 132.

4. John Lemly, "Masks and Self-Portraits in Jonson's Late Poetry," *ELH* 44 (1977): 248–66; Anne Barton, *Ben Jonson, Dramatist* (Cambridge: Cambridge University Press, 1984), 300–20.

5. Patterson, 134–35.

6. On the dates of the religious poems, see Donaldson, 125–27 n. At least two of the classical translations can be assigned to the Jacobean period: Jonson modeled *For.* 3 on the Horatian ode translated as *Und.* 85 and mentioned *Und.* 90, his translation of Martial, to William Drummond (*Conv. Dr.* 15–16).

7. There are eight occurrences of the word "grace" in *Epigrammes*, six in *The Forrest*, and thirty-one in *Under-wood*. In addition, Jonson refers to "graces" as a set of human traits or to the classical figures of the Graces eleven times in *Under-wood* and uses related words ("ungraced," "gracefull") uncommon or absent in his other books of poetry. See Steven L. Bates and Sidney D. Orr, *A Concordance to the Poetry of Ben Jonson* (Athens: Ohio University Press, 1978), 303–4.

8. Lawrence Venuti provides another account of Jonson's decision to abandon Petrarchan poetry in "Why Jonson Wrote not of Love," *Journal of Medieval and Renaissance Studies* 12 (1982): 195–220.

9. Jonson first used the phrase "black jawes" in the prologue to *Poetaster* (1601), when Envy makes a perverse appeal to the audience: "Here, take my snakes among you, come, and eate / And while the squeez'd juice flowes in your blacke jawes, / Help me to damne the Authour" (Herford and Simpson, 4:204: 44–46). The Author ends the "apologeticall dialogue" appended to the play by dismissing Nasutus and resolving to write for a fit audience though few: "Leave me. There's something come into my thought, / That must, and shall be sung, high, and aloofe, / Safe from the wolves black jaw, and the dull asses hoofe" (Herford and Simpson, 4:324).

10. Patterson regards this poem as part of a subtext of defiance and subversion central to the entire collection (131).

11. For a thorough discussion of Jonson's attitudes toward painting, see Mary L. Livingston, "Ben Jonson: The Poet to the Painter," *Texas Studies in Literature and Language* 18 (1976): 381–92.

12. The present location of the portrait is unknown. David Piper published a photograph and a brief analysis of the painting in *The Development of the British Literary Portrait up to Samuel Johnson, Proceedings of the British Academy* 54 (1968): 51–106. See Plate VIII.

13. Susanne Woods, "Ben Jonson's Cary-Morison Ode: Some Observations on Structure and Form," *Studies in English Literature* 18 (1978): 57–74; Paul Fry, *The Poet's Calling in the English Ode* (New Haven and London: Yale University Press, 1980); Annabel Patterson, *Censorship and Interpretation*, 139–43.

14. Ian Donaldson, "Jonson's Ode to Sir Lucius Cary and Sr. H. Morison," *Studies in the Literary Imagination* 6 (1973): 139–52; Mary I. Oates, "Jonson's 'Ode Pindarick' and the Doctrine of Imitation," *Papers on Language and Literature* 11 (1975): 126–48. Donaldson and Oates note that Jonson warns himself against self-indulgent bitterness in the "Ode. To Himself" and the Cary-Morison ode, both written in 1629.

15. Michael Van Cleave Alexander, *Charles I's Lord Treasurer: Sir Richard Weston, Earl of Portland (1577–1635)* (Chapel Hill: University of North Carolina Press, 1975), 170–80.

16. Lemly, 248–66.

17. Norman K. Farmer, Jr., *Poets and the Visual Arts in Renaissance England* (Austin: University of Texas Press, 1984), 28–30.

18. Quoted by Christopher Brown, *Van Dyck* (Ithaca: Cornell University Press, 1982), 145 n.

19. For a discussion of several "memorial portraits" of aristocratic women, see Jonathan Goldberg, *James I and the Politics of Literature* (Baltimore: The Johns Hopkins University Press, 1983), 97–100. These portraits juxtapose the public record of family history with private emblems of love and death: a skull, a husband-lover's glove dropping toward the outstretched hand of his dying wife. Each of the portraits also addresses the history of the dying woman by portraying her twice, as she lived and as she lay dying. Van Dyck's portrait of Lady Venetia Digby presents only the private image of the lady and the blown rose.

20. Brown, 146.

21. Digby described the painting as an image of his wife "as Prudence, sitting in a white dress with a coloured wrap and a jewelled girdle. Under her hand are two white doves, and her other arm is encircled by a serpent. Under her feet is a plinth to which are bound, like slaves, Deceit with two faces; Anger with a furious countenance, meagre Envy with her shabby locks; Profane Love, blindfolded, his wings clipped, his bow broken, arrows scattered and torch extinguished; with other naked figures the size of life. Above is a glory of singing Angels, three of them holding the palm and wreath above the head of Prudence as a symbol of her victory and triumph over the vices, and the epigram, taken from Juvenal, *Nullum numen abest si sit Prudentia* [The prudent will not look in vain for Heaven's help]." Quoted by Brown, 146. See also Oliver Millar, *Van Dyck in England* (London: National Portrait Gallery, 1982), 48–50.

22. Millar, 48; Brown, 146.

23. Millar, 50. Jonson may have referred to this act of copying when he wrote, in "The Picture of the Body," "But painter, see thou do not sell / A copy of this piece, nor tell / Whose 'tis" (*Und.* 84.3.29–31).

24. Kenelm Digby, *Two Treatises, in the One of Which, the Nature of Bodies; in the Other, the Nature of Mans Soule, is looked into* (Paris, 1644; London, 1645). See Farmer, 29.

25. The most comprehensive account of Cavalier attitudes and art remains Earl Miner, *The Cavalier Mode from Jonson to Cotton* (Princeton: Princeton University Press, 1971). See also Joseph Summers, *The Heirs of Donne and Jonson* (New York: Oxford University Press, 1970).

Select Bibliography

Adams, Hazard. *Philosophy of the Literary Symbolic.* Tallahassee: University Presses of Florida, 1983.

Alexander, Michael Van Cleave. *Charles I's Lord Treasurer: Sir Richard Weston, Earl of Portland (1577–1635).* Chapel Hill: University of North Carolina Press, 1975.

Altieri, Charles. *Act and Quality: A Theory of Literary Meaning and Humanistic Understanding.* Amherst: University of Massachusetts Press, 1981.

Akrigg, G. P. V. *Jacobean Pageant: The Court of King James I.* New York: Atheneum, 1967.

Aulus Gellius. *The Attic Nights.* Translated by John C. Rolfe. 3 vols. London: William Heinemann, 1927.

Austin, J. L. *How to Do Things with Words.* New York: Oxford University Press, 1962.

Babb, Howard. "The 'Epitaph on Elizabeth, L. H.' and Ben Jonson's Style." *Journal of English and Germanic Philology* 62 (1963): 738–44.

Bacon, Francis. "Of Followers and Friends." In *Francis Bacon: A Selection of his Works,* edited by Sidney Warhaft. New York: Odyssey Press, 1965.

Baldwin, T. R. *Shakespere's Small Latine and Lesse Greeke.* 2 vols. Urbana: University of Illinois Press, 1944.

Barish, Jonas. "Feasting and Judgment in Jonsonian Drama." *Renaissance Drama,* n.s., 5 (1972): 3–35.

———. *Ben Jonson and the Language of Prose Comedy.* Cambridge, Mass.: Harvard University Press, 1969.

Barton, Anne. *Ben Jonson, Dramatist.* Cambridge: Cambridge University Press, 1984.

Bates, Steven L., and Sidney D. Orr. *A Concordance to the Poems of Ben Jonson.* Athens: Ohio University Press, 1978.

Beaurline, Lester A. "Ben Jonson and the Illusion of Completeness." *PMLA* 84 (1969): 51–59.

———. "The Selective Principle in Jonson's Shorter Poems." *Criticism* 8 (1966): 64–74.

Bell, Ilona. "Circular Strategies and Structures in Jonson and Herbert." In *Classic and Cavalier: Essays on Jonson and the Sons of Ben,* edited by Claude J. Summers and Ted-Larry Pebworth, 157–70. Pittsburgh: University of Pittsburgh Press, 1982.

Blissett, William, Julian Patrick, and R. W. Van Fossen, eds. *A Celebration of Ben Jonson.* Toronto: University of Toronto Press, 1973.

Bloom, Harold. *The Anxiety of Influence.* New York: Oxford University Press, 1973.

Braden, Gordon. *The Classics and English Renaissance Poetry.* New Haven: Yale University Press, 1978.

Bradshaw, Graham. "Three Poems Ben Jonson Did Not Write: A Note on Jonson's Christian Humanism." *ELH* 47 (1980): 484–99.

Brady, Jennifer. "'Beware the Poet': Authority and Judgment in Jonson's *Epigrammes.*" *Studies in English Literature* 23 (1983): 95–112.

———. "Jonson's 'To King James': Plain Speaking in the *Epigrammes* and the *Conversations.*" *Studies in Philology* 82 (1985): 380–90.

Brock, D. Heyward. *A Ben Jonson Companion.* Bloomington: Indiana University Press, 1983.

———. "Jonson and Donne: Structural Fingerprinting and the Attribution of Elegies XXXVIII–XLI." *Papers of the Bibliographical Society of America* 71 (1978): 519–27.

Brock, D. Heyward, and James M. Welsh. *Ben Jonson: A Quadricentennial Bibliography, 1947–1972.* Metuchen, N.J.: Scarecrow Press, 1974.

Brodhurst, Francis. "Elizabeth Hardwycke, Countess of Shrewsbury." *Derbyshire Archaeological Society Journal* 30 (n.d.): 231–36.

Brower, Reuben. *Mirror on Mirror: Translation, Imitation, Parody.* Cambridge, Mass.: Harvard University Press, 1974.

Brown, Christopher. *Van Dyck.* Ithaca: Cornell University Press, 1982.

Cain, William E. "Mirrors, Intentions, and Texts in Ben Jonson." *Essays in Literature* (Macomb, Ill.) 8 (1981): 11–23.

———. "Self and Others in Two Poems by Ben Jonson." *Studies in Philology* 80 (1983): 163–82.

———. "The Place of the Poet in 'To Penshurst' and 'To My Muse.'" *Criticism* 21 (1979): 34–48.

Camden, William. *Remaines of a Greater Worke Concerning Britain.* London: G. E. for Simon Waterson, 1605. Reprinted East Ardsley, Wakefield: EP Publishing, Ltd., 1974.

Carlson, Peter. "Judging Spectators." *ELH* 44 (1977): 443–57.

Castiglione, Baldesar. *The Book of the Courtier.* Translated by Charles S. Singleton. Garden City, N.Y.: Anchor Books, 1959.

Cervantes, Miguel. *Don Quixote.* Translated by J. M. Cohen. Baltimore: Penguin Books, 1950.

Clark, Ira. "Ben Jonson's Imitation." *Criticism* 20 (1978): 107–27.

Cope Jackson. *The Theatre and the Dream: From Metaphor to Form in Renaissance Drama.* Baltimore: The Johns Hopkins University Press, 1973.

Corbett, Margery, and R. W. Lightbown. *The Comely Frontispiece.* London: Routledge and Kegan Paul, 1979.

Council, Norman. "Ben Jonson, Inigo Jones, and the Transformation of Tudor Chivalry." *ELH* 47 (1980): 159–75.

Cubeta, Paul M. "Ben Jonson's Religious Lyrics." *Journal of English and Germanic Philology* 62 (1963): 96–110.

———. "'A Celebration of Charis': An Evaluation of Poetic Strategy." *ELH* 4 (1958): 163–80.

———. "A Jonsonian Ideal: 'To Penshurst.'" *Philological Quarterly* 42 (1964): 14–24.

Culler, Jonathan. *Structuralist Poetics.* Ithaca: Cornell University Press, 1975.

Curtius, Ernst. *European Literature and the Latin Middle Ages.* Translated by Willard Trask. New York: Harper and Row, 1953.

Danby, John. *Elizabethan and Jacobean Poets.* London: Faber and Faber, 1965. Published in 1952 as *Poets on Fortune's Hill.*

De Luna, B. N. *Jonson's Romish Plot: A Study of 'Catiline' and Its Historical Context.* London: Oxford University Press, 1967.

Demetrius. *On Style.* Translated by W. Rhys Roberts. Cambridge, Mass.: Harvard University Press, 1953.

Derrida, Jacques. "Differance." In *Speech and Phenomena and Other Essays on Husserl's Theory of Signs.* Translated by David B. Allison, 129–60. Evanston, Ill.: Northwestern University Press, 1973.

Dessen, Alan. *Jonson's Moral Comedy.* Evanston, Ill.: Northwestern University Press, 1971.

Di Cesare, Mario A., and Ephim Fogel, eds. *A Concordance to the Poems of Ben Jonson.* Ithaca: Cornell University Press, 1978.

Donaldson, Ian. "Jonson and the Moralists." In *Two Renaissance Mythmakers: Christopher Marlowe and Ben Jonson,* edited by Alvin B. Kernan, 146–64. Baltimore: The Johns Hopkins University Press, 1977.

———. "Jonson's Ode to Sir Lucius Cary and Sir H. Morison." *Studies in the Literary Imagination* 6 (1973): 139–52.

Doughtie, Edward. "Ferrabosco and Jonson's 'The Houre-glass.'" *Renaissance Quarterly* 22 (1969): 148–50.

Dubrow, Heather. "The Country-House Poem: A Study in Generic Development." *Genre* 12 (1979): 53–80.

Duncan, Douglas J. M. *Ben Jonson and the Lucianic Tradition.* Cambridge: Cambridge University Press, 1979.

Durant, David. *Bess of Hardwick: Portrait of an Elizabethan Dynast.* London: Weidenfeld and Nicolson, 1977.

Dutton, Richard P. *Ben Jonson: To the First Folio.* Cambridge: Cambridge University Press, 1983.

Eccles, Mark. "Ben Jonson and the Spies." *Review of English Studies* 13 (1937): 385–97.

Edwards, Philip. *Threshold of a Nation.* Cambridge: Cambridge University Press, 1979.

Eliot, T. S. "Ben Jonson." In *Essays on Elizabethan Drama*, 65–82. New York: Harcourt Brace, 1956.

Elsky, Martin. "Words, Things, and Names: Jonson's Poetry and Philosophical Grammar." In *Classic and Cavalier: Essays on Jonson and the Sons of Ben*, edited by Claude J. Summers and Ted-Larry Pebworth, 91–104. Pittsburgh: University of Pittsburgh Press, 1982.

Empson, William. *Seven Types of Ambiguity*. New York: Meridian Books, 1955.

Enck, John J. *Jonson and the Comic Truth*. Madison: University of Wisconsin Press, 1957.

Esler, Anthony. *The Aspiring Mind of the Elizabethan Younger Generation*. Durham: Duke University Press, 1966.

Farmer, Norman K., Jr. *Poets and the Visual Arts in Renaissance England*. Austin: University of Texas Press, 1984.

Ferry, Anne. *All in War with Time: Love Poetry of Shakespeare, Donne, Jonson, Marvell*. Cambridge, Mass.: Harvard University Press, 1975.

Fike, Francis. "Ben Jonson's 'On My First Sonne.'" *The Gordon Review* 11 (1969): 205–20.

Fish, Stanley. "Authors-Readers: Jonson's Community of the Same." *Representations* 7 (1984): 26–58. A shorter version of this essay is included in *Lyric Poetry: Beyond New Criticism*, edited by Chaviva Hŏsek and Patricia Parker, 132–47. Ithaca and London: Cornell University Press, 1985.

Fisher, Alan. "Jonson's Jokes." Paper presented at 1984 Pacific Northwest Renaissance Conference, Seattle, Washington.

Ford, Herbert L. *Collation of the Ben Jonson Folios, 1616–31–40*. Oxford: Oxford University Press, 1932.

Foucault, Michael. *The Order of Things*. New York: Random House, 1970. His translation of *Les Mots et les Choses*, Paris: Editions Gallimard, 1966.

Fowler, Alistair. "The Silva Tradition in Jonson's *The Forrest*." In *Poetic Traditions of the English Renaissance*, edited by Maynard Mack and George deForest Lord, 163–80. New Haven: Yale University Press, 1982.

Freehafer, John. "Leonard Digges, Ben Jonson, and the Beginning of Shakespeare Idolatry." *Shakespeare Quarterly* 21 (1970): 63–75.

French, R. W. "Reading Jonson: *Epigrammes* 22 and 45." *Concerning Poetry* 10 (1977): 5–11.

Friedberg, Harris. "Ben Jonson's Poetry: Pastoral, Epigram, Georgic." *English Literary Renaissance* 4 (1974): 111–36.

Fry, Paul. *The Poet's Calling in the English Ode*. New Haven and London: Yale University Press, 1980.

Gardiner, Judith Kegan. *Craftsmanship in Context: The Development of Ben Jonson's Poetry*. The Hague: Mouton, 1975.

Galloway, David, ed. *The Elizabethan Theatre II*. London: Macmillan, 1970.

Garrison, James. "Time and Value in Jonson's 'Epistle to Elizabeth, Countess of Rutland.'" *Concerning Poetry* 8 (1975): 53–58.

Geertz, Clifford. *The Interpretation of Cultures*. New York: Basic Books, 1973.

Goldberg, Jonathan. *James I and the Politics of Literature*. Baltimore: The Johns Hopkins University Press, 1983.

Goldsworthy, William. *Ben Jonson and the First Folio*. London: C. Palmer, 1931.

Gordon, D. J. "Poet and Architect: The Intellectual Setting of the Quarrel between Ben Jonson and Inigo Jones." *Journal of the Warburg and Courtauld Institutes* 12 (1949): 152–78. Reprinted in D. J. Gordon, *The Renaissance Imagination*, edited by Stephen Orgel, 77–101. Berkeley: University of California Press, 1975.

Gray, Hanna. "Renaissance Humanism: The Pursuit of Eloquence." In *Renaissance Essays*, edited by Paul O. Kristeller and Philip Wiener, 199–216. New York: Harper and Row, 1968.

Greenblatt, Stephen. *Renaissance Self-Fashioning from More to Shakespeare*. Chicago: University of Chicago Press, 1980.

Greene, Thomas. "Ben Jonson and the Centered Self." *Studies in English Literature* 10 (1970): 325–48.

———. "The Flexibility of the Self in Renaissance Literature." In *The Disciplines of Criticism*, edited by Peter Demetz, Thomas Greene, and Lowry Nelson, Jr., 241–64. (New Haven: Yale University Press, 1968).

———. *The Light in Troy: Imitation and Discovery in Renaissance Poetry*. New Haven: Yale University Press, 1982.

Greg, W. W. "The First Folio and Its Publishers." *Studies in the First Folio, Shakespeare Association Studies*. London: Oxford University Press, 1924.

———. *The Shakespeare First Folio: Its Bibliographical and Textual History*. Oxford: Oxford University Press, 1955.

Grube, G. M. A. *A Greek Critic: Demetrius on Style*. The Phoenix, supplementary volume 4. Toronto: University of Toronto Press, 1961.

Guibbory, Achsah. "The Poet as Mythmaker: Ben Jonson's Poetry of Praise." *Clio* 5 (1976): 322–39.

Gunn, Thom, ed. *Ben Jonson*. Poet to Poet Series. Baltimore: Penguin, 1974. Reprinted in Thom Gunn, *The Occasions of Poetry*, 106–7. San Francisco: North Point Press, 1985.

Hardison, O. B. *The Enduring Monument*. Chapel Hill: University of North Carolina Press, 1962.

Hartman, Geoffrey. " 'The Nymph Complaining for the Death of her Faun': A Brief Allegory." In *Beyond Formalism*, 173–92. New Haven: Yale University Press, 1970.

———. "Monsieur Texte." In *Saving the Text: Literature / Derrida / Philosophy*, 1–32. Baltimore: The Johns Hopkins University Press, 1981.

———. "Wordsworth, Inscriptions, and Romantic Nature Poetry." In *From Sensibility to Romanticism: Essays Presented to Frederick A. Pottle*, edited by Frederick W. Hilles, 389–414. New Haven: Yale University Press, 1965.

Hay, Millicent V. *The Life of Robert Sidney, Earl of Leicester (1563–1626)*. Washington: The Folger Shakespeare Library, 1984.

Haydn, Hiram. *The Counter-Renaissance*. New York: Scribners, 1950.

Helgerson, Richard. *Self-Crowned Laureates: Spenser, Jonson, Milton, and the Literary System*. Berkeley: University of California Press, 1983.

Herendeen, W. H. "'Like a Circle Bounded in Itself': Jonson, Camden, and the Strategies of Praise." *Journal of Medieval and Renaissance Studies* 11 (1981): 137–67.

Herrick, Robert. *The Complete Poetry of Robert Herrick.* Edited by J. Max Patrick. New York: Doubleday, 1963.

Hibbard, G. R. "The Country House Poem in the Seventeenth Century." *Journal of the Warburg and Courtauld Institutes* 19 (1956): 159–74.

———. *The Elizabethan Theatre IV.* Hamden, Conn.: Shoe String Press, 1974.

Hobsbaum, Philip. "Ben Jonson in the Seventeenth Century." *Michigan Quarterly Review* 16 (1977): 405–23.

Hollander, John. *Vision and Resonance: Two Senses of Poetic Form.* New York: Oxford University Press, 1975.

Honigmann, E. A. J. *The Stability of Shakespeare's Text.* Lincoln: University of Nebraska Press, 1965.

Horace. *Odes and Epodes.* Translated by C. E. Bennett. Cambridge, Mass.: Harvard University Press, 1927.

———. *Satires, Epistles, and Ars Poetica.* Translated by H. R. Fairclough. Cambridge, Mass.: Harvard University Press, 1929.

Howard-Hill, T. H. *Ralph Crane and Some Shakespeare First Folio Comedies.* Charlottesville: Bibliographical Society of the University of Virginia, University Press of Virginia, 1972.

Hudson, Hoyt. *The Epigram in the English Renaissance.* Princeton: Princeton University Press, 1947.

Huizinga, Johan. *Homo Ludens: A Study of the Play-Element in Culture.* Boston: Beacon, 1960.

Hunter, George K. *John Lyly: The Humanist as Courtier.* Cambridge, Mass.: Harvard University Press, 1962.

Hunter, Joseph. *History of Hallamshire.* Sheffield, 1869.

Ihalainen, Ossi. "The Problem of Unity in Ben Jonson's 'Epitaph on Elizabeth, L. H.'" *Neuphilologische Mitteilungen* 80 (1979): 238–44.

Jackson, Gabriele B. *Vision and Judgment in Ben Jonson's Drama.* New Haven: Yale University Press, 1968.

Javitch, Daniel. *Poetry and Courtliness in Renaissance England.* Princeton: Princeton University Press, 1978.

John, Lisle C. "Ben Jonson's 'To Sir William Sidney, on his Birthday.'" *Modern Language Review* 52 (1957): 168–76.

Johnston, George B. *Ben Jonson, Poet.* New York: Columbia University Press, 1945.

Jones, Robert C. "The Satirist's Retirement in Jonson's 'Apologetical Dialogue.'" *ELH* 34 (1967): 447–67.

Jonson, Ben. *Ben Jonson.* Edited by C. H. Herford, Percy Simpson, and Evelyn Simpson. 11 vols. Oxford: Clarendon Press, 1925–52.

———. *The Complete Poetry of Ben Jonson.* Edited by William B. Hunter, Jr. New York: W. W. Norton, 1968.

———. *Poems.* Edited by Ian Donaldson. Oxford: Oxford University Press, 1975.

————. *Workes of Benjamin Jonson.* London: William Stansby, 1616. Reprinted in facsimile, with introduction by D. Heyward Brock. London: Scolar Press, 1976.

Jorgens, Elise. *The Well-Tun'd Word: Musical Interpretations of English Poetry 1597–1651.* Minneapolis: University of Minnesota Press, 1982.

Jowett, John. "New Created Creatures: Ralph Crane and the Stage Directions in *The Tempest.*" *Shakespeare Survey* 36 (1983): 107–20.

Judkins, David C. *The Non-Dramatic Works of Ben Jonson: A Reference Guide.* Boston: G. K. Hall, 1982.

Kamholtz, Jonathan. "Ben Jonson's *Epigrammes* and Poetic Occasions." *Studies in English Literature* 23 (1983): 77–94.

————. "Ben Jonson's Green World: Structure and Imaginative Unity in *The Forrest.*" *Studies in Philology* 78 (1981): 170–93.

Kay, W. David. "*Bartholomew Fair:* Ben Jonson in Praise of Folly." *English Literary Renaissance* 6 (1976): 115–26.

————. "Jonson's Urbane Gallants: Humanistic Contexts for *Epicoene.*" *Huntington Library Quarterly* 39 (1975–76): 251–66.

————. "The Shaping of Ben Jonson's Career: A Reexamination of Facts and Problems." *Modern Philology* 67 (1970): 224–37.

————. "The Christian Wisdom of Ben Jonson's 'On My First Sonne.' " *Studies in English Literature* 11 (1971): 125–36.

Kelly, T. J. "Jonson's 'Celebration of Charis.' " *Critical Review* (Melbourne) 17 (1974): 120–26.

Kennedy, J. Gerald. "Parody as Exorcism." *Genre* 13 (1980): 161–70.

Kernan, Alvin B., ed. *Two Renaissance Mythmakers: Christopher Marlowe and Ben Jonson.* Baltimore: The Johns Hopkins University Press, 1977.

Kerrigan, William. "Ben Jonson Full of Shame and Scorn." *Studies in the Literary Imagination* 6 (1973): 199–207.

Kerrigan, William. "The Articulation of the Ego in the Renaissance." In *The Literary Freud: Mechanisms of Defense and the Poetic Will,* edited by Joseph H. Smith, 261–308. *Psychiatry and the Humanities,* vol. 4. New Haven: Yale University Press, 1980.

Kiremidjian, G. K. "The Aesthetics of Parody." *Journal of Aesthetics and Art Criticism* 28 (1969): 231–42.

Knights, L. C. *Drama and Society in the Age of Jonson.* London: Chatto & Windus, 1937.

Knoll, Robert E. *Ben Jonson's Plays: An Introduction.* Lincoln: University of Nebraska Press, 1964.

Kristeller, Paul O. *Renaissance Thought II: Papers on Humanism and the Arts.* New York: Harper and Row, 1965.

Kristeller, Paul O., and Philip Wiener, eds. *Renaissance Essays.* New York: Harper and Row, 1968.

Kronenfeld, Judith Z. "The Father Found: Consolation Achieved Through Love in Ben Jonson's 'On My First Sonne.' " *Studies in Philology* 75 (1978): 64–83.

Lanham, Richard. *The Motives of Eloquence.* Berkeley: University of California Press, 1976.

Leavis, F. R. *Revaluation: Tradition and Development in English Poetry.* London: George W. Stewart, 1947. Reprinted New York: Norton, 1963.

Leclercq, R. V. "The Reciprocal Harmony of Jonson's 'A Celebration of Charis.'" *Texas Studies in Literature and Language* 16 (1975): 626–50.

Leggatt, Alexander. *Ben Jonson: His Vision and His Art.* London: Methuen, 1981.

Lemly, John. "Masks and Self-Portraits in Jonson's Late Poetry." *ELH* 44 (1977): 248–66.

Levine, J. A. "The Status of the Verse Epistle before Pope." *Studies in Philology* 59 (1962): 658–84.

Levy, F. J. *Tudor Historical Thought.* San Marino, Calif.: The Huntington Library, 1967.

Lipking, Lawrence. *The Life of the Poet: Beginning and Ending Poetic Careers.* Chicago: University of Chicago Press, 1981.

Livingston, Mary L. "Ben Jonson: The Poet to the Painter." *Texas Studies in Literature and Language* 18 (1976): 318–92.

———. "Ben Jonson's Rhetoric of Love." *Kenyon Review* 3, no. 2 (1982): 35–41.

Logan, George M. "Substance and Form in Renaissance Humanism." *Journal of Medieval and Renaissance Studies* 7 (1977): 1–34.

McClung, William. *The Country House in English Renaissance Poetry.* Berkeley: University of California Press, 1977.

McClure, Norman E., ed. *The Letters of John Chamberlain.* 2 vols. Philadelphia: The American Philosophical Society, 1939.

McConica, J. K. *English Humanists and Reformation Politics.* Oxford: Oxford University Press, 1965.

McEuen, Kathryn. *Classical Influences on the Tribe of Ben.* Cedar Rapids, Iowa: Torch Press, 1939.

Mack, Maynard. "The Muse of Satire." *Yale Review* 41 (1951–52):80–92.

Maclean, Hugh. "'A More Secret Cause': The Wit of Jonson's Poetry." In *A Celebration of Ben Jonson,* edited by William Blissett, Julian Patrick, and R. W. Van Fossen. Toronto: University of Toronto Press, 1973.

———. "Ben Jonson's Poems: Notes on the Ordered Society." In *Essays in English Literature from the Renaissance to the Victorian Age, Presented to A. S. P. Woodhouse, 1964,* edited by Millar Maclure and F. W. Watt, 43–68. Toronto: University of Toronto Press, 1964.

McPherson, David. "Ben Jonson's Library and Marginalia: An Annotated Catalogue." *Studies in Philology (Texts and Studies 1974)* 71, no. 5 (December 1974).

Maddison, Carol. *Apollo and the Nine.* Baltimore: The Johns Hopkins University Press, 1960.

Major, John J. "A Reading of Jonson's 'Epitaph on Elizabeth, L. H.'" *Studies in Philology* 73 (1976): 62–86.

Manley, Frank, ed. *John Donne: The Anniversaries.* Baltimore: The Johns Hopkins University Press, 1963.

Marcus, Leah. "'Present Occasions' and the Shaping of Ben Jonson's Masques." *ELH* 45 (1978): 201–25.

Marotti, Arthur. " 'Love Is Not Love': Elizabethan Sonnet Sequences and the Social Order." *ELH* 49 (1982): 396–428.

———. "All About Jonson's Poetry." *ELH* 39 (1972): 208–37.

Martial. *Epigrams*. Translated by W. C. A. Ker. 2 vols. New York: G. P. Putnam's Sons, 1920.

Martz, Louis. *The Poetry of Meditation*. New Haven: Yale University Press, 1962.

Mason, H. A. *Humanism and Poetry in the Early Tudor Period*. London: Routledge and Kegan Paul, 1959, reprinted 1980.

Matchett, William. *The Phoenix and the Turtle: Shakespeare's Poem and Chester's "Love's Martyr."* The Hague: Mouton, 1965.

Maus, Katherine. *Ben Jonson and the Roman Frame of Mind*. Princeton: Princeton University Press, 1984.

Medine, Peter. "Object and Intent in Jonson's 'Famous Voyage.' " *Studies in English Literature* 15 (1975): 97–110.

Millar, Oliver. *Van Dyck in England*. London: National Portrait Gallery, 1982.

Mills, Laurens. *One Soul in Bodies Twain: Friendship in Tudor Literature and Stuart Drama*. Bloomington: Indiana University Press, 1937.

Miner, Earl. *The Cavalier Mode from Jonson to Cotton*. Princeton: Princeton University Press, 1971.

Molesworth, Charles. " 'To Penshurst' and Jonson's Historical Imagination." *Clio* 1, no. 2 (1972): 5–13.

Mortimer, Anthony. "The Feigned Commonwealth in the Poetry of Ben Jonson." *Studies in English Literature* 13 (1973): 69–79.

Munro, John, ed. *The Shakspere Allusion-Book*. London: Oxford University Press, 1932.

Murphy, G. N., and William C. Slattery. "Meaning and Structure in Jonson's 'Epitaph on Elizabeth, L. H.' " *Re: Arts and Letters* 2 (1969): 1–3.

Newton, Richard. " 'Ben. / Jonson': The Poet in the Poems." In *Two Renaissance Mythmakers: Christopher Marlowe and Ben Jonson*, edited by Alvin B. Kernan, 165–95. Baltimore: The Johns Hopkins University Press, 1977.

Newton, Richard. "Ben Jonson and the (Re)invention of the Book." In *Classic and Cavalier: Essays on Jonson and the Sons of Ben*, edited by Claude J. Summers and Ted-Larry Pebworth, 31–58. Pittsburgh: University of Pittsburgh Press, 1982.

Nichols, J. G. *The Poetry of Ben Jonson*. London: Routledge and Kegan Paul, 1969.

Oates, Mary I. "Jonson, Congreve, and Gray: Pindaric Essays in Literary History." *Studies in English Literature* 19 (1979): 387–406.

———. "Jonson's 'Ode Pindarick' and the Doctrine of Imitation." *Papers on Language and Literature* 11 (1975): 126–48.

Orgel, Stephen. *The Jonsonian Masque*. Cambridge, Mass.: Harvard University Press, 1965.

Orgel, Stephen, and Roy Strong, eds. *Inigo Jones: The Theatre of the Stuart Court*. 2 vols. London: Sotheby, Parke Bernet; Berkeley: University of California Press, 1973.

Parfitt, George A. E. "Compromise Classicism: Language and Rhythm in Ben Jonson's Poetry." *Studies in English Literature* 11 (1971): 109–23.

———. "Ethical Thought and Ben Jonson's Poetry." *Studies in English Literature* 9 (1969): 123–34.

———. "The Poetry of Ben Jonson." *Essays in Criticism* 18 (1968): 18–31.

———. *Ben Jonson: Public Poet and Private Man.* New York: Barnes and Noble, 1977.

Parry, Graham. *The Golden Age Restor'd: The Culture of the Stuart Court, 1603–42.* Manchester: Manchester University Press, 1981.

Partridge, A. C. *Orthography in Shakespeare and Elizabethan Drama.* Lincoln: University of Nebraska Press, 1955.

Partridge, Edward. "Jonson's *Epigrammes:* The Named and the Nameless." *Studies in the Literary Imagination* 6 (1973): 153–98.

———. *The Broken Compass: A Study of the Major Comedies of Ben Jonson.* London: Chatto & Windus, 1958.

Patterson, Annabel. *Censorship and Interpretation: The Conditions of Writing and Reading in Early Modern England.* Madison: University of Wisconsin Press, 1984.

Patterson, Annabel. "Lyric and Society in Jonson's *Under-wood.*" In *Lyric Poetry: Beyond New Criticism,* edited by Chaviva Hōsek and Patricia Parker, 148–63. Ithaca: Cornell University Press, 1985.

Pearlman, E. "Ben Jonson: An Anatomy." *English Literary Renaissance* 9 (1979): 364–93.

Peterson, Richard S. "Virtue Reconciled to Pleasure: Jonson's 'A Celebration of Charis,'" *Studies in the Literary Imagination* 6 (1973): 219–68.

———. *Imitation and Praise in the Poems of Ben Jonson.* New Haven: Yale University Press, 1981.

Petrarca, Francesco. *Le Familiari.* Edited by Vittorio Rossi. Florence: Sansoni, 1934.

———. *Petrarch's Secret.* Translated by W. H. Draper. London, 1911.

Pierce, Robert B. "Ben Jonson's Horace and Horace's Ben Jonson." *Studies in Philology* 39 (1981): 20–31.

Pigman, G. W., III. "Versions of Imitation in the Renaissance." *Renaissance Quarterly* 33 (1980): 1–32.

———. "Suppressed Grief in Jonson's Funeral Poetry." *English Literary Renaissance* 13 (1983): 203–20.

Piper, David. *The Development of the British Literary Portrait up to Samuel Johnson. Proceedings of the British Academy* 54 (1968): 51–106. Reprinted as separate pamphlet, London: Oxford University Press, 1968.

Pratt, Mary Louise. *Toward a Speech Act Theory of Discourse.* Bloomington: Indiana University Press, 1977.

Putney, Rufus. "'This So Subtile Sport': Some Aspects of Jonson's Epigrams." *University of Colorado Studies.* Series in Language and Literature 10. Boulder: University of Colorado Press, 1966.

Puttenham, George. *The Arte of English Poesie.* Edited by Baxter Hathaway. Kent, Ohio: Kent State University Press, 1970.

Rathmell, J. C. A. "Jonson, Lord Lisle, and Penshurst." *English Literary Renaissance* 1 (1971): 150–60.

Rawson, Maude. *Bess of Hardwick and Her Circle.* New York: John Lane Co., 1910.

Revard, Stella P. "Pindar and Jonson's Cary-Morison Ode." In *Classic and Cavalier: Essays on Jonson and the Sons of Ben,* edited by Claude J. Summers and Ted-Larry Pebworth, 17–30. Pittsburgh: University of Pittsburgh Press, 1982.

Ribeiro, Alvaro. "Sir John Roe: Ben Jonson's Friend." *Review of English Studies* n.s. 24 (1973): 153–64.

Roberts, Josephine A., ed. *The Poems of Lady Mary Wroth.* Baton Rouge: Louisiana State University Press, 1983.

Rollin, Roger B. "The Anxiety of Identification: Jonson and the Rival Poets." In *Classic and Cavalier: Essays on Jonson and the Sons of Ben,* edited by Claude J. Summers and Ted-Larry Pebworth, 139–56. Pittsburgh: University of Pittsburgh Press, 1982.

Rosenthal, M. L., and Sally M. Gall. *The Modern Poetic Sequence.* Oxford: Oxford University Press, 1983.

Ryan, Lawrence. "Art and Artifice in Erasmus' *Convivium Profanum.*" *Renaissance Quarterly* 31 (1978): 1–17.

Sale, Roger. *Literary Inheritance.* Amherst: University of Massachusetts Press, 1984.

Schafer, Roy. *A New Language for Psychoanalysis.* New Haven: Yale University, 1976.

———. *Language and Insight: The Sigmund Freud Memorial Lectures 1975–1976, University College, London.* New Haven and London: Yale University Press, 1978.

———. *The Analytic Attitude.* New York: Basic Books, 1983.

Schelling, Felix. "Ben Jonson and the Classical School." *PMLA* 13 (1898): 221–49.

Schoenbaum, Samuel. "Shakespeare and Jonson: Fact and Myth." In *Elizabethan Theatre II,* edited by David Galloway, 1–19. London: Macmillan, 1970.

Sennett, Richard. *The Fall of Public Man.* New York: Alfred A. Knopf, 1977.

Shafer, Robert. *The English Ode to 1660: An Essay in Literary History.* Princton: Princeton University Press, 1918.

Shakespeare, William. *Complete Works,* Edited by Alfred Harbage. 1969 revision of the Pelican text. Reprinted New York: Viking Press, 1977.

———. *Pericles.* Edited by F. D. Hoeniger. London: Methuen, 1963.

———. *The Tempest.* Edited by Frank Kermode. London: Methuen, 1964.

Sharpe, Robert. "Jonson's 'Execration' and Champman's 'Invective': Their Place in Their Authors' Rivalry." *Studies in Philology* 42 (1945): 555–63.

Sidney, Philip. *An Apologie for Poetrie.* In *Elizabethan Critical Essays,* edited by G. Gregory Smith, 1 : 148–207. Oxford: Oxford University Press, 1904.

Sidney, Robert. *The Poems of Robert Sidney.* Edited by P. J. Croft. Oxford: Oxford University Press, 1984.

Siegel, Jerrold. *Rhetoric and Philosophy in Renaissance Humanism.* Princeton: Princeton University Press, 1968.

Simpson, Evelyn. "Jonson and Donne: A Problem of Authorship." *Review of English Studies* 15 (1939): 274–82.

Skelton, Robin. "The Masterpoet and the Multiple Tradition: The Poetry of Ben Jonson." *Style* 1 (1967): 225–46.

Smith, Barbara Herrnstein. *Poetic Closure.* Chicago: University of Chicago Press, 1968.

Smith, Bruce. "Ben Jonson's *Epigrammes:* Portrait-Gallery, Theater, Commonwealth." *Studies in English Literature* 14 (1974): 91–110.

Spanos, William. "The Read Toad in the Jonsonian Garden: Resonance in the Nondramatic Poetry." *Journal of English and Germanic Philology* 68 (1969): 1–23.

Spencer, T. J. B. "Ben Jonson on his beloved, The Author Mr. William Shakespeare." In *The Elizabethan Theatre IV,* edited by G. R. Hibbard, 22–40. Hamden, Conn.: Shoe String Press, 1974.

Spenser, Edmund. *The Poems of Edmund Spenser.* Edited by J. C. Smith and E. De Selincourt. London: Oxford University Press, 1912.

Stallybrass, Basil. "Bess of Hardwick's Buildings and Building Accounts." *Archaeologia* 64 (1913): 347–98.

Stone, Lawrence. *The Crisis of the Aristocracy, 1558–1641.* Oxford: Clarendon Press, 1965.

Strout, Nathaniel. "Jonson's Use of a Name in 'Epitaph on Elizabeth, L. H.'" *English Language Notes* 17 (1979): 30–33.

Struever, Nancy. "Humanities and Humanists." *Humanities in Society* 1, No. 1 (1978): 25–34.

———. *The Language of History in the Renaissance.* Princeton: Princeton University Press, 1970.

Summers, Claude J., and Ted-Larry Pebworth. *Ben Jonson.* Boston: G. K. Hall & Co., 1979.

Summers, Claude J., and Ted-Larry Pebworth, eds. *Classic and Cavalier: Essays on Jonson and the Sons of Ben.* Pittsburgh: University of Pittsburgh Press, 1982.

Summers, Joseph H. *The Heirs of Donne and Jonson.* New York: Oxford University Press, 1970.

Surtz, Edward, S. J. *The Praise of Pleasure.* Cambridge, Mass.: Harvard University Press, 1957.

Sweeney, John Gordon, III. *Jonson and the Psychology of Public Theater.* Princeton: Princeton University Press, 1985.

Tayler, Edward W. *Nature and Art in Renaissance Literature.* New York: Columbia University Press, 1964.

Taylor, Dick, Jr. "The Third Earl of Pemrboke as a Patron of Poetry." *Tulane Studies in English* 5 (1955): 41–67.

Thompson, Craig, ed. *The Colloquies of Erasmus.* Chicago: University of Chicago Press, 1965.

Tilley, M. P. *A Dictionary of the Proverbs in England in the Sixteenth and Seventeenth Centuries.* Ann Arbor: University of Michigan Press, 1950.

Tracey, James. *Erasmus: The Growth of a Mind.* Geneva: Droz, 1972.

Trevor-Roper, Hugh R. *Religion, the Reformation and Social Change.* London: Secker and Warburg, 1984.

Trimpi, Wesley. *Ben Jonson's Poems: A Study of the Plain Style.* Stanford, Calif.: Stanford University Press, 1962.

Trinkaus, Charles. *In Our Image and Likeness: Humanity and Divinity in Renaissance Thought.* 2 vols. Chicago: University of Chicago Press, 1970.

Turner, Victor. "African Ritual and Western Literature: Is a Comparative Symbology Possible?" In *The Literature of Fact,* edited by Angus Fletcher. New York: Columbia University Press, 1976.

van den Berg, Kent T. *Playhouse and Cosmos: Shakespearean Theater as Metaphor.* Newark: University of Delaware Press, 1985.

———. "Theatrical Fiction and the Reality of Love in *As You Like It.*" *PMLA* 90 (1975): 885–93.

Van Deusen, Marshall. "Criticism and Ben Jonson's 'To Celia.'" *Essays in Criticism* 7 (1957): 95–103.

Venuti, Lawrence. "Why Jonson Wrote not of Love." *Journal of Medieval and Renaissance Studies* 12 (1982): 195–220.

Waddington, Raymond P. "'A Celebration of Charis': Socratic Lover and Silenic Speaker." In *Classic and Cavalier: Essays on Jonson and the Sons of Ben,* edited by Claude J. Summers and Ted-Larry Pebworth, 121–38. Pittsburgh: University of Pittsburgh Press, 1982.

Waelder, Robert. "The Principle of Multiple Function." *Psychoanalytic Quarterly* 15 (1936): 45–62.

Walker, D. P. "Musical Humanism in the Sixteenth and Early Seventeenth Centuries." *Music Review* 2 (1941): 1–13, 111–21, 220–27, 288–308; 3 (1942): 55–71.

Walker, Ralph S. "Ben Jonson's Lyric Poetry." *Criterion* 13 (1933–34): 430–48.

Walton, Geoffrey A. *Metaphysical to Augustan: Studies in Tone and Sensibility in the Seventeenth Century.* London: Bowes & Bowes, 1955.

Wayne, Don E. *Penshurst: The Semiotics of Place and the Poetics of History.* Madison: University of Wisconsin Press, 1984.

Wedgwood, C. V. *Poetry and Politics under the Stuarts.* Ann Arbor: University of Michigan Press, 1964.

Weever, John. *Epigrammes in the Newest Cut and Oldest Fashion,* ed. Ronald B. McKerrow. Stratford-upon-Avon: at the Shakespeare Head, 1922. First published by Sidgwick and Jackson, Ltd., 1911.

Weinberg, Bernard. "Translations and Commentaries of Demetrius, *On Style* to 1600." *Philological Quarterly* 30 (1951): 353–79.

Weinberger, G. J. "Jonson's Mock-encomiastic 'Celebration of Charis.'" *Genre* 4 (1971): 305–28.

Weller, Barry. "The Rhetoric of Friendship in Montaigne's *Essais.*" *New Literary History* 9 (1977–78): 503–23.

Wells, Susan. "Jacobean City Comedy and the Ideology of the City." *ELH* 48 (1981): 37–60.

Westrup, J. A. "Foreign Musicians in Stuart England." *Musical Quarterly* 27 (1941): 70–89.

Whigham, Frank. *Ambition and Privilege: The Social Tropes of Elizabethan Courtesy Theory.* Berkeley: University of California Press, 1984.

Whipple, T. K. *Martial and the English Epigram from Sir Thomas Wyatt to Ben Jonson. University of California Publications in Modern Philology* 10. Berkeley: University of California, 1925. Reprinted New York: Phaeton Press, 1970.

White, Robert B., Jr. "A Reading of Jonson's 'Epitaph on Elizabeth, L. H.'" *Notre Dame English Journal* 9 (1973–74): 9–14.

Wickham, Glynne. "Shakespeare's 'Small Latine and less Greeke.'" In *Shakespeare's Dramatic Heritage*, 84–112. New York: Barnes and Noble, 1969.

Williams, E. Carleton. *Bess of Hardwick*. London: Longmans Green, 1969.

Williams, Franklin B., Jr. "Commendatory Verses: The Rise of the Art of Puffing." *Studies in Bibliography* 19 (1966): 1–14.

Williams, Gordon. *Tradition and Originality in Roman Poetry*. Oxford: Clarendon Press, 1968.

Williams, Raymond. *The Country and the City*. New York: Oxford University Press, 1973.

Williamson, George. *The Proper Wit of Poetry*. Chicago: University of Chicago Press, 1961.

Williamson, J. H. *The Myth of the Conqueror: Prince Henry Stuart, A Study in 17th Century Personation*. New York: AMS Press, 1978.

Wilson, Edmund. "Morose Ben Jonson." In *The Triple Thinkers*, 213–32. New York: Oxford University Press, 1948.

Wilson, Gayle E. "Jonson's Use of the Bible and the Great Chain of Being in 'To Penshurst.'" *Studies in English Literature* 8 (1968): 77–89.

Wilson, John Dover. "Ben Jonson and *Julius Caesar*." *Shakespeare Survey* 2 (1949): 36–43.

Winn, James A. *Unsuspected Eloquence: A History of the Relations between Poetry and Music*. New Haven: Yale University Press, 1981.

Winner, Jack. "The Public and Private Dimension of Jonson's Epitaphs." In *Classic and Cavalier: Essays on Jonson and the Sons of Ben*, edited by Claude J. Summers and Ted-Larry Pebworth. Pittsburgh: University of Pittsburgh Press, 1982.

Winters, Yvor. "The Sixteenth-Century Lyric in England: A Critical and Historical Reinterpretation." *Poetry* 53 (1939): 258–72, 320–35; 54 (1939): 35–51. Reprinted in *Elizabethan Poetry: Modern Essays in Criticism*, edited by Paul J. Alpers, 93–125. New York: Oxford University Press, 1967.

Winzeler, Charlotte. "Curse upon a God." *Brigham Young University Studies* 5 (1964): 87–94.

Woods, Susanne. "Ben Jonson's Cary-Morison Ode: Some Observations on Structure and Form." *Studies in English Literature* 18 (1978): 57–74.

———. "The Context of Jonson's Formalism." In *Classic and Cavalier: Essays on Jonson and the Sons of Ben*, edited by Claude J. Summers and Ted-Larry Pebworth, 77–90. Pittsburgh: University of Pittsburgh Press, 1982.

Woolf, Daniel R. "Erudition and the Idea of History in Early Modern England." Paper presented at the 1985 Pacific Northwest Renaissance Conference, Vancouver, British Columbia.

Wykes, David. "Ben Jonson's 'Chast Booke,'—The *Epigrammes*." *Renaissance and Modern Studies* 13 (1969): 76–87.

Young, R. V., Jr. "Style and Structure in Ben Jonson's Epigrams." *Criticism* 17 (1975): 201–22.

———. "Jonson, Crashaw, and the Development of the English Epigram." *Genre* 12 (1979): 137–52.

Zitner, Sheldon P. "The Revenge on Charis." In *The Elizabethan Theatre IV*, edited by G. R. Hibbard, 127–42. Hamden, Conn.: Shoe String Press, 1974.

Index